Remarkable Service

Remarkable service ^{SM}

A guide to winning and keeping customers for
servers, managers, and restaurant owners

THE CULINARY INSTITUTE OF AMERICA

John Wiley & Sons, Inc.
New York • Chichester • Weinheim
Brisbane • Singapore • Toronto

LEAD WRITER

Ezra Eichelberger

LEAD EDITOR

Gary Allen

CONTENT TEAM

Sheridan Dowling
Gerard Fischetti
Mary Frankini
Ralph Johnson
Philip Papineau
Tom Schmitter
Carmine Stanzione
John Storm

CONTRIBUTORS

Ken Carlson
Stephen Giunta
Anke Holtmann
Heinz Holtmann
Reuben Katz
Kari Kinder
Steven Kolpan
Bryan Miller
John Nihoff
Konstantin Sembos
Brian Smith
Rich Vergili
Charlene Von Eikh
Michael Weiss
Henry Woods

CIA EDITORIAL TEAM

Tim Ryan, *Executive Vice President*

Dr. Fred Mayo, *Associate Vice President and
    Dean of Liberal and Management Studies*

Mary Cowell, *Editorial Director*

Susan Deresky, *Editorial Assistance*

Mary Donovan, *Senior Editor*

Jessica Bard, *Photo Editor/Producer*

Jennifer Armentrout, *Editor/Writer*

Lorna Smith, *Photographer*

Elizabeth Corbett Johnson, *Photo Studio Manager*

Dawn Altomari-Rathjen, *Assistant Producer and
    Food/Prop Stylist*

Susan Wright, *Production Assistant*

Denise Swidey, *Production Assistant*

All interior photography by Lorna Smith
Line illustrations by Terri Sileno
Cover photograph by Louis Wallach
Historical images from Corbis Images, Culver Pictures, and
    Omni-Photo Communications

This book is printed on acid-free paper.
Copyright © 2001 by The Culinary Institute of America
All rights reserved.

Published simultaneously in Canada.
No part of this publication may be reproduced, stored in a retrieval system or transmitted in any form or by any means, electronic, mechanical, photocopying, recording, scanning or otherwise, except as permitted under Sections 107 or 108 of the 1976 United States Copyright Act, without either the prior written permission of the Publisher, or authorization through payment of the appropriate per-copy fee to the Copyright Clearance Center, 222 Rosewood Drive, Danvers, MA 01923, (978) 750-8400, fax (978) 750-4744. Requests to the Publisher for permission should be addressed to the Permissions Department, John Wiley & Sons, Inc., 605 Third Avenue, New York, NY 10158-0012, (212) 850-6011, fax (212) 850-6008, E-Mail: PERMREQ @ WILEY.COM
This publication is designed to provide accurate and authoritative information in regard to the subject matter covered. It is sold with the understanding that the publisher is not engaged in rendering professional services. If professional advice or other expert assistance is required, the services of a competent professional person should be sought.

Library of Congress Cataloging-in-Publication Data:
Remarkable service: a guide to winning and keeping customers for servers, managers, and restaurant owners /
    by The Culinary Institute of America.
        p.   cm.
    Includes bibliographical references and index.
    ISBN 0-471-38022-9 (pbk. : alk. paper)
    1. Food service management. I. The Culinary Institute of America.
TX911.3.M27 R453 2000   00-023097
647.95'068—dc21

Printed in the United States of America.
10 9 8 7 6 5 4 3 2

Contents

Foreword

Remarkable Service is a simple concept, one that should be achievable with no more dramatic cost than that of a welcoming smile, knowledge of the menu, and the willingness to pay attention to your guests for the entire time that they are in your dining room. Unfortunately, what people should do and what they do in fact is not the same. Thus, in surveying customers over the last twenty years, we have found service problems to be the weak link in the restaurant industry.

Therefore, I am gratified that the industry is beginning to see the need for dining room personnel to be recognized as 'real professionals.' This book, with its grounding in Nine Basic Principles of Service, demonstrates the underpinnings of a style of professional service that can only enhance the entire industry, both in terms of respect with which it is held and the revenues it can generate. It behooves every member of the restaurant's staff to try to make the customer's experience as rewarding as possible, so that the customer comes back again as a source of ongoing revenue, as opposed to working against you as a source of bad word-of-mouth. In the front lines, of course, is the professional server.

The service side of the industry is where the chef stood some twenty years ago. In the two decades that have passed, chefs have gone from virtual unknowns to important, even famous figures, within the restaurant industry and in the much larger public arena as well. As culinary training in this country has matured, so has the professional standing of the chef. The same standards for professionalism and training on the service side can and will make an enormous difference to the entire restaurant industry.

A really complete knowledge of what you are doing and a sense of what is important is a prerequisite for professionalism. If you have been trained in every aspect of what is being done in the kitchen and you know how to act appropriately, that is the most important thing. As this book emphasizes, to be 'remarkable,' service must be not just knowledgeable, efficient, well timed, consistent, informative, and trustworthy, but hospitable as well. What do we mean by 'hospitable'? The dictionary says it means 'given to generous and cordial reception of guests.' In short, the service professional must make the customer feel at home. It means being friendly and courteous, as any good host would. Of course, to be remarkable, service must exceed expectations and delight the guest.

It is vital to realize the importance of your job and to take pride in it. Professional dining room staff ought to embody a sense of honor, in the same way that other acknowledged professionals do, whether they be lawyers, doctors, teachers, or accountants. You must have a basic knowledge of the skills you need to perform the tasks that you are expected to render. If you are a true professional, then you know what you must do to provide Remarkable Service. You must learn as much as you can about your profession, your dining room, and your colleagues and their work in the kitchen. You'll feel good about yourself, the restaurant, and your guests. At that point, you will know that you are doing the right thing.

Tim Zagat

Introduction

Statistics abound in the food service profession. Every part of the business is measured. The current numbers reported by organizations such as the National Restaurant Association (NRA), showing steady and continual growth in restaurant sales, should make food professionals happy.

The NRA also reported in its 1996 consumer survey that half the Americans contacted were cooking fewer meals at home than they were in 1994. But even as these figures show the positive side of the industry, other findings suggest that the needs or demands of that growing number of customers are not being met.

Although the majority of customers have no complaints about their dining experiences, among those who take the time and effort to formally complain, service is the most frequently mentioned area.

At a Restaurant Industry Summit held in New York in the summer of 1999, the ZagatSurvey revealed its finding that 62 percent of customer complaints—nationwide—were about service. Complaints about the quality of the food ranked well down on the list, with only 11 percent. This survey was based on responses from fifty thousand customers from a wide range of settings.

RESTAURANT CUSTOMER COMPLAINTS

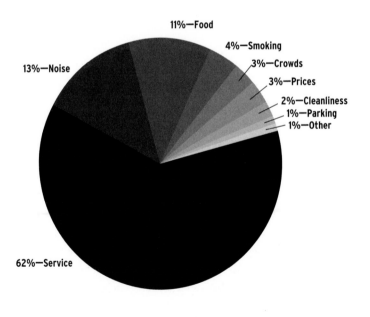

Used with permission from ZagatSurvey®-Restaurant Conference, ©1999, ZagatSurvey, New York

SERVICE BREAKDOWN

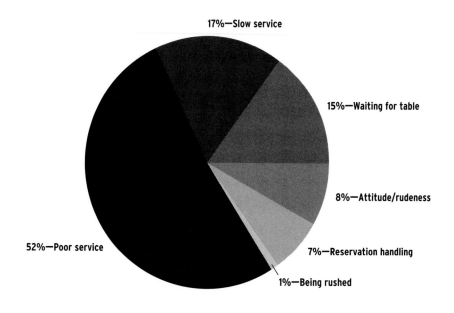

17%—Slow service

15%—Waiting for table

8%—Attitude/rudeness

7%—Reservation handling

1%—Being rushed

52%—Poor service

Used with permission from ZagatSurvey®-Restaurant Conference, ©1999, ZagatSurvey, New York

The Zagat report echoed previous surveys conducted by the National Restaurant Association that put the percentage of customer complaints dealing with service issues at 60 percent. Within that group of complaints, most cited the speed of service as the problem, followed by the inattentiveness of the wait staff.

Restaurant guests may not comment on good service—they expect that food and beverages will be brought to the table efficiently and unobtrusively. But when something goes wrong, diners certainly notice, and they feel moved to comment.

The goal of this book is to turn every comment into a compliment. The delivery of Remarkable Service is the only way to ensure a steady stream of positive remarks. "Remarkable Service" refers to a system that not only is worthy of praise but also is above and beyond expected levels. Remarkable Service engenders the word-of-mouth promotion that no amount of money can buy.

Common sense suggests that any restaurant would want to keep regular customers coming back. That's good not only in general terms but also in financial terms. According to Tom Feltenstein of Feltenstein Partners, a consulting firm in

Palm Beach, Florida, "If you can get your average customer to make one more visit per month, you almost double your sales." A high level of service is the key to maintaining repeat business. Service affects sales.

Any restaurant interested in maximizing sales must look at service as an important part of the business plan. To create Remarkable Service every successful establishment needs to develop a service program. This book provides the foundation for such a program.

In this book we describe the attributes of Remarkable Service and the standards that such service must meet or exceed. Like principles, attributes can be difficult to define. Everyone knows courteous service when experiencing it, but how to set guidelines for courtesy? For this reason, we have used numerous examples or vignettes throughout the text. These examples are drawn from the experience of the authors and come from real-life events. Through these stories from the field, the sometimes abstract principles become clear.

Not all aspects of great service are based on abstract concepts. There are right and wrong ways of doing things. No matter what the setting, from the most informal to the height of fine dining, there are dos and don'ts. These rules and their rationales are clearly explained.

The book is also designed to be a reference work on all aspects of front-of-the-house service, from setting up an appropriate reservations system to equipment identification. Even the most veteran server, faced with a new situation, can use this book as a source for solutions.

The numbers tell us that sales nationwide are hitting new heights as more people have more meals outside the home. The figures also tell us that those diners are looking for better service when they have that meal. Any establishment that can deliver consistent Remarkable Service is bound to garner a larger piece of the growing market. This book can lay the foundation for achieving that goal.

CHAPTER one

The Nine Basic Principles of Hospitality and Service

Attributes of Remarkable Service

Remarkable Service:

- Is welcoming, friendly, and courteous
- Is knowledgeable
- Is efficient
- Is well timed
- Is flexible

- Is consistent
- Communicates effectively
- Instills trust
- Exceeds expectations

To entertain a guest is to be answerable for his happiness so long as he is beneath your roof.
— *Anthelme Brillat-Savarin, 1825*

The Nine Basic Principles of Hospitality and Service may seem to refer to different kinds of acts, but in fact they constitute a code of service that encompasses taking care of the guest or customer. Providing service is at the heart of any business, from auto repair to hairdressing to restaurants. The more intimate the customer's involvement, the more crucial this factor is to the success of the business. Dining is a very personal activity, with many emotional as well as rational factors. A high level of caring for the comfort of guests—Remarkable Service, in other words—is the distinctive attribute of the best dining establishments. Remarkable Service makes guests feel comfortable, and it makes dining out enjoyable.

> **"I DECIDED TO TRY BREAKFAST AT THE COUNTER OF A NEW DINER IN MY NEIGHBORHOOD. Everything was fine, nothing special; it was just a diner, after all. About a week later I went back, and the waitress repeated my entire order from the first visit, including crisp bacon, and asked if I wanted the same thing. Now that's a very special diner! And I'm a regular customer because I wasn't just another guy at the counter."**

To comply with Brillat-Savarin's dictum, servers must not only physically provide the food and drinks guests desire but also ensure the guests' enjoyment by providing a haven from annoyances that might spoil enjoyment of the meal, such as loud music or the clattering of dishes. Remember, servers must not only cater to the expressed needs of the guests but anticipate unspoken needs as well.

In addition to being a guide to practical, how-to issues of service, the Nine Basic Principles of Hospitality and Service also underlie the less tangible aspects of service. Less tangible does not mean less important. In fact, attention to these details is exactly what characterizes Remarkable Service. In today's competitive market, the quality of the service is as important as the food—sometimes even more important—in determining how well a restaurant will fare, whether it's a high-end dining palace or a neighborhood diner.

Remarkable Service Is Only as Good as It Looks, or First Impressions Matter

"You only have one chance to make a good first impression" has become the mantra for quality-oriented service businesses. In the restaurant business, judgments that can alter the entire dining experience are made by guests within minutes of their arrival. A good server never forgets this oft-quoted but still valid adage.

When a restaurant—including the physical plant, decor, furnishings, equipment, and staff—presents a clean and neat appearance, it banishes any worries guests might have about sanitary conditions in the part of the restaurant they can't see, the kitchen. Even a single grease stain on the carpet, a crumb on a chair, or a spot on the wall can turn guests off about the meal they came expecting to enjoy. Stubbed-out cigarette butts on the sidewalk or dirty windows send a very powerful negative message to would-be customers.

The Nine Basic Principles of Hospitality and Service will be referred to throughout this book. Since they represent various aspects of service and share the goal of making the guest feel comfortable, it should come as no surprise when two or more of the principles overlap. Together they all form a code of service.

Remarkable Service Is Welcoming, Friendly, and Courteous

A warm, friendly welcome assures guests that they can relax and enjoy their meal. By the same token, a warm good-bye makes guests feel appreciated and encouraged to return.

Good servers are sensitive to guests' needs, not only as to the dishes served but also in terms of the entire dining experience. Few guests come to a restaurant to chat with the service staff; most want to converse with their companions. Regular customers may develop an informal relationship with the staff; some may even think of the restaurant as their second dining room or home away from home. Good manners smooth uncertain social interactions, subconsciously informing people that they have nothing to fear. Courteous behavior creates an atmosphere of comfort, so guests know what to expect.

Remarkable Service Is Knowledgeable

Guests often request information about menu items or wines. Servers who are knowledgeable about the menu (ingredients and preparation of the menu items, presentation, wines, and the like) can provide the help they need to order from the menu and the wine list. Servers can—and should—list specials of the day and other dishes not on the menu to help guests make informed decisions about their meal. Guests cannot order dishes they don't know exist.

A remarkable server not only has to know how to answer the guest's question but also must guess what the guest really wishes to find out. For example, a guest asks what is in the spinach-and-goat-cheese quiche. While the server could reply, "Spinach and goat cheese," which is technically accurate, it is far from hospitable and doesn't tell the customer what he wants to know, which is probably if there is garlic or onion in the quiche. The server should tell the guest what else is in the dish, especially if there is garlic or onion or nuts, which some customers have allergies or aversions to.

Remarkable Service Is Efficient

Efficiency is important to the servers and to the restaurant for obvious reasons; for one, more work can be done (and more money made) with less effort. And when guests see the servers working quickly, smoothly, and easily, they feel at ease. Disorganization and unseemly haste are contagious.

Inefficient technique wastes everybody's time. It interrupts the flow of the meal and erodes the environment of trust. Attention to the mise en place (having everything in its place), an intelligent economy of motion, and a cooperative attitude all make the server's job easier to perform.

Remarkable Service Is Well Timed

Remarkable servers anticipate the dining needs of the guests. This means providing just the right items or services before the guests even realize they need them.

- Orders should be taken within a reasonable time after the guests are seated and have had time to peruse the menu.

- Flatware should be in place before the guest needs it; nothing is more frustrating for a guest than to look at dessert and not have a fork or spoon to eat it with.

- Guests should not have to wait a long time between courses. Careful timing of the delivery of each course ensures that guests will get their food while it is at its freshest and at its ideal temperature.

- Guests should not have to ask for refills of water or iced tea, bread or butter.

- Coffee should not sit cooling in front of the guests while they wait for cream and sugar to be brought to the table. Cream and sugar should precede the coffee or tea.

- The check should be delivered smoothly, quietly, and unobtrusively when the guests have finished and indicated that they are ready to pay.

- Guests should never be made to feel rushed. However, when guests are in a hurry—when they need to be in theater seats by curtain time, for example, or when they are traveling—whatever is needed to pace the meal should be done so that the guests can enjoy their meal in the time at their disposal.

> "WHILE DRIVING CROSS-COUNTRY I STOPPED FOR A QUICK BREAKFAST. The informal restaurant I entered obviously catered to travelers, as it was located just off the exit of a major interstate highway. I sat down, and the server offered to pour coffee—decaf or regular—and gave me the menu. As soon as I had lifted my eyes from the menu the server was there to take my order. In just a matter of minutes the breakfast was in front of me— hot and perfectly prepared. The server also put down the check at the same time as my meal, saying, 'I'll be happy to bring you anything else, but I am giving you the check now in case you're in a hurry.' I didn't feel rushed; I felt well served. The service perfectly fit the circumstances."

Remarkable Service Is Flexible

Remarkable Service consists of more than adhering to a set of principles. Sometimes the rules must be bent a little. A guest might ask, for example, for an appetizer and a salad instead of an appetizer and an entrée or to have the courses out of the menu sequence, such as a salad after the entrée instead of before. Some guests prefer to pour the wine themselves for their table. This happens frequently in wine country; it is an easy request to accommodate. If two guests are deeply involved in a conversation, common sense suggests that one should be served from the right and one from the left. Sound judgment provides the best guides as to when and where flexibility is called for.

Remarkable Service Is Consistent

People go to a restaurant the first time for many different reasons. They come back for only one: They like the restaurant, its food, and its service. Making good use of the Nine Basic Principles of Hospitality and Service can induce someone to come back to the restaurant once, but consistently high-quality food and service is the only way to bring in repeat business. Uneven service does not encourage return visits. A single episode of bad service, even when no fault of the server—two cooks called in sick, the refrigerator broke down—will discourage the people who experienced it from coming back. Word of mouth will do the rest. The key to long-term success is Remarkable Service, delivered to every guest, every day, every week, every month, every year.

Remarkable Service Communicates Effectively

The art of communication consists of transmitting just the right amount of information exactly when it is needed. When a server describes specials that don't appear on the menu or offers suggestions about additional dishes or beverages that might enhance the dining experience, the diner is well served. The waiter might suggest a side dish to go with a steak, for instance: "Many of our guests like to have a blooming rose with their steak. It's a deep-fried whole onion that opens up like a rose when it's cooked."

"WE WERE HALFWAY THROUGH OUR MAIN COURSE, AND MY WINEGLASS WAS EMPTY, though everyone else had plenty. I didn't want to order another bottle of wine. I must have been sending some kind of signal, because the waiter came to me and told me they had a wine by the glass that would be just perfect with my steak."

Remarkable servers recognize what guests want to know and provide the information in an unobtrusive manner. Rather than an ostentatious flaunting of knowledge, which can make guests uncomfortable and irritated because they feel condescended to, a tactful delivery of the facts best serves the purpose.

While some guests respond well to humor, others prefer more distance. Remarkable servers adapt their communication style to the situation and the guests with whom they are speaking. The type of establishment very often determines the form and style of conversation between servers and guests. Diners, family places, bistros, and white-tablecloth restaurants all develop different communication styles.

Remarkable servers are always "reading the table" for clues about what guests might need. A guest turns his head, for example, and the alert server is at his elbow instantly to see what he needs—an extra side dish, an extra plate to share food, or more cheese.

Effective communication is accomplished by other means as well. Uniforms set a tone for a restaurant, establishing at a glance a style of communication that both servers and guests understand. Polo shirts and khakis convey a casual feel, while long French aprons denote a higher level of formality.

Remarkable Service Instills Trust

A state of trust must be established between the server and the guest. The guest wants to feel secure that menu items are described accurately and that health and sanitary codes are observed. For example, when guests order decaffeinated coffee, they have only the server's word that they are, in fact, getting decaffeinated coffee. If a guest notices that the coffee machine has only two carafes, both with a brown handle, which indicates regular coffee, rather than orange or green, which usually indicates decaffeinated, doubts take shape that can undermine the relationship of trust established during the rest of the meal. Similarly, if a guest who is allergic to garlic asks if a dish contains garlic and is told no, eats it, and wakes up in the middle of the night with palpitations, that guest is not going to return to that restaurant. A bond of trust is central to return business.

Remarkable Service Exceeds Expectations

Repeat customers expect the same basic level of service each time they visit, but remarkable servers are constantly seeking ways to better the experience. The best service is constantly improving service. Little touches, such as recalling a guest's name or offering a toy to a child, are sure to be remembered. When something goes wrong, such as a reservation mix-up, an apology is called for, but the manager's offer of a complimentary glass of wine is doubly appreciated, precisely because it exceeds expectations.

A Brief History of Table Service

The Nine Basic Principles of Hospitality and Service may seem straightforward, but they have not always been the rules of the profession. Table service is a noble profession, one that has had a long and varied history, and it has been shaped by that history.

Table service evolved with changes in social structure, architecture, and the foods that were served. By comparing the foods and ways our ancestors ate, especially when they dined in banquets, with our own customs, today's dining habits, whether in formal dining rooms, bistros, or family restaurants, can be better understood—even some of the bizarre jargon used in today's kitchens and dining rooms, which has its roots in the past.

THE ANCIENT WORLD: GREECE

The earliest written descriptions of recognizably Western dining scenes are found in the Old Testament and in Homer's *Odyssey* and *Iliad*. In reading these accounts,

Greek banquet (©Bettmann/Corbis)

it is obvious that it was the status of the diners that counted. Until fairly recent times, writers (for the most part) did not write about ordinary, everyday life. They wrote for and about the rich and powerful, describing banquets and special occasions attended by people of high social status.

By 400 BCE the Greek banquet had become standardized, with a fixed structure for the dishes served and the manner in which they were to be served. Banquets were generally held in private homes, as the Greeks had very few public eating places. Dining rooms were small, containing couches for the guests. Rooms were described by the number of couches they contained. Usually these feasts took place in a five-couch room, with a small table in front of each couch.

A basket containing a selection of breads made of wheat or barley was placed on each table. Servants brought large dishes from the kitchen, and guests chose their favorite portions, tossing scraps, shells, and bones onto the table.

MIXING-BOWLS, OR *KRATERES.*

Krater. Wine mixed with water tableside in a krater, a large clay pot with a wide mouth, was served with the desserts.
(Courtesy of Culver Pictures)

The meal was divided into three parts. The first part or course might include fruit, poultry, salted seafood, and small savory meat dishes, much like the Greek *mezze* of today. These light dishes were followed by heartier fare—fresh seafood and roasted meats, such as lamb or baby goat.

After this course, the tables were removed with all the bones and other debris, and new tables were brought out. Servants circulated with towels and basins of warm water scented with precious oils for the guests to clean their hands.

Desserts were then served. These might include dried and fresh fruits, cheeses, nuts, and small pastries or other confections. Wine mixed with water tableside in a krater, a large clay pot with a wide mouth, was served with the desserts. Diluted wine was considered healthier than water, and drunken behavior (during the early stages of the meal, at least) was discouraged.

After the desserts the soiled tables were removed once again, signaling the end of the meal and the beginning of the symposium, a convivial party with a mix of literary and philosophical discussions, music, and performances by acrobats and female dancers, accompanied by the drinking of unmixed wine.

THE ANCIENT WORLD: ROME

The Romans adopted a great deal of Greek culture, including the culinary arts, taking Greek ideas about the meal merely as a starting point. They used more-complex recipes, more-elaborate presentations, more kinds of seasonings and more of them, and more imported ingredients.

Roman families often dined together. There were strict rules governing the position of each diner, based upon status. The head of the household always had the most prestigious spot. Guests also took their places according to status. Just to be invited to dine often signaled sought-after social recognition. Who was invited by whom, who accepted an invitation, and to whom one appealed for an invitation said much about power in ancient Rome.

Roman banquet
(Courtesy of Culver Pictures)

The Roman dining room was called a *triclinium*; it contained three couches, each for three diners, arranged in a **U** shape. Diners rested on their left sides, their left elbows propped up on cushions. The legs of the second diner on the couch were behind the cushion on which the first diner rested, and the legs of the third were behind the cushion of the second. This left the right hand free to choose from the platters of food, carried from the kitchen on discuses. Each guest ate from a red pottery bowl or dish, such as the then-famous Samian ware.

A Roman dinner consisted of three courses. The first, the *gustum*, was similar to our hors d'oeuvre. It was served with *mulsum*, a light wine mixed with honey. The *gustum* was followed by the *mensa primae*, or first table, as in the sequence of the Greek banquet. Red wine mixed with water accompanied the *mensa primae*. The next course was the *mensa secundae*, or second table. This course included a dessert of fruits and sweets—and the first unwatered wines of the meal. This was the time for entertainment and for serious drinking to begin, as in the Greek symposium.

The Middle Ages Through the Renaissance

The hierarchy of power and status was reflected in medieval banquets as well. In Anglo-Saxon times meals were large-scale affairs, taking place in the main hall of a castle; there were no rooms reserved solely for dining. Although some tables were permanent, most consisted of boards laid across heavy trestles or sawhorses (the origin of the modern sense of *board* as "daily meals," as in "room and board") and dismantled after the meal. Tables were arranged in a **U**, and the head of the household and honored guests sat at a table elevated on a dais. The table was covered with a white cloth and an overcloth called a sanap in English.

Salt cellar with Neptune and Tellus by Benvenuto Cellini
(©Bettmann/Corbis)

The first thing to go on the table was the salt cellar, which was placed before the most important person, salt being of immense value in the Middle Ages. The status of those who were to eat could be determined by where they sat in relation to the salt. High-status diners ate above the salt, others below. Only those above the salt were seated on chairs. The rest sat on benches that were, in effect, miniature versions of the trestle tables at which they ate.

The most important implement on the table was a carving knife. Carving was a manly art, and at first it was reserved for the carver, a person of exalted rank. Later this task was given over to the "officer of the mouth," the highest-ranking servant. A

The carver (Courtesy of the New York Public Library Picture Collection)

concern with courtliness and manners, if not sanitation, demanded that the officer of the mouth "set never on fish, beast, or fowl more than two fingers and a thumb." Diners brought along their own knives. They used them to cut foods into pieces small enough to be eaten conveniently with the hands or conveyed directly into the mouths on the point of the knife.

The tables used in French banquets were covered with a large cloth called the *nappe*. The top was kept clean, but the sides where it hung down were used for wiping the hands (made especially greasy by the absence of forks). Occasionally *manuturgia*, or hand towels, were made available.

The French word *nappe* is the source of the English word *napery*, meaning "table linens." *Napkin* is a diminutive form, and *apron* is an altered form of *napron*. Likewise, the culinary term *napper* is used to describe coating or covering food with sauce.

Food was served from common bowls, called messes. It was scooped, or dragged, to large dishes or to trenchers, either *tranchoirs* (slabs of stale bread used as plates) or *tailloirs* (large wooden or metal plates), which were shared by two or three diners.

In France, as in England, wealthy households had a large number and variety of silver bowls, basins, pitchers, and other serving vessels. Ordinary folk, on the other hand, might have no more than a pewter mug. The display of wealth through service ware was only one of the ways that the host's status was expressed at the table.

In the late fourteenth century people began to think of food and its service as worthy of study and respect. In France, Taillevent (Guillaume Tirel, 1312–1395), cook to Charles V and Charles VI, collected and codified medieval cooking in his book *Le Viandier*. *Le Ménagier de Paris*, modeled on *Le Viandier* and written by an elderly gentleman for his young bride, outlined the bourgeois repertoire.

In the mid-fifteenth century Platina of Cremona (Bartolomeo Sacchi), librarian to Pope Sixtus IV and a learned epicure, published *De Honesta voluptate et valutudine* (On Honest Indulgence and Good Health). In it, Platina discussed proper manners, table etiquette, table settings, nutrition, and more. It also contained recipes. *De Honesta*

Caterina de Medici (1519-89), an Italian princess from the famous Florentine family, married the Duc d'Orleans, later Henri II of France. She introduced a more refined style of dining, including the use of the fork and the napkin. Her Florentine chefs influenced French chefs as well, most particularly in the use of spinach. (Courtesy of Culver Pictures)

voluptate altered the way the wealthy, who still ate with their hands, thought about eating and manners. Written in Latin, it was translated into many languages, including Italian, French, and English, and had tremendous impact.

Although not all historians agree, some trace the origins of classic fine dining to a single aristocratic family of the sixteenth century, the Medicis of Florence. When Catherine de Medici (1519–1589) married the future King Henri II of France in 1533, she brought as part of her entourage a small army of Italian cooks, chefs, servants, and wine experts.

Catherine introduced fine dining and its appropriate service to France; her cousin, Marie de Medici (1573–1642), wife of King Henri IV, continued that culinary mission. François La Varenne, one of the greatest chefs of France, received his training in the kitchen of Henri IV. While Taillevent looked to the past for inspiration, La Varenne's book *Le Cuisinier françois* (1651) showed signs of a more modern approach to cooking, foreshadowing *Le Guide culinaire* of Escoffier, still 250 years in the future.

The new table manners that began with Platina were expanded during the reigns of the Medici cousins. Among the table refinements brought to France by the Medicis (and which later spread to the rest of Europe) were:

- Washing hands before sitting down at the table—an old custom that had fallen into disuse
- Using a fork to select food from a platter
- Passing the best morsels of food to others at the table
- Not blowing on hot food

THE FORK AND OTHER EATING UTENSILS

The fork was used in Italy long before it appeared in France or England. The fourteenth-century monarch Charles V did not use forks, nor did the Duc de Bourgogne list forks in his household inventory of 1420. Bartolomeo Scappi's 1570 book *Cuoco secreto di Papa Pio Quinto* (Cooking Secrets of Pope Pius V) contains the first known illustration of a fork.

The title page of the 1604 edition of Vincenzo Cervio's *Il Trinciante* (The Server), printed in Venice, shows a wood engraving of meats being roasted on spits and carved tableside. Of the two diners pictured, one seems to be examining a morsel skewered on the point of a knife, while the other sits patiently, his two-pronged fork awaiting the next slice of roasted bird. The illustration is an early-seventeenth-century glimpse of table manners in the midst of change.

In early-sixteenth-century England Henry VIII initiated formal, luxurious dining, and under the rule of his daughter Elizabeth I in the latter half of the century the practice flourished. Men and women were seated alternately at the table. Husbands and wives shared a plate, but it was a true plate, not a trencher of stale bread. (Trenchers survive today only in our term *trencherman*, meaning "an enthusiastically big eater.")

Table manners came to be expected of refined people. Books about table manners and the right way to serve became popular. Forks were recommended for serving portions of meat (which by that time were beginning to be carved by women at the table), although the use of forks as eating implements was still not mentioned. The spoon was the primary table utensil. Diners brought their own spoons to dinner. Silver was reserved for the wealthy, which in those times tended to mean nobility. Other spoons were made of tin-plated iron or, for the very poor, wood. Lord Braithwaite's Rules for the Governance of the House of an Earl (1617) listed spoons and knives as essential but did not mention forks.

Thomas Coryate (ca. 1577–1617) was a traveler and onetime jester in the court of James I. He had traveled to Italy, where he became convinced of the usefulness of the fork.

Coryate's English countrymen remained unconvinced, and for his efforts to win acceptance of the new device, they mocked him with the nickname Furcifer, a specially coined word combining the Latin word for fork with one of the devil's names. Indeed, as late as 1897 sailors in the British navy were not permitted to use forks, which were considered an affectation.

In Asia chopsticks had been in use long before forks. As Margaret Visser reports in *The Rituals of Dinner*, "Once people become accustomed to fingers remaining clean throughout the meal, napkins used for serious cleansing seem not only redundant but downright nasty. Father João Rodrigues observed in the seventeenth century that the Japanese were 'much amazed at our eating with the hands and wiping them on napkins, which then remain covered with food stains, and this causes them both nausea and disgust.'"

> **CORYATE WROTE HOME FROM ITALY IN 1611:**
>
> "[The Italians] always at their meales use forke when they cut their meat for while with their knife which they hold in one hand they cut the meate out of the dish, they fasten their forke, which they hold in their other hand, upon the same dish; so that whatsoever he be that sitting in the company of any others at meale, should unadvisedly touch the dish of meate with his fingers which all at the table doe cut, he will give occasion of offense unto his company, as having transgressed the lawes of good manners, insomuch that for his error he shall at least be brow beaten, if not reprehended in wordes."

During the reign of Queen Anne in the early eighteenth century, napkins and the increased use of forks made it possible to use finer napery. Table setting began to be seen as an art in itself. Books on the subject, including the first titles about napkin folding, began to appear.

Meanwhile, the dining room had begun to be a place of pomp. A brigade system of officers of the household, complete with uniforms (which even included swords for the highest-ranking servants), was created, not to serve in the trenches but to wait on the trenchermen. The first service manual of this brigade, *L'Escole parfaite des officiers de bouche* (The Perfect School of the Officers of the Mouth) (1662), explained, "Give the best portions to the most esteemed guests, and if they are of great importance, give them an extra portion."

Service à la française (French service) had its origins in the court of Louis XIV, a grandson of Marie de Medici and Henri IV, who reigned during the latter half of the seventeenth century and the first part of the eighteenth century. The meal was divided into three separate parts, or services. The first and second services consisted of soups, game, and roasts; the third service was dessert. The sequence was much the same as it had been in ancient Greece and Rome. As guests entered the dining room they found the first course, the entrée, already in place. Hot food was kept warm on réchauds, or heating units. After the dishes in the first service were finished, the guests left the table while it was cleaned and reset for the second service.

Service à la française had some distinct disadvantages. The tables were overloaded, and not merely with food. Réchauds, centerpieces, flower baskets, and candelabras filled every available inch. Despite the use of réchauds, the food was often cold, or at best had lost its freshness. With so many dishes served, most guests limited themselves to one or two and rarely had an opportunity to sample the rest.

THE EIGHTEENTH CENTURY

Up to the end of the eighteenth century, lavish meals and presentations were confined almost exclusively to the aristocracy. This was especially true in France. With the start of the French Revolution in 1789, the political and social landscape of not only France but England and the rest of Europe changed. With these vast changes came a democratization of dining. No longer were chefs cooking only in the homes of the rich and powerful. With the toppling of the French monarchy and nobility, their chefs had no choice but to ply their trade in other venues. The development of restaurants in France was not due solely to the French Revolution, but this event spurred the growing need for eateries available to the increasing numbers of the middle class.

Coffeehouses had been around, both in France and in England, since the second half of the seventeenth century; they began as places for businessmen to meet. Lloyd's of London, the insurance firm, was originally Lloyd's coffeehouse (founded 1687), a place where ship's captains, shipowners, merchants, and insurance brokers met to discuss the day's events, art, literature, and politics—and gamble on the chances of ships reaching their destinations safely. The Café Procope in Paris was a popular gathering place for intellectuals. It opened at its current location, across the street from the Comédie-Française theater, in 1686 and is the oldest surviving coffeehouse in Paris.

The first real restaurants in France appeared about twenty years before the French Revolution; they proliferated after that as the nobility's former chefs sought employment. In 1782 A. B. Beauvilliers opened the restaurant La Grande Taverne de Londres. The term *restaurant* already existed in France, but it previously referred only to small establishments that sold broth or bouillon, that is, restoratives. Beauvilliers had spent time working in England, especially during the Revolution, when association with French nobility might have endangered his life. Beauvilliers contributed the à la carte (literally, "from the card") menu, offering his guests the opportunity to choose from a number of menu items, as opposed to the fixed-menu table d'hôte of the past.

Antonin Carême (1784–1833) lived during the crest of the social changes brought about by the Revolution. He represented the grandest statement of the old, court-based cuisine, inspired by the vigor of a new society in transition. Carême was one of the last practitioners of service à la française. It was a perfect frame for the exhibition of his art.

Antonin Carême (1784–1833) became known as the founder of the *grande cuisine* and was responsible for systematizing culinary techniques. He had a profound influence on the later writing of Escoffier, and was known as the "chef of kings, king of chefs." Pictured above is one of Carême's stylized presentations, for which he was noted. (Courtesy of the Art Archive)

THE NINETEENTH CENTURY

Carême's preference for the grandeur of service à la française could not slow the shift to a more guest-centered form of service. In 1808 Grimod de la Reynière published his *Manuel des amphitryons*, a guidebook for table service. He used an archaic term

GEORGES AUGUSTE ESCOFFIER

Georges Auguste Escoffier (1847-1935) was a renowned chef and teacher and the author of *Le Guide Culinaire*, a major work codifying classic cuisine that is still widely used. His other significant contributions include simplifying the classic menu in accordance with the principles advocated by Carême, and initiating the brigade system. (See "The Kitchen Brigade System" later in this chapter.) Escoffier's influence on the foodservice industry cannot be overemphasized. (Courtesy of Culver Pictures)

for host (after Amphitryon, who was the husband of Alceme, the mother of Hercules in Greek mythology) for the person in charge of the dining room, in place of the old expressions "officer of the mouth" and "carver." The motto for service staff, according to Reynière, was "The host whose guest is obliged to ask for anything is a dishonored man."

This change in focus from host to guest was echoed in 1825 in the *Physiologie du goût* (The Physiology of Taste) by Anthelme Brillat-Savarin (1755–1826). Félix Urbain-Dubois's *La Cuisine classique* (1856) took this approach to service another step forward. It introduced service à la russe (Russian service) to European dining rooms. Food was served hot from the kitchen rather than from an immense display where all the dishes, prepared well ahead of time, had been sitting for maximum visual effect.

If service à la française expected diners to be impressed by the host's largesse (even if the food was served lukewarm), service à la russe ensured that each guest's meal was served at its peak. The burden of guaranteeing the guest's enjoyment was shifted to the host (or the host's staff). In a sense, Urbain-Dubois had rediscovered the best aspect of classic Greek, Roman, and medieval table service: piping hot dishes rushed out of the kitchen for the guest's delectation.

From this point on, the development of European, and especially French, cuisine became a series of small refinements. The formats of table d'hôte, service à la française, and service à la russe were continuously fine-tuned.

Cesar Ritz (left) teamed with Auguste Escoffier to make the Savoy in London (above) the epitome of fine dining in the late 1800s. (©Bettmann/Corbis)

Delmonico's in lower Manhattan led New York's fine-dining scene in the latter part of the nineteenth century. (©Corbis)

THE NEW WORLD

Just as the landscape of Europe was transformed by the Industrial Revolution, the United States changed drastically in the late 1800s. The factories springing up brought immigrants and workers from the farms and created greater concentrations of people in urban areas. These working groups had to be fed, and restaurants and services were created to meet the needs of these people.

Factories ran on schedules in which mealtimes were strictly defined, so quickly prepared and served meals were necessary. The birth and rise of counter service, where one wait staff member could serve dozens of individual diners, followed that need. The opening in New York in 1902 of Horn and Hardart's coin-operated food vending service, where prepared food items were behind glass doors whose latches were released when the right number of tokens or coins was put in the slot, was a logical step in the development of fast food.

The Industrial Revolution also brought the advent of steam-powered machinery. Steam ushered in a new era of transportation, and with the pounding of the Golden Spike in 1869 the North American continent was spanned by rail. Goods and people could move relatively quickly and easily from the Atlantic to the Pacific. To meet the restaurant needs of this emerging group of train travelers, the Santa Fe Railroad added a string of restaurants owned and operated by Fred Harvey. These Harvey House restaurants hired all-female wait staff. Harvey made the move so that the gentility of the female wait staff would influence the sometimes rowdy behavior of the male patrons.

Although Americans were a people on the move, they were also a people with a wide diversity of ethnic backgrounds. From the middle of the 1800s through the twentieth century, each wave of immigrants gave the culture new foods, new flavors, and new ways of preparing foods. This melting pot is evident in every city on the continent, where a Chinese restaurant may be next to a classic French bistro, which may be next to an Italian trattoria.

Harvey House
(Courtesy of the Kansas State Historical Society, Topeka, Kansas)

With the wide variety of cuisines came a varied selection of eateries. Today high-end dining establishments, or white-tablecloth restaurants, are succeeding alongside bistros, family dining restaurants, and fast-food chains, and the National Restaurant Association predicts continued growth in the industry as more and more people eat out. Each of these styles of restaurant has a defined mode of service, but in all cases the principles of Remarkable Service can be applied.

CHAPTER two

Styles of
Table Service:
Classic to Modern

Like many words, *service* has several meanings. Traditionally, the group of dishes comprising a given part of a meal was called a service, as in tea service. *Service* can also signify the utensils necessary to serve a part of a meal. *Service* in this sense encompasses the ensemble of objects used at the table: linens, plates, glasses, flatware, and holloware (candlesticks and deep vessels of metal or ceramic, such as bowls, pitchers, and coffeepots). For our purposes, however, *service* refers to the manner of presenting a meal to the guest.

What Is Table Service?

There are many styles of table service: French, Russian, English, American, butler, buffet, counter, and self-serve or cafeteria. Overall, the type of service offered at a restaurant is determined, ultimately, by the market the restaurant is trying to reach. No one style of service is better than any other. Each form of service meets the specific needs and demands of individual circumstances. Any combination of styles may be used if consistent with the restaurant's concept.

In the past forty years, restaurant service has changed as dramatically as the food being served, especially in America. During the first half of the century, American fine-dining restaurants tried to emulate European manners. French service was considered the most elegant, followed by Russian and English. American service evolved from these European forms of service, utilizing aspects of all three styles in varying combinations. The style of service, as much as the menu, decor, uniforms, table settings, and ambience, should be consistent with the type of cuisine that a restaurant offers. Today's dining is less stratified and formal than in the past; it reflects the shift in values that has characterized society and consequently table service.

The Classic Menu

Today's restaurant menu is a list of suggested dishes, but the basic sequence of courses in a menu goes back to that of the ancient Greeks, which had as its goal to match the food to the sensory requirements of the diners. In order for each course to be enjoyed, the Greeks believed, it should not be overpowered by the preceding course. And so cold foods were served before warm foods and light foods before heavy foods, with the meal building to a climax at the main course, then gradually relaxing to lighter foods. This basic pattern has endured, no matter how copious or complex the dishes.

Even the classic courses essentially follow those simple guidelines. Though rarely—if ever—served today in their entirety, they are:

Hors d'oeuvre (appetizer): A small portion—the word means literally "outside the work of the menu"—meant to awaken the appetite. Special utensils, such as caviar spoons (of gold, horn, or mother-of-pearl), oyster forks, or snail tongs, may be needed.

Potage (soup): Clear soup, such as bouillon or consommé, served in a two-handled bouillon cup with a bouillon spoon, or a thicker soup, served in a soup plate with a soup spoon.

Bouillon spoon and bouillon cup

Soup spoon and soup bowl

Oeufs (eggs): An omelet or poached or scrambled eggs.

Farineux (starches): Generally pasta, such as spaghetti, ravioli, or gnocchi, or sometimes risotto. String pastas, such as spaghetti, are served in Italy in a bowl with a fork set on the right; in America, they are usually served on a plate, with a fork on the left and a tablespoon on the right.

Poisson (fish): Usually an individual portion of fish. A fish fork and fish knife are provided for boning the fish on the plate.

Entrée (light meat): A small portion of poultry, beef, pork, or lamb, garnished but served without vegetables when followed by a relevé.

Sorbet (ice): Served between main courses to refresh the palate. (The sorbet course is sometimes used as an intermezzo, or intermission, during which a speech could be given.)

Relevé (meat): Traditionally, roast meat served with sauce, potatoes, and vegetables. This meat course follows, or replaces, the entrée.

Rôti (roast): The main event. Usually roasted game, often served with a small green salad.

Légumes (vegetables): Vegetables, usually served with a sauce.

Salade (salad): Any assortment of dressed greens.

Rôti froid (cold meat): A small portion of cold meat, such as ham or cold roast chicken, or fish.

Entremets (sweets): Dessert; service might require forks and spoons, parfait spoons, or the like.

Savory (savory): This course, served only in Britain, is a tidbit served hot on toast, such as Welsh rarebit or grilled chicken livers and bacon.

Fromage (cheese): An assortment of cheeses brought from table to table on a platter or a cheese cart.

Fruit (fruit): Fresh, dried, or candied fruit.

Digestif/tabac (beverages/tobacco): Coffee, tea, cordials, brandies, and cigars. Service requires spoons, cream and sugar, and ashtrays.

A CLASSIC MENU: SEVENTEEN COURSES

Appetizer (hors d'oeuvre)

Soup (potage)

Eggs (oeufs)

Starch (farineux)

Fish (poisson)

Light meat (entrée)

Ice (sorbet)

Meat (relevé)

Roast (rôti)

Vegetables (légumes)

Salad (salade)

Cold meat (rôti froid)

Dessert (entremets)

Savory (savory)

Cheese (fromage)

Fruit (fruit)

Beverages/tobacco

(digestif/tabac)

A MODERN AMERICAN CLASSIC MENU

Cold appetizer

Soup

Fish

Sorbet

Meat

Salad

Dessert/coffee

COMMON MENU IN AMERICAN RESTAURANTS

Appetizer (cold or hot)

Salad

Main course

Dessert/coffee

A common approach today is to adjust the order of the classic menu, serving the sweets after the savory, if any, and cheese course. Also, in Europe coffee is served as a separate course after dessert, while most Americans prefer coffee with dessert. It may be appropriate to ask the guests when they would like to have their coffee served.

The Modern Menu

Social changes, from a more egalitarian spirit to a lifestyle that leaves little time available to devote to fine dining, have led to a reduced number of courses in the modern menu. Several types of menus have evolved: the so-called à la carte menu, the table d'hôte menu, the prix fixe menu, and the menu dégustation.

THE À LA CARTE MENU

Guests generally create their own meal from the dishes offered on the full menu, ordering à la carte, literally, "from the card" or menu.

Dishes are individually priced, and guests may structure their meal in any way they choose. Often a dessert menu is presented separately at the end of the meal.

THE TABLE D'HÔTE MENU

Some restaurants also have a table d'hôte menu, which offers a limited choice of dishes within each category, for a set price determined by the entrée. Generally no additional choices from the à la carte menu and no substitutions, such as salad for potatoes, are allowed.

A choice of desserts may be specified, or dessert may be picked from the dessert menu.

THE PRIX FIXE MENU

A prix fixe menu offers a set meal at a set price, usually with no choices, though occasionally there are some, with a supplemental charge for a luxury item such as lobster or caviar. Sometimes a glass of wine is included in the price. Most of the time the price of a prix fixe menu is relatively low because it reduces production costs by permitting the kitchen to operate at a predetermined pace and flow. If the dishes were ordered à la carte, the bill would be considerably higher. The guest is expected to pay for the entire menu whether or not he orders all the dishes.

A LA CARTE MENU

WOOD-FIRED PIZZAS   Small 4.50   Large 6.75

* Mediterranean-Style Vegetable pizza

STARTERS

Grilled Chicken Skewer with Soy-Lime Sauce   5.00

Smoked Shrimp with Horseradish and Dill-Yogurt Sauce   6.00

Wood Oven–Roasted Clams in "Casino"-Style Broth   5.50

Seafood Sausage with Tomato and Leek Sauce   5.50

* Morel Risotto with White Truffle Oil   6.00

* Crispy Potato and Vegetable Napoleon   4.50

SOUPS AND SALADS

Potato-Olive Soup Garnished with Tomato Marmelade   4.00

Shrimp and Chicken Gumbo   4.50

Curried Carrot Soup with Ginger Cream   4.00

A Taste of Each—Our Soup Sampler   4.50

* Local Organic Mesclun with Choice of Creamy Blue Cheese,
Lemon-Thyme Vinaigrette, or Balsamic Vinaigrette   4.00

* Salad of Baby Lettuces with Apples, Walnuts, and Coach Farm
Goat Cheese Dressing   4.50

Italian-Style "Pancake" with Fresh and Roasted Vegetable Salad   5.00

MAIN COURSES

"Pho"—Vietnamese-Style Beef Consommé Full of Noodles, Herbs,
and Chilies   9.50

Monkfish Bouillabaise with Local Potatoes and Braised Fennel   12.00

Roasted Pork Tenderloin with Black Bean Sauce, Mango-Tomatillo Salsa,
and Grilled Vegetables   11.50

Salmon and Potato Rösti with a White Wine–Vegetable Demi-glace   14.50

Grilled Prosciutto-Wrapped Quail with Roasted Shallots and Figs   12.00

* Braised Celery Hearts with Herbed Risotto—Sauce of Roasted Shallots
and Chanterelle Mushrooms   10.00

Grilled Beef Tenderloin with Mushroom Ragout   16.50

*INDICATES VEGETARIAN SELECTIONS

TERRINA RUSTICA DI MONTAGNA
*"Pork Terrine from the Mountains"—Pork, Veal, and Pistachios Served
with Salsa Rossa, Salsa Verde, and Seasonal Greens*

ANTIPASTO FREDDO ASSORTITO
Assorted Seasonal Cold Antipasti

CARPACCIO DI MANZO CON RUCOLA E PARMIGIANO REGGIANO
Thin-Sliced Raw Sirloin of Beef with a Zesty Lemon Dressing, Shaved Parmigiano, and Arugula

ZUPPETTA DI COZZE CON ROSMARINO
Mussels Steamed in Olive Oil, Garlic, White Wine, and Rosemary

RISOTTO DEL GIORNO
Risotto of the Day

STRACCIATELLA ALLA ROMANA
Egg Drop Soup—Roman-Style

TORTELLI CON LA ZUCCHA
*Large Tortelli Filled with Butternut Squash, Amaretti, Mostarda di Frutta,
Parmigiano Reggiano, and Sage Butter*

RAVIOLI CON FONDUTA E SALSA DI FUNGHI
*Small Ravioli Filled with Piemontese-style Fontina Fondue in a Sauce of Mushrooms
and Parmigiano Reggiano*

LINGUINE CARBONARA
Linguine in a Traditional Roman Sauce of Eggs, Pancetta, Black Pepper, and Parsley

SECONDI PIATTI

OSSOBUCO CON PORCINI   *28.00*
Veal Shank Braised with Porcini Mushrooms, Tomatoes, and Marsala Wine

MANZO ALL PIZZAIOLA   *28.00*
*Pan-Fried Steaks "Pizza-maker's Style" with a Sauce of Tomatoes,
Garlic, and Fresh Oregano*

QUAGLIE RIPIENE AL FORNO   *29.50*
Quail with Sausage, Herb, Pine Nut, and Raisin Stuffing with Oven-Roasted Potatoes

MERLUZZO IN CROSTA DI PANGRATTATO SU LETTO DI PATATE   *27.00*
*Fresh Atlantic Cod Marinated in Virgin Olive Oil, Rosemary, and Garlic,
Roasted on a Bed of Thin-Sliced Potatoes with a Crust of Bread Crumbs*

APOLPETTINI DI VITELLO CON SALSA D'AGLIO E PEPERONI   *27.50*
Veal and Pork Patties with a Garlic and Roasted Red Pepper Sauce

MAIALE FARCITO CON SALVIA E FONTINA IN CROSTE DI ERBE   *26.00*
Pork Filets Stuffed with Fontina, Eggplant, and Sage with an Herb Crust

CRÈME DE ÉCHALOTES

Cream of shallots

SALADE DE FONDS D'ARTICHAUTS ET TOMATES,
VINAIGRETTE DE FRAMBOISE

Artichoke heart and baby tomato salad with raspberry vinaigrette

BAR AUX CHANTERELLES EN CROÛTE,
SAUCE CHAMPIGNON AUX POIREAUX CONFITS

Sauteed chanterelle-crusted tilebass with mushroom sauce and butter-stewed leeks

CRÈME DE PÊCHES

Peaches in a light custard

CAFÉ, THÉ

Coffee, tea

$55

THE MENU DÉGUSTATION

Some restaurants offer a menu dégustation, or tasting menu. Small portions of numerous dishes, chosen by the chef (sometimes in consultation with the guest) and often served with paired wines, make up a multiple-course meal. Usually the menu dégustation is served only to the whole table and has to be ordered in advance.

Service Styles

Any one of several styles of table service may be followed, or, at times, a combination may be employed. The most common styles for seated dining are French, Russian, butler, English and family service, and room service. Other serving styles include buffet, cafeteria, take-out (or home replacement), and counter service.

There is some controversy regarding the elements included in French service versus Russian service. These styles have evolved, and the clear distinctions between the elements have blurred over time. For instance, the use of the guéridon is discussed in the text as part of French service, but there are food service professionals who would place it under Russian service.

FRENCH SERVICE

Based upon the banquet style of sixteenth-century France but first appearing in the court of Louis XIV circa 1680, French service, or service à la française, is the most elaborate and labor intensive of all serving styles. Traditionally in French service, a meal was divided into three separate services, or courses—the first, the second, and the entremets, or dessert. Much of the food was cooked or finished tableside from a voiture, or cart, or from a guéridon, or side table, in the dining room.

ADVANTAGES OF TABLESIDE SERVICE	DISADVANTAGES OF TABLESIDE SERVICE
Elegant, leisurely, and personalized service	Highly trained staff required; high labor cost
Entertaining (boning fish, carving meat, flambéing at tableside)	Expensive equipment required
Showcases the food and preparation	Less turnover
High average check	Seating capacity reduced by need for guéridon space

In tableside service, the guéridon is center stage in the service act. The table is often equipped with a réchaud, or heating element, and a cloche, or large silver dome, for covering food. The fuel is usually alcohol or bottled butane. The voiture (the word means literally "carriage" or "car"), on the other hand, is mobile. It is a decorative cart equipped with a heating unit and a hinged cover to keep prepared foods hot, although cold foods can also be served from a voiture. A voiture is large enough to hold an entire roast. In practice, voiture service refers to the plating of a precooked main course at the guest's table from a voiture.

When guests entered the dining room, the first course was already set up (the word *entrée* can be traced to this entry into the dining room). In the first and second services, hot items were carried to the dining room on silver platters and placed on the guéridon. After the guests finished a service, they got up and left the table while it was cleaned and reset for the next service. This second course was the relevé. The first two services consisted of between ten and forty items, including soup, game, and roasted meat. The third service, the entremets, was dessert.

GUÉRIDON SERVICE

Contemporary guéridon service generally requires two servers to deliver and prepare the food, as well as a captain to seat guests and take orders and a sommelier to assist in wine selection and to serve the wine. This courtly style of service can be entertaining for guests, but it has some distinct drawbacks in our more cost-conscious (and less decorous) era. The cost of equipment, staff, and space required to serve at tableside is very expensive, prohibitively so for most restaurants.

Some fine-dining restaurants employ a modified form of guéridon service in which food is fully or partially cooked in the kitchen, placed on a platter, and carried to the dining room by a waiter. The platter is then placed on a guéridon and the food is plated. This allows some tableside showmanship with less labor.

PLATTER SERVICE

Russian service, or service à la russe, currently considered platter service in America, is used mostly for banquets. It is less showy than French service, but it is quicker and no less elegant. Speed replaces showmanship, although skill is involved. The main goal of platter service is to ensure that the guest receives fully cooked, hot food served in a smooth and swift fashion. It is especially suited to banquets or wherever it is necessary to serve many people attractively presented food quickly but without sacrificing the personal touch.

In platter service, the food is fully cooked and arranged and garnished on large platters in the kitchen. Using the right hand, the server sets in the empty plates from the guest's right, beginning with the first woman seated at the host's left and moving clockwise around the table. Then a server carries the platters of food to the dining room and presents them to the table. Next, holding the platter with the left hand and serving the food with the right, the server stops at the left of each guest, displays the food, and serves the desired portion. The server transfers the food from the platter to the guest's plate with a serving fork on top of a serving spoon.

The server with the platter moves around the table counterclockwise, beginning with the first woman seated at the host's right. Note that service is done from the opposite sides of the guest, as compared with French and other service styles.

Butler service is often used for passing hors d'oeuvre at cocktail parties.

BUTLER SERVICE

Butler service procedures are basically the same as for Russian service, except that the guests serve themselves with utensils provided from the platter, which is held by the waiter with both hands.

Beginning with the woman at the host's left, the butler offers from the left, moving counterclockwise around the table.

ADVANTAGES OF BUTLER SERVICE	DISADVANTAGES OF BUTLER SERVICE
Personalized service	Space between chairs for platter width required
Guests may choose portion size and quantity of sauces	Poor portion control; may run out of items
	Can be time-consuming

ENGLISH SERVICE AND FAMILY SERVICE

In restaurants, English service is usually reserved for private rooms or special group dinners. All food is fully cooked in the kitchen. Plates are preset. The host generally serves soup, if any, into bowls, which are then passed around the table. The host, or perhaps the maître d'hôtel, carves the meat or plates the main dish and passes it to a guest, who in turn passes it along the table. Side dishes arrive from the kitchen on large serving platters and guests help themselves.

In another scenario, serving dishes are placed on a sideboard, from which the server plates the food, then presents it to the guests. The server moves clockwise around the table when clearing used plates.

Family style is similar to English style, except that the foods are placed on the table in large serving dishes and the guests help themselves.

Variations on this less formal style of serving are becoming popular in the United States, especially at restaurants and grills that want to create a familylike ambience. It is also found in resorts, on small cruise ships, and in Pennsylvania Dutch country farmhouse restaurants.

ADVANTAGES OF ENGLISH SERVICE	DISADVANTAGES OF ENGLISH SERVICE
Casual, communal atmosphere	Not elegant
Guests can have second helpings	No portion control
Friendly but not necessarily skilled servers required	No plate presentation

AMERICAN SERVICE

By far the most widespread style of service, American service is usually found in bistro/trattoria and casual restaurants. It is often employed in fast-turnover, high-volume operations as well. It also is frequently used for banquets because large numbers of guests can be handled quickly by a limited number of service personnel.

Procedures vary depending on the service needs. In American service, all cooking and plating of food are completed in the kitchen. A waiter picks up the plated food, carries it to the dining room, and sets in the plate in front of the guest from the right with the right hand. This allows two or three plates to be held in the left hand and arm while serving with the right. For small parties (fewer than six guests), women are served first, moving clockwise around the table, then men. For larger parties (six or more), the woman to the left of the host is served first. The server moves clockwise around the table, finishing with the host. If there is no obvious host, the server may begin with any woman.

Some restaurants prefer service to be from the left, with the left hand, in which case, the server moves around the table counterclockwise. For small parties women are served first, then men. For larger parties, the woman to the right of the host is served first, then the server moves counterclockwise around the table, finishing with the host. House policy determines where to start when there is no host or no apparent host.

The practice in the United States of serving from the guest's left with the left hand is believed to have originated in American homes with limited service staff. The maid would serve the plates from the sideboard, clearing a dirty plate from the right with the right hand, then immediately serving the next course with the left before returning to the sideboard.

ADVANTAGES OF AMERICAN SERVICE	DISADVANTAGES OF AMERICAN SERVICE
Informal	Less personalized service
Portion control and reduced food costs	Guests cannot choose portion size
Limited skill and less space required	

SUMMARY OF SERVING STYLES					
Style	Activity	From Guests' Side	Waiter's Hand	Move Around Table	Begin With
Guéridon	Set	Right	Right	Clockwise	Woman at host's left
Platter, preset plate	Set	Right	Right	Clockwise	Woman at host's left
Platter	Serve	Left	Right	Counterclockwise	Woman at host's right
English and American	Set	Right	Right	Clockwise	Woman at host's left
Clearing dirty china	Clear	Right	Right	Clockwise	Woman at host's left
Butler	Set	Left	Left	Counterclockwise	Woman at host's right
Butler	Serve	Right	Both	Clockwise	Woman at host's left

ROOM SERVICE

Quality room service demands a high degree of anticipation of the guest's needs since, unlike service in a dining room, everything to complement the meal must be brought to the guest's room in one trip. Salt and pepper, cream and sugar, lemon wedges, or even side orders should be double-checked before leaving the room service kitchen.

BUFFET SERVICE

French, Russian, English, and American service are styles for seated dining where the food is brought to the guest. The buffet table is like a miniature marketplace, attractively arranged to display the food offered. The guest goes to the food. A

ADVANTAGES OF BUFFET SERVICE	DISADVANTAGES OF BUFFET SERVICE
Impressive display of food	Guests may not be able to identify foods
Guests can mingle	Long waiting lines
Guests have more choice	Little portion control; food can run out
Flexibility (one or more long lines or separate stations)	Additional equipment (platters, chafing dishes, sauceboats, serving utensils, tables) required
Less service staff required	Not as elegant as being served

buffet is often employed for simple, fast, and economical service when a large number of people must be served in a short amount of time.

Buffet service is generally found at parties and other casual functions. Hot and cold foods are set out on long tables, sometimes with serving staff standing behind. This is an efficient way to serve large groups because people can serve themselves what they want when they want it.

Guests generally pay a set price and help themselves as they pass from one selection to the next along the buffet line. Buffet service requires a smaller number of service personnel than other service styles, but the rate of food consumption is high, and the greater food expense may outweigh the lower cost of labor. This expense is somewhat offset by placing inexpensive dishes at the beginning of the line (guests tend to fill their plates early, so they have less appetite for the more expensive ones later).

As with any style of service, buffet service should be logical and convenient for the guest. Cold foods should be first in the line, hot foods last, also because that way the food is still hot when the guest sits down to eat. Accompanying sauces for self-service should have an underliner and be placed near the guests' side of the table to minimize dripping on the table. Portion sizes can be controlled and the line kept moving by having servers along the buffet to assist guests with plating. A carver is often stationed at the end of the line to serve roasted meats, such as baked ham, prime rib, or turkey.

Food safety is always a concern with buffet service. Food may be left out for long periods of time and is handled by many people. One strategy to minimize problems is the so-called sneeze guard, a transparent plastic shield hanging above the food just below face level. Some people, however, find it tacky. And, of course, nothing can stop customers from leaning over the food, mixing utensils, or reusing a soiled plate.

OTHER TYPES OF SERVICE

Brunch

Brunch is often a combination of American service and buffet service. The emphasis is on informality, with some plating of foods.

Cafeteria Service

Most cafeterias are self-service. Guests select their own food and carry it to the table. Some cafeterias have servers who plate the food chosen by the guest, thereby controlling portion size. Attendants are generally needed for busing tables, although self-busing is common.

ADVANTAGES OF TAKE-OUT SERVICE	DISADVANTAGES OF TAKE-OUT SERVICE
Convenience and lower cost than a restaurant	Loss of control of quality and sanitation
Can serve more covers each night	Can interrupt flow of dining room service

Take-out or Home Meal Replacement Service

During the last decade, take-out, or home meal replacement (HMR) service, as it's coming to be known, has become the fastest-growing segment of the food industry. It is found mainly in delis, gourmet shops, and supermarkets. Some experts attribute the popularity to aging baby boomers, who now stay home to care for their own babies yet want restaurant-quality food. Other reasons range from the time pressures on families where both partners work, a disinclination to cook on weeknights, and more adventuresome palates.

Even upscale restaurants are providing meals for the office and the home. Bistros/trattorias and casual establishments offer a range of options. A recent twist on this service style has resulted from the rapid growth in the use of the Internet. In a matter of minutes customers can look at the menus of dozens of available restaurants. Orders can be placed via e-mail (usually right from the Web page) and food is either prepared for take-out or delivered directly to the customer.

Clearly, HMR involves a new and different definition of table service than in the past. Restaurateurs in particular need to understand and make allowances for the differences in perceived comfort between eating at home and being served in a restaurant.

Counter Service

Fast turnover is the goal of counter service. Patrons are served with a minimum of conversation and movement. Pictures of prepared food items are often displayed on the menu or walls to speed decision making.

A server may have from eight to twenty guests to serve at any one time, and may repeat the process ten times in an eight-hour shift. Everything should be within reach. The counter should be close to the production area so that orders can be placed, picked up, and served quickly. Rhythm and timing must

be established between kitchen personnel and service staff to ensure a smooth, trouble-free operation. Of course, this kind of coordination is essential in any restaurant, but with counter service the guest can see the entire process.

Counter service has seen a rapid growth in sophistication in recent years. The rise in popularity of tapas and sushi bars has paralleled the greater interest in more adventuresome dining practices in the United States. Service and presentation can provide a relaxed, casual environment that suits modern tastes.

Types of Restaurants

Restaurants can be divided into three basic styles. The service should always be warm and welcoming, but the accoutrements may vary. The type of restaurant one chooses is the result of several different considerations. The kind of food to be served is important, but it is not the only factor. The price range, the level of service, and the ambience of the room all play a role.

The three general categories discussed here cover the majority of restaurants, although the variety within the categories is great. The variations within the family-style restaurant are apparent to anyone who has been to a shopping mall. Within most malls there may be several dining venues. Each would classify itself as a family-style restaurant but each is completely different. Even within one establishment you might find two types of dining. For instance, one establishment may have a portion of the restaurant dedicated to fine dining and another part a more casual bistro. The casualness of the establishment should not reflect a casual attitude toward customer service, however. Customer satisfaction is not the domain of one type of restaurant or one style of service.

Fine dining: Restaurants that offer luxurious and comfortable surroundings, usually including good-quality tabletop silver, china, crystal, and linen. A maître d'hôtel directs the dining room and the staff of captains, waiters, and buspersons. The menu offers many choices, and the wine list is appropriately extensive and well paired to the food. A sommelier may be on hand to help guests. The pace of service is leisurely; a meal may last three hours or more.

Fine dining

Bistro/trattoria

Bistro/trattoria: Restaurants that range from white-tablecloth establishments, with a range of food styles, to animated and bustling bare-bones places serving simple fare and beverages. The original bistro or trattoria—a family-run establishment serving simple foods—has been all but abandoned in the United States. The terms now refer to any simple, cozy restaurant.

Casual/family: Family-style restaurants, diners, theme restaurants, and the like. The principles of good service apply here as well, although servers may be less experienced than in other types of restaurant.

Casual/family

Conclusion

Ultimately, there are only two types of service: good service and bad service. Bad service is available in thousands of flavors. But the main points of good service are always the same:

KEY POINTS

- All foods are served at their appropriate temperatures: hot foods served hot on hot plates, cold foods served cold on cold plates.
- All foods and beverages are served in a timely, courteous, sanitary manner.

Dining Room Organization and Personnel

In a very real sense, all the employees of a restaurant are hosts, serving their guests. Every task, no matter how small, is carried out for one reason: to make the guest's experience as pleasant as possible. If the servers are not neat, clean, and professional-looking, the guests will choose to eat elsewhere.

Personal Qualities of the Professional Server

In order to succeed, the professional server must have certain physical and behavioral characteristics.

PHYSICAL TRAITS

The first (and possibly most lasting) impression a professional server can make is through his or her appearance; it should be a positive one. The uniform, be it a tuxedo, khakis, or a stylized costume, is a badge of professionalism and should be worn with pride. It should be neat, clean, and fresh-looking at all times. Good grooming is a must for anyone working in a restaurant. Well-groomed people look clean because they are clean.

- Their hair is neatly cut and combed.
- Their nails are clean and trimmed, with clear or no nail polish.
- Their teeth are clean, brushed and flossed.
- Their clothing fits properly.
- Their shoes are shined and in good condition (no run-down heels).

Servers must also have impeccable personal hygiene. Daily showers and the use of deodorants are a must. Since servers are in close proximity with so many people, they should wash their hands frequently, about every half hour if possible. Like dentists, they should not have bad breath or a perceptible odor of onion, garlic, or cigarette smoke on their breath. Colognes and perfumes can conflict with delectable food aromas, so they should be avoided.

BEHAVIORAL TRAITS

The most important behavioral characteristic a professional server can possess is the ability to deal with people. No amount of superficial polish or knowledge can take the place of this innate trait. Maintaining a high level of personal concern for the customer is not always easy, though. Some customers are cranky and demanding while they expect the people who wait on them to be unfailingly pleasant and efficient. Everyone has a bad day occasionally, but professional servers should never let their bad days be seen by the guests.

Other desirable traits include:

Knowledge: The professional server is familiar with the menu and beverage list and knows ingredients, preparation methods, proper service temperature, and garnishes. This information can be particularly helpful in dealing with special requests, such as substitutions. The professional server knows the restaurant's hours of operation as well as its special services and facilities. The professional server also is informed about events taking place in the region and local sites of interest. Reading books and periodicals about wine and food helps the professional server learn to appreciate their complexities and become better informed—and, not so incidentally, more impressive and reassuring in discussions with guests. Attending wine tastings, going to cooking demonstrations, and taking service classes are other ways to expand horizons.

Proficiency: People who want to advance in their career—whatever it is—have to be willing to work constantly at extending their skills and improving them by practice. Moving through a crowd with a tray of beverages, properly opening sparkling and still wines and decanting red wines, and delivering drinks without spilling them are skills acquired with practice.

Attentiveness: It is important to pay attention, not to daydream at work or lapse into absent-mindedness. A good server is alert to the needs of the guests. Being aware of the current state of the dining room while anticipating what is about to occur calls for considerable skill. Judging when more wine should be poured, when the table needs to be cleared, and how orders should be coordinated require that a server's attention stay focused on the job at hand.

Preparedness: The knowledgeable server has everything prepared ahead of time, before service begins. Putting off work that can be done in advance results in having to do it later, when time should be spent on the customer. The hospitality industry is not a business for procrastinators. Having all the required equipment on hand (matches or a lighter, an extra pencil or pen, a corkscrew) helps to make servers more professional-looking.

Efficiency: Getting the same work done but with less effort and better results is what is meant by efficiency. Planning trips to the kitchen and service area and avoiding empty-handed trips between the dining room and the kitchen save steps. The time saved by being well organized can be spent on better serving the customer.

Persuasiveness: Before the actual service of the meal begins, the professional server "sells" guests on what to order. Even as they enter the dining room, the professional server determines whether to try to sell them expensive dishes or extras or to suggest those that are more of a bargain. Most guests are not familiar with the entire menu, so a good server can steer them away from certain menu items and toward others. If done subtly, this selling will be appreciated by the guests.

Loyalty: Showing loyalty and working together with all of the restaurant's staff presents the restaurant as a competent and confident entity. The server is the most visible representative of a unified effort to provide good service to the guest. The kitchen should never be blamed for delays, for instance; the servers and the kitchen staff are both working to achieve the same goal: pleasing the guests. Part of loyalty is also a sense of proprietorship, that is, of "ownership" of one's job. Professional servers who see themselves this way work together for the common good.

Honesty: Honesty is fundamental. During the course of a regular business day, each member of the dining room staff has countless opportunities to deceive both the restaurant and the guests. The appearance as well as the quality of honesty instill trust.

Politeness: A professional server is polite, ready to assist in any way that relates to the customer's comfort. This includes such mundane tasks as opening doors; helping guests with chairs, packages, coats, and dropped items; correcting glare from lights or the sun; and adjusting the sound level of music if necessary. When a guest asks for directions (to the coatroom or rest room) it is rude to point rather than showing the way or giving simple directions. Polite words and considerate actions indicate a regard for the well-being of others, fellow employees as well as guests. Crude but commonly used expressions such as "Coming through!" or "Watch your back!" should be avoided.

Dependability: Dependability is a desirable trait for individuals in any profession. Dependable people can be relied on to accomplish what they promise, to fulfill their commitments, and to be at work on time. Dependability is a major factor that employers consider in hiring.

Composure: A good server is unobtrusive. The front of the house is not a place for chatting. Service personnel should speak only about business, about the job at hand. Unless the customer initiates a conversation, the only subjects of discussion with a guest should be the meal and its service.

Sensitivity: The professional server is sensitive to the needs of the guest. For example, for many guests a meal is a time to linger and to engage in conversation. For others, particularly at breakfast or lunch, a meal is only an interruption in a series of other events, not an end in itself.

Tact: Tact, the innate ability to say or do the right thing at the right time without giving offense to others, is rare but important for anyone dealing with the public. It can, however, be cultivated. The professional server sometimes has to be a diplomat, negotiating between the guest and the chef.

Good servers cultivate these behavioral traits, recognizing them as the essential tools of their trade. Good servers also know that they do not work alone—they are part of a team, an integrated staff of restaurant personnel. Every restaurant has its own structure, its own way of organizing its staff. These structures vary from restaurant to restaurant. No single structure is best for all restaurants, but the structures share common elements, which can be traced back to the traditional service structure.

Restaurant Personnel for Classic Service

As menus and styles of service have changed over the years, so has the structure of the dining room staff. The medieval position of officer of the mouth has been replaced by that of maître d'hôtel, which in many places has been replaced by the position of general manager, dining room manager, or simply host. The titles may change, but the responsibilities, though perhaps changed in some details, remain constant. The entire dining room staff is always functioning as host for the guest.

In an organization of any size, it is important for all involved to know to whom they report and to whom their supervisors report. It is equally important to understand the nature of the job and the characteristics that must be developed in order to advance in the hospitality industry or elsewhere.

Every restaurant has a dining room brigade of some sort, based, however distantly, on the classic model. A dining room brigade is designed to serve the guests efficiently, according to the type and price level of the menu, the style of service, and the physical structure of the restaurant. The more expensive and elaborate the menu, the greater the number of service staff required and expected. In a more casual setting, there are fewer staff members on hand, and there is less expectation of services.

Many of the positions serve as training posts for the positions above them. Employees frequently fill in for others: A captain may work one day a week as maître d'hôtel, the front waiter as captain, and so on.

The front-of-the-house staff must also work closely with the back-of-the-house or kitchen staff. Customers want consistency in the quality of the food they are served. On repeat visits they want their orders prepared in the same manner, served in the same quantity, and sometimes served by the same waiter.

The work of the kitchen staff is vital to the success of a restaurant, since its style and service evolve from the menu. The preparation of food must be organized and scheduled for ease of operation. There must be standards of quality, style, and quantity.

From an operational standpoint, uniformity of food preparation is central to efficient, cost-effective, and smooth performance. Failure to adhere to portion standards raises food costs, undermines the profit structure, and makes proper inventory control virtually impossible to maintain.

Following are descriptions of the classic dining room and classic kitchen brigades.

The Classic Front-of-the-House Dining Room Brigade: Job Titles and Job Descriptions

Maître d'hôtel (general manager): Traditionally, the manager of the house, with responsibility for the entire operation. In modern bistros or casual restaurants, this position is filled by either the manager or the host. Informally referred to as the maître d', he is responsible for the overall management of services in the dining room, including the bar, as well as public relations in the dining room and the maintenance of the physical plant of the dining room.

Chef de salle (dining room manager): Traditionally, the manager of the dining room, though the French term is rarely used today. The maître d'hôtel is in charge of the dining room service.

Organization

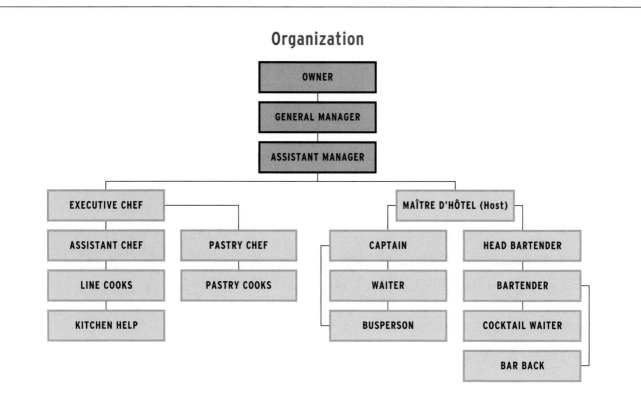

Chef de rang (captain): Also known as the chief of station. Usually in charge of service in a particular section of tables. Takes the order from the guests and assists the commis de rang (front waiter) in serving the food. A captain has more interaction with the guests than any other service staff person. As host of the station, the chef de rang should rarely leave it. If necessary, the front waiter can leave the floor to check the status of an order in the kitchen or retrieve drinks from the bar. A headwaiter may have the responsibilities of a maître d'hôtel, a manager of the dining room, or a chief of station in the dining room, depending on the restaurant.

Trancheur (carver): Though the position is rare now, this person rolls a voiture or cart and prepares plates with the meat and accompaniments, such as smoked salmon or roasted meats. In a modern fine-dining restaurant, these functions are performed by the captain.

Sommelier (wine steward): Responsible for the creation of the wine list, for maintenance of the wine inventory (that is, the purchasing and storage of wines), for recommending wines to guests, and for wine service.

Fine Dining Restaurant

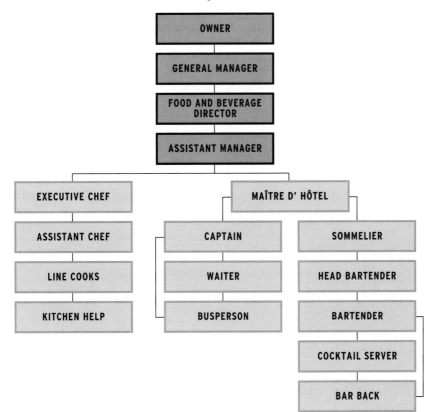

Commis de rang (front waiter): Second in command of the station after the captain. Takes the order from the captain or assists the captain in taking the order, relays it to the kitchen, and serves the food with the assistance of the captain. May assist the commis de suite (back waiter) in bringing the food from the kitchen.

Commis de suite (back waiter): Also known as food runner. Brings drinks and food to the front waiter, sets up the guéridon as needed, helps clear, and generally assists the front waiter.

Commis de débarrasseur (bus person): Responsible for stocking side stands and guéridons, and for cleaning during the preparation time prior to service. While employed primarily to clear the tables of soiled items, bus persons often assist with bread and water service.

Receptionniste (receptionist): Greets and occasionally seats the guests, takes phone reservations, and looks after the front desk area. In casual restaurants, this position often replaces those of maître d'hôtel and captain.

The Classic Back-of-the-House Brigade System: Job Titles and Job Descriptions

Chef de cuisine (executive chef): In charge of the kitchen; ultimately responsible for the menu, quality, consistency, and cost control. Has a staff, including a sous chef and any one of a number of assistant station chefs, also called line chefs or chefs de partie. The executive chef works together with the maître d'hôtel to develop the appropriate style of service and provides detailed menu information for training the service staff. To avoid confusion and reduce the noise in the kitchen, the executive chef decides how special orders are to be requested.

Chef (chef): Responsible for the actual production of the menu to the standards established by the executive chef.

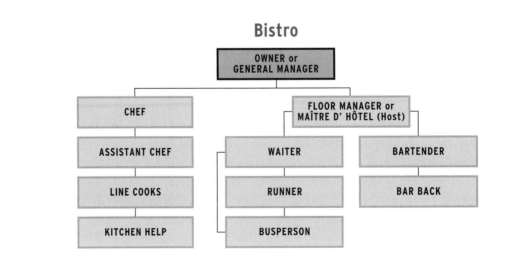

Sous chef (sous chef): Assists the chef.

Chef de partie—rôtisseur (rôtisseur): Prepares and cooks all roasts.

Chef de partie—poissonier (poissonier): Prepares and cooks fish.

Chef de partie—saucier (saucier): Prepares all sautéed dishes and related sauces.

Chef de partie—garde manger (garde manger): Prepares cold appetizers, salads, terrines, and hors d'oeuvres.

Chef de partie—entremetier (entremetier): Prepares hot appetizers, vegetables, and pastas and other starches.

Chef de partie—tournant (tournant): Also called switch cook or roundsman. Works with any station and may be used to fill in on another's day off.

Pâtissier (pastry chef): Responsible for all desserts.

Chef de partie—aboyeur (aboyeur): Also called expediter. Calls out the orders and coordinates the plates for pickup.

Casual (Chain)

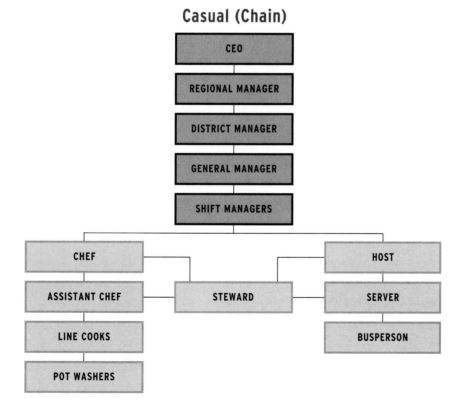

One way to better understand the hierarchy of a restaurant as a total unit is to use an organization chart. For charts for each of the three styles of restaurants discussed in this book, see pages 45–47.

Conclusion

The characteristics that define a good server include knowledge, proficiency, attentiveness, preparedness, efficiency, persuasiveness, loyalty, honesty, politeness, dependability, composure, sensitivity, and tact. If a single word had to be chosen to describe the sum of the personal characteristics that define the professional server, it would have to be *caring*. Obviously, caring is not, by itself, enough. The professional server must master necessary skills.

The front and the back of the house are staffed by brigades, each with a chain of command. Each position has responsibilities and skills that must be mastered. In each brigade there is the potential for working one's way up to the top of that chain of command.

THE Front Door

The front door is the very first contact guests have with a restaurant. The sparkling clean glass door of the restaurant may be the first thing that they see. If they happen to be driving by, a clean parking lot with well-maintained shrubbery may be first. These first impressions play a big part in determining whether or not a guest chooses to visit a new restaurant.

Sometimes guests are making a return visit to a restaurant. How they are treated—whether in the way reservations are taken, by the first greeting, by the manner in which they are seated, or by the style in which the staff makes accommodations for special requests—in large part defines the quality of their dining experience. This is the moment when the host establishes a warm and welcoming relationship with the guest.

Reservations

If a restaurant accepts reservations, the customer's first contact may be with a reservationist. In many restaurants, reservations are handled either in person just inside the front door (at the reception desk, the maître d'hôtel's podium, or the front desk) or over the phone. In some places phone reservations are made to a reservations department that is not even a part of the dining room. Indeed, it might not even be in the same building—reservations are easily taken over the Internet. No matter how the reservation process is managed, physically it is the restaurant's first opportunity to impress the guest with first-class service.

It is the responsibility of management to make sure that everyone who might be called upon to take a reservation is trained not only in the use of the reservation system but in proper etiquette and telephone technique.

PHONE ETIQUETTE

The reservationist's demeanor on the telephone is every bit as important as that of the maître d' in the dining room. If the receptionist is rude and disgruntled, the caller will come away with negative feelings. If, on the other hand, the receptionist sounds pleasant and helpful, the guest will look forward to a good experience.

The very first thing a reservationist can do to make a guest feel welcome is to answer the phone within the first three rings.

Every restaurant should have a standard greeting for anyone who answers the phone, stating the time of day, the name of the restaurant, and the first name of the person speaking. This should be written down. For example: "Good morning, An American Bounty. Adam speaking."

Putting people on hold can be annoying, but it is often unavoidable. The person answering the phone should always ask politely, "May I put you on hold?" and wait for a reply. It is very rude to cut people off before they have a chance to answer. If it might be a long wait, callers should be asked if they can be called back.

If a caller asks to speak with a particular employee, the person answering the phone should ask, "May I say who is calling?"

Reservationists should be familiar with the names of important or repeat customers. If a name is not familiar, it should be written down and used while speaking with the guest. It is a small but important courtesy. Everyone is an important guest or potential repeat guest.

LOVE THY BEST CUSTOMERS

Best guests deserve special treatment, and there is no excuse for greeting a regular guest with "And how do you spell your name?" The maître d' should meet periodically with the reservationists to review the names of important clients so that they can be welcomed personally on the phone. Caller ID can help identify guests before they identify themselves. This allows time to search through a card file or computerized customer database for preferences and to be prepared for the guest's requests. With a database, the reservationist can also see information about the caller's last visit, favorite table, favorite waiter, and so on.

For these reasons it is advisable to have as few people as possible taking reservations. If someone other than the regular reservationist books a table, he or she should be informed so that nothing (and no one) falls through the cracks.

Some restaurants hold a table or two in reserve in case a regular customer calls at the last minute or in the event of an error in reservations, but this is a luxury that few restaurants can afford.

WHY TAKE RESERVATIONS?

In restaurant heaven, all restaurants would be so busy every day that they could operate on a first-come-first-served basis and do away with reservations altogether. Considerate customers would call restaurants in advance to ask what time would be convenient to arrive so as not to overburden the chef and service staff. That, alas, is not the reality. It often seems that everyone on the planet wants to dine between 8:00 and 8:30 on Saturday evening. Consequently, most restaurants must take reservations.

WHEN RESERVATIONS ARE UNNECESSARY

In some cases reservations may not be needed.

Some restaurants take customers in the order in which they arrive at the front door. Guests sometimes have to wait for a table, which adds to the mystique of the restaurant. This works for such places as K-Paul's Louisiana Kitchen in New Orleans, the Carnegie Deli in New York City, and Le Bar Lyonnaise in Philadelphia. In addition, many casual and ethnic restaurants dispense altogether with the formality of a reservations system.

WHEN RESERVATIONS MIGHT BE NECESSARY

Fine-dining and bistro restaurants need to weigh the advantages and disadvantages of taking reservations. It may take guests thirty minutes or more by car or public

ADVANTAGES OF A NO-RESERVATIONS POLICY	DISADVANTAGES OF A NO-RESERVATIONS POLICY
Reduces personnel needed to staff the phones	Crowds can scare away potential customers—that is, the Yogi Berra syndrome can kick in: "Nobody goes there anymore, it's too crowded"
Maximizes table use through constant turnover	The service staff may feel compelled to rush diners to free up tables
Eliminates the no-show problem and lends a more casual aura to an establishment	Customers may get tired of waiting and leave or tell their friends not to bother; also, some customers will not patronize a restaurant if they are not guaranteed a table
Increases bar sales—even if guests waiting for tables do not buy a drink, a busy bar creates a lively ambience and attracts more bar business	The decibel level can mount as guests waiting at the bar sip their drinks
People standing outside give passersby the impression that this is an "in" place	Additional space is needed for people to wait, especially in cold weather

transportation to get to some restaurants, so such restaurants cannot expect guests to make such a long trip on the off chance that they may find a table. Reservations become a must. Also, the logistics of running a fine-dining restaurant require knowing in advance roughly how many guests to expect.

TAKING RESERVATIONS

Restaurants need to have a reasonable idea of how many diners to expect on a given day. A reservation system can help with staffing, purchasing, menu planning, and cost estimates. Of course, it is impossible to be exact—some customers inexplicably and without notice fail to appear or show up late, while spur-of-the-moment arrivals can increase numbers at unexpected times.

RESERVATIONS FOR EFFICIENCY

The primary goal of the reservationist is to fill the dining room to capacity while staggering the timing of the seatings to ensure the best service from the kitchen and dining room staff. Several people may take reservations, but they may not all understand the complications involved in attaining this goal.

ADVANTAGES OF ACCEPTING RESERVATIONS	DISADVANTAGES OF ACCEPTING RESERVATIONS
Makes some guests feel more comfortable to have a guaranteed table	Requires extra staff to work the reservation desk and make reconfirmation calls
Helps a restaurant estimate customer flow, which is better for kitchen and dining room staffs as well as guests	Creates a no-show problem, which skews sales projections and estimates
Allows more efficient table assignments	Requires extra effort on the part of customers who might otherwise just drop in to a restaurant at the last minute
Allows a restaurant to become familiar with customers' names and eating preferences	
Makes it easier to deal with special requests (birthdays, special menus, allergies, etc.), since they can be handled at the time of reservation rather than after the customer arrives	
Permits logging the phone numbers of guests for future promotions or in case they leave something behind	
Some restaurants use both reservation methods—reservations may be required only for large groups, for example	

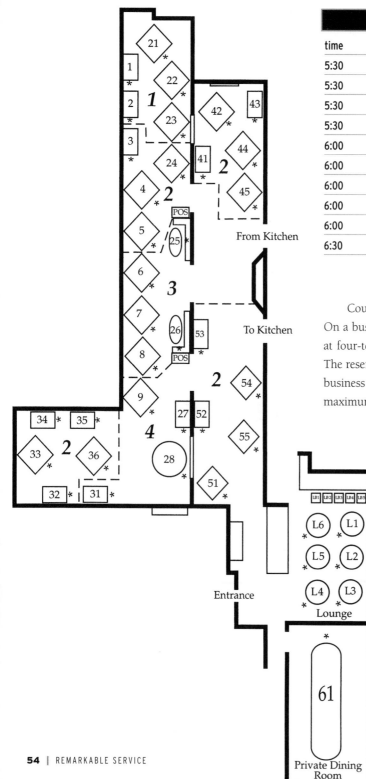

SAMPLE CHART				
time	number	name	phone	table
5:30	2–3			
5:30	2			
5:30	4			
5:30	4			
6:00	2–3			
6:00	2			
6:00	4			
6:00	4			
6:00	6			
6:30	2–3			

Counting chairs is as important as counting tables. On a busy night one does not want to book all deuces at four-tops (except on Valentine's Day, for example). The reservationist should try to accommodate as much business as the staff can efficiently serve. To make the maximum seating capacity clear, it can be helpful to print the times and number of covers in the reservation book in advance.

If this information is written in advance, then any reservationist knows instantly that if he or she takes a reservation for three people at a table for four, revenue has been lost for the restaurant. If, however, three people can be comfortably seated at a deuce, revenue has been increased. Computer systems can be programmed in a similar manner, but the reservationist still needs to be aware of the possibilities for flexibility of the room.

Combining this list with a floor plan of the room and writing in the times the tables are reserved or seated helps keep track of which tables are available (and at what times) for a second or third seating.

Informing the chef of the total number of guests expected does not provide enough information to prepare for the evening's business. For example, a restaurant seats 130 and has 253 reservations. The chef might think that means two seatings—and send part of the staff home early. However, if the restaurant has a theater crowd, there might be 125 guests between 6:00 and 6:30, 50 between 8:00 and 9:30, and 78 between 10:00 and 11:30. A chart tells the kitchen to allow for some prep time before the late-night rush.

TIMING IN THE DINING ROOM

Restaurants, no matter what the type, need to have an idea about how long the average customer stays in order to stagger seatings to achieve a smooth flow in the dining room and kitchen. Many factors need to be taken into account: the menu, the number of courses offered, the style of service, the type of client attracted at different times of day, the ambience of the restaurant.

How long does it take for a couple or a larger group to dine? An hour and a half? Two hours? Three hours? Dining time varies with the type of restaurant. For example, at casual grills or bistros (or for a business lunch crowd), guests could

	deuce	3	4	5	6	7-10	total
TRAFFIC CHART							
6:00	HH I	II	IIII				34
6:30	HH IIII	I	HH IIII	I	II	1-10, 1-7	91
7:00							0
7:30	II		I				8
8:00	II		I		I		14
8:30	III	I	II	I			22
9:00			I				4
9:30	I						2
10:00	HH I						12
10:30	III		II				14
11:00	III		HH				26
11:30	II		II		I	1-8	26
						Total	253

easily be in and out in forty-five to ninety minutes. At some renowned fine-dining shrines around the country, on the other hand, dinner could last all evening.

At casual restaurants, times are shorter, about an hour for a party of two to six, two to two and a half hours for larger groups.

RESERVATION SYSTEMS

Different restaurants have different reservation systems, and many different types of reservation books are available. Since parties do not always arrive together, a common practice is to draw half a circle around the number in the party when some arrive, and complete the circle when the full party is seated. Situations change quickly, so it is best to use pencil in the actual reservation book. Several computer programs are also available to help with this and other aspects of reservation taking.

Cancellations should be noted distinctly in the reservation book so that any staff member can quickly determine which tables are available. The reservationist simply makes a pencil line through the name (so it is still legible) and writes "cxl" or "cncl" in the table number column. It is best to avoid erasing the names, unless that is the only available method to maximize seating.

A seating chart marked with each waiter's designated tables is a useful tool at the front desk. It can assist in seating parties in alternating stations so that one waiter does not get "slammed." Some managers keep the seating chart covered with clear plastic, marking the tables with a china marker and erasing as necessary with a wipe of a paper towel.

On the day of service, the reservation list becomes a waiting list. As guests arrive, the receptionist should take their names and discreetly note some physical characteristic to help remember them later (blue blazer, lapel pin in jacket). Judgmental descriptions should be avoided (looks like a toad, soiled tie), and the receptionist should never give the impression of being confused or disorganized, no matter how harassed.

As a rule, restaurants want to seat to full capacity. Achieving this goal can be difficult if reservations are accepted on the basis of the time requested by the party without considering the number in the party.

For example, a guest calls asking for a reservation for the same evening. The reservationist first asks, "For what time?" and the guest answers, "Seven P.M." If the guest is not immediately informed that no table is available at that time, he will assume that he can be accommodated. If the reservationist then asks how many are in the party, the guest says two, and the reservationist sees that only tables for four are available at seven o'clock, it's too late—there is no graceful way to try to move the time. The party of two has to be seated at a table for four, costing the restaurant fifty percent of the table's potential income.

Once the date of the reservation is established, the reservationist's next question should be "For what time?" followed by "How many in your party?" This sequence gives the reservationist the flexibility to suggest a time when a table for two will be available.

TAKING THE RESERVATION

The reservation procedure should be standardized to eliminate confusion and overlooked items. Use of a checklist by the reservationist guarantees that all essential information is secured. The checklist should include the following:

☐ **DATE AND TIME:** First, note the date and time. If the date and time requested are not available, discuss alternative times. If there is a waiting list, offer that, explaining the procedure to the caller, namely, that if there is a cancellation, he or she will be called. Be sure to ask for a phone number where he or she can be reached.

☐ **NUMBER:** Second, ask how many are in the party. This allows you to consider tables that are available before taking the caller's name, permitting the most efficient use of available seating and maximizing the dining room's capacity.

☐ **SMOKING OR NONSMOKING:** Third, ask if smoking or nonsmoking is preferred. The number of seats in each section is limited, and most guests have strong feelings about this.

☐ **NAME AND TELEPHONE NUMBER:** Fourth, take the caller's name, last name first, then initial. Ask for a daytime telephone number where you can call to reconfirm. (Some restaurants ask guests to reconfirm.)

☐ **SPECIAL REQUESTS:** Always allow the caller to make special requests. Some guests prefer certain tables or servers, have dietary restrictions, or may wish to order a special dessert (such as a birthday cake) or wine. When such requests can be honored, they should be noted here.

☐ **RESERVATION NUMBER:** If a computerized system is used for reservations, be sure to give the guest the reservation number, in case any changes are needed later on. These numbers are also helpful in finding solutions when errors have been made.

☐ **DATE AND TIME OF RESERVATION AND RESERVATIONIST'S NAME:** Note when the reservation was taken and by whom. This information can be useful in reconstructing details that the guest or restaurant may have confused. Leave your initials next to the party's name in case questions arise.

OVERBOOKING

No-shows are always a risk, but overbooking is a big gamble. People have certain expectations about seating, especially at fine-dining and bistro/trattoria restaurants. Restaurants that have a consistent no-show problem may want to accept a few extra customers on the expectation that seats will go unoccupied, but there is always the chance that everybody will show up. That is a nightmare no maître d' wants to experience.

It is unwise to play those odds. The potential damage from turning away guests who have reservations is too great. It is better to book the dining room to capacity and replace any no-shows with last-minute calls or spur-of-the-moment arrivals.

SPECIAL REQUESTS

Guests at any kind of restaurant may ask for a particular table, a high chair, a cake, Champagne, and so on. A guest may have dietary restrictions. These requests should be noted clearly, and management should be informed. They often mean a great deal to the customer, so every effort should be made to accommodate such requests cheerfully. If the request seems especially unusual or difficult, the reservationist should explain to the guest that it will be noted as a request and that every effort will be made to honor the request.

Some restaurants add a special touch to the reservations system by putting out a table card with the customer's name.

Occasionally someone will call with a request for something special to be given to another guest. Unless the customer is well known to the establishment, many misunderstandings can arise in such transactions. A safer approach is to recommend a gift certificate. For a sample order form, see Appendix B (page 258).

SPECIAL SERVER REQUESTS

Guests sometimes ask to be served by a particular waiter. While this is not always possible because of scheduling or station assignments, a good host will try to accommodate such requests. Professional servers often develop their stations as if they were their own businesses—acting as entrepreneurs in promoting their own repeat customers.

SPECIAL TABLE REQUESTS

At fine-dining restaurants and bistros, one of the most common requests, especially from regular customers, is for a particular table. Usually the reservation desk cannot make guarantees on the spot, but the person on duty can note the request for the maître d'. When such a table request is made, the reservationist should immediately check to see if that table has been booked already for the seating time requested or within the average time in which the table is occupied. A good host should try to fulfill such requests whenever possible (especially if given sufficient notice), because of the bond of loyalty they can create between the guest and the restaurant.

Sometimes a particular table has a spectacular view or some other distinguishing and desirable feature. Some restaurant managers, finding that these specific tables are always in demand, add a surcharge when they are reserved. In order to increase the desirability of those tables (and defuse any resentment a guest might feel at being charged an extra fee), the restaurant generally offers something special—perhaps an unusual dessert or bottle of wine—to make the evening more memorable.

"HAPPY BIRTHDAY TO YOU..."

Acknowledging birthdays is an excellent way to engender goodwill with customers. Noting anniversaries and other special events is important, too. With computerized reservation systems, it is possible to have important birthdays and anniversaries pop up automatically. The reservationist should convey the information to the staff. In addition, the front desk should be familiar with taking cake orders, including the quantities needed for different party sizes, prices, and so on.

SEE PAGE 259

Restaurants should establish a cancellation policy for cakes and special requests. This might include a deposit (made by credit card) or a clear written arrangement stating what happens if the reservation is canceled on short notice (such as the day of the party). Some restaurants charge for the entire cake and suggest that the client pick it up. Others sell the cake by the slice to regular customers and charge the person who ordered it a partial fee of 25 to 50 percent of the original cost. For a typical order form, see page 259. It should be written in triplicate, with one copy going to the chef, one to the reservation book, and one to the customer.

An inexpensive but effective way to make a birthday presentation (especially at the last minute) is to pipe "Happy Birthday" and the guest's name on the rim of a plate in meringue, then brown it lightly in the salamander. (Tempered chocolate can be used instead of browned meringue.) The guest can order any dessert, which is served with a candle on the specially prepared plate.

Sparklers should never be used indoors—they are toxic, smelly, and messy as they leave ash and can pose a serious risk of fire or burns.

GROUP RESERVATIONS

In sizable restaurants, a banquet manager may be on staff to book all large parties; this position would be a luxury for most medium-size establishments.

Large groups (10 to 20 percent of a restaurant's seating capacity) require meticulous handling. In order to allow smooth flow in the dining room and the kitchen, consider the following suggestions:

- Recommend that the party arrive early, before the bulk of the other customers, or later, when the crowds are dwindling.

- Try to establish a set menu in advance, one that is satisfactory for both the guests and the staff. The kitchen can handle set menus more quickly and efficiently than à la carte for groups. If the group is small (5 to 10 percent of seating capacity), the menu could have several options per course. If the group is large (more than 15 percent of seating capacity), it is best to offer a fixed menu. Guests will enjoy faster service, too.

- Consult with the guest to preselect wines that complement the meal. Thus an adequate quantity of wines, readily available at the correct temperature at the correct time, is ensured.

- Print a menu for each guest.

- Establish a plan for gratuities and payment of the check. Gratuities for large groups range from 15 to 20 percent.

- It is advisable to take a deposit of at least 25 to 50 percent when the reservation is made. Some restaurants require payment in full in advance; others divide the bill into three equal payments spread out from the time of the reservation to the completion of the event. This practice protects the restaurant in the event that some guests do not show up. The number of guests in the group must be reconfirmed the day of the party. There could be a per-person charge for no-shows. All terms should be in the contract or written agreement.

Juggling reservations for a large group along with normal reservations can be a complex matter. The clearer the details beforehand, the more enjoyable the experience for all. When booking large groups, remember that they tend to linger longer (possibly overlapping into a second seating), take up a number of tables, often disturb other guests, and generally take longer to be served cocktails, order (if they have a choice), and eat. On the other hand, they often spend more, buying additional bottles of wine or dessert wine. Groups may also introduce your restaurant to new guests, who could become regulars—which is one reason why guests in a group should be treated with the same care and attention as individual guests.

Some holidays, notably Easter, Mother's Day, Thanksgiving, and New Year's Eve, require some additional planning. Many restaurants resort to a simple prix fixe menu with set seatings, while others require a more detailed reservation than usual, essentially a contract (see page 260).

How to Deal with No-Shows and the Chronically Late

Restaurants can make reservations for guests, but they cannot force them to show up at the restaurant on time—or at all. No-shows and late arrivals are frustrating, and they can be very costly to a restaurant. What can a restaurant do?

RECONFIRMING RESERVATIONS

Many restaurants try to minimize no-shows and latecomers by reconfirming reservations on the appointed day. A staff member might begin working the phones in the afternoon, calling all reserved customers to ask if they still intend to come. This may help somewhat, although even reconfirmed reservations have been known to result in no-shows. Jean-Jacques Rachou, chef and owner of La Côte Basque in Manhattan, for example, says that on Saturday night his restaurant can have a no-show rate of more than 30 percent. "And these are people we have called at home just hours before," he adds.

Some maître d's contend that many no-shows are caused by inept reservation taking. For example, if a guest wants to come at 8 P.M. and is offered only 9 P.M. or 9:30 P.M., the chances of a no-show rise dramatically. A reservationist should feel out the customer to determine if there might be another solution, even dining in the cocktail lounge (if there are tables) or at the bar itself. If a customer reluctantly accepts an unsatisfactory reservation, it is almost certain that he or she will start calling other restaurants to see if something better is available—and may forget to call back to cancel.

Sometimes guests are no-shows without realizing it, through no fault of their own. Their reservation may have been written on the wrong day, for instance. If reservations have not been confirmed a day ahead, it is good practice to call no-shows the next day. By being asked if the restaurant has made a mistake, the guests do not feel guilty but gain an appreciation for the importance of reservations. Such guests will probably be more considerate about cancellations in the future.

André Soltner, former chef and owner of the famed Lutèce, believes that many diners make reservations weeks in advance at four or five top restaurants, then decide at the last minute where they want to go, without notifying the other restaurants. "What is really bad," Mr. Soltner says, "is when a customer calls many times trying to get a reservation on a fully booked night only to arrive and see empty tables in the room. The customer gets angry and thinks I am playing games with him, when the empty tables could be a result of latecomers or no-shows. It really makes me feel stupid."

Mr. Soltner's colleagues still chuckle over the time several years ago when he became enraged by a man who failed to honor a reservation for eight on a Saturday night. Mr. Soltner called him at 4 A.M. and said: "Sir, this is the owner of Lutèce. We are still waiting for you."

DEPOSITS

The best insurance against no-shows is a deposit, and many restaurants now require deposits for major holidays, special events, and large groups. On the other hand, such deposits can result in bookkeeping headaches for restaurant operators—aside from the ill will they may create. Consequently, a manager may prefer to persuade diners to cancel reservations at least an hour in advance so that the restaurant has a chance to fill the vacancy. That takes some finesse.

Another approach used by some restaurants is a reservation contract. The guest receives, then fills out and returns, a contract that includes date, time, number in party, and all credit card information. Some restaurants even require photocopies of both sides of the guest's credit card.

Some restaurateurs find these practices too confrontational and decline to try them. Gordon Sinclair, owner of Gordon's in Chicago, has used a simpler, less alienating approach. He has his reservationists ask, "Will you agree to call us if you change your plans?" when taking reservations. This phrasing involves the guest rather than threatening some form of retaliation. It still manages the situation, but the guest feels respected, not suspected.

In the late 1980s a group of restaurants around the country that had been hurt by no-shows asked American Express if it could help with the problem. In the early 1990s the company began a program called the Guaranteed Restaurant Reservations Program. Essentially, clients are asked to use their American Express credit cards to guarantee reservations for large groups or holidays (the two worst no-show situations). The program is now being offered to restaurants that accept American Express cards.

When a customer calls to reserve a table of ten, for example, the restaurant asks for the person's full name, American Express billing address, card number, and expiration date. Clients are told that they do not have to reconfirm but that if they decide to cancel, they must do so at some specified time before their reservation. If a party fails to show up under the American Express program, within forty-eight hours a per-person charge is added to the American Express account ($10 in some areas of the country, $25 in others). "Not all customers are actually charged," says Deborah Freundlich, a spokesperson for the American Express program, "but having that card number is amazingly motivating.

"Large tables are the biggest problem for restaurants," Ms. Freundlich adds. "If someone doesn't show up, it affects the whole layout of the dining room."

Restaurateurs who use the program report that it drastically reduces no-shows. American Express says that customers generally go along with it. Only about 10 percent refuse, the company reports.

Gordon Sinclair notes that when a guest is asked for a credit card number to secure a table, precise language is important. "You can't pause when you are asking, because the client might start thinking about it. For example, you say, 'We need a credit card to guarantee your table. What credit card would you like to use?' If you pause in the middle, the client might start asking questions about the policy. Don't give them a chance to demur."

According to Henny Santo, owner of Sign of the Dove, in Manhattan, his restaurant has a no-show rate of about 15 percent. "You really can't do much about people who have not put down any kind of deposit. With the American Express program where we take a credit card number, the no-show rate is zero. There is something about getting a credit card number—even if you are not going to use it—that makes people at least call to cancel."

Priscilla Martel, who for thirteen years owned and ran the dining room at Restaurant du Village, a small country restaurant in Chester, Connecticut, says that she had a more personal relationship with customers, and no-shows were far less frequent than elsewhere. "It can happen, but not usually with the local people who are the bulk of our clients. On the other hand, a small restaurant [forty-five seats] does not have the flexibility to protect itself by overbooking slightly."

Asking guests to secure their reservation with a credit card or to confirm a reservation on the day of their visit may seem a simple matter, but it is often perceived as an inconvenience by the guests. A friendlier, less confrontational method is for the

A resource book for the reservationist to answer guests' questions should be accessible at the reception desk and placed near any phones used to take reservations. This should be updated on a monthly basis. Information might include:

- Description of the cuisine
- Wine and beverage information
- Price range of the menu
- Accepted methods of payment
- Children's menu
- Chef's name
- Maître d's name
- Hours of operation
- Handicapped facilities
- Guest dress code
- Directions to the restaurant from various areas
- Parking facilities
- Public transportation
- Taxi phone numbers
- Emergency phone numbers (police, fire department, EMT)
- Area hotel accommodations
- Area restaurants
- Special events in the area
- Cake order forms
- Incident report forms
- A log of problems encountered, including complaints, accidents, food-borne illness and maintenance problems (ServSafe forms)

restaurant to call beforehand to confirm the reservation. This may not be necessary for regular customers, who are more likely to call in the event of a cancellation.

No single method for preventing no-shows is ideal for all restaurants or all guests. Each manager must use judgment and tact and consider the record of no-shows in a particular situation when deciding on the best approach.

The Reception Desk

As a matter of routine, the reception desk should be equipped with a reservation book, a seating chart, copies of the menu and wine list, a backup telephone answering machine, a hospitality handbook, an up-to-date telephone directory and maps (for answering customer questions), public transportation maps and schedules (if applicable), plenty of pens and pencils (constantly disappearing in dining rooms), and employee home phone numbers. (Home phone numbers should never be given out. If requested, call the employee and have him or her call back.)

Not essential but thoughtful things to have at (or near) the reception desk are giveaway maps of the area (which can be obtained at no cost from the chamber of commerce), inexpensive umbrellas that can be given to guests in the event of an unexpected downpour, and a wheelchair.

In addition, the front desk should have a list with the manager's name, the number of waiters on duty, and the number of people working in the kitchen. (In the event of an emergency, the fire department needs to know how many people are in the building.)

IF THE SYSTEM CRASHES

Sometimes it seems as if Murphy's Law was written specifically for restaurants, where mishaps are legendary. The introduction of computers gave Murphy an even more powerful opportunity to wreak havoc. In the event of a power failure (or any other crash of the restaurant's point-of-sale system) an emergency backup system should be kept at the reservation desk. This might include a flashlight and extra candles, a printed copy of the reservation list, sequentially numbered guest checks, a sales tax chart, a battery-powered calculator, backup batteries, and a manual credit card machine with a supply of forms.

LOGBOOK

A valuable tool for comparing business from season to season and from year to year is a logbook that records the number of covers, seating times, and any special problems. A good logbook enables management to look at holiday experiences the year before, for example, to determine volume, peak seating times, and other considerations to plan better for the current year.

The maître d' should make daily entries in the reservation log detailing the manager on duty, the expected number of covers, the final number of covers, the number of waiters and kitchen crew, lost and found items, sundry incidents and names of people involved, even weather conditions. Weather is one of the biggest reasons guests are late or fail to show up. The previous year's data can be noted in the current logbook for quick comparison.

LOOKING GOOD

The receptionist/host is also responsible for maintaining presentable menus and wine lists. Stained, crumpled, or worn menus send an undesired signal to the guests. They might think, "If the menus look this bad, what must the kitchen look like?"

Rest rooms should be checked every half hour by one of the front-door personnel or management. The cleanliness of rest rooms is always a high-priority item among respondents in restaurant surveys. Judging the cleanliness and neatness of the rest rooms should not be left solely to the discretion of a porter or bus person.

THINGS TO DO AT THE RECEPTION DESK	THINGS NOT TO DO AT THE RECEPTION DESK
Make a good first and last impression; look happy	Chew gum, eat or drink, slouch, read the newspaper, or do crossword puzzles
Answer the phone within three rings	Make nonessential personal calls or engage in unnecessary chitchat with the staff
Greet guests within thirty seconds of their arrival—make eye contact with them, thank them for coming, and repeat the guests' names	Stare at the reservation book rather than looking at the guests when they arrive, or hide behind the desk or use it as a barrier
Recognize regular guests and become familiar with guests' names, especially those of regular guests	Assume that the guests approaching the reservation desk are—or are not—with each other
Pay attention to guests who are waiting for a table—explain why they are waiting and keep them updated as to the status	Leave the desk
Scan the room for problems and alert appropriate staff	Appear stressed or hassled to the guests
Continually review the reservation plan and status of tables for the next seating, making every attempt to maximize seating while maintaining even service	

GREETING ARRIVING CUSTOMERS

Unlike the greeting on the phone, the greeting at the door should not be standardized, or it can begin to sound insincere (especially if a guest hears the same greeting addressed to other guests). There should be several ways to welcome the guests, usually starting with something along the lines of "Good evening, Mrs. Kinder, welcome to American Bounty." While the greeting should vary slightly from guest to guest, it should always include the guest's name if known.

The guests' reception is more pleasant if it includes an offer to take coats, hats, umbrellas, or shopping bags, rather than sending the guests to the checkroom. The coats should be handed to the coat check person in exchange for the claim check. This way the guests don't have to wait for their coats to be hung up. The claim checks should be given to the coat's owner or to the men of the party, unless some other preference is indicated.

If the receptionist doesn't recognize the guest, asking "What was the name of the reservation?" is friendlier than "Did you have a reservation?" If no reservation was made and seating is available, the guest's name should be asked and written in the reservation book.

People have names, and they should be used. Referring to customers as "the table of four" is rude, as is referring to people who arrive unannounced as "walk-ins." The guest's name should be written down in the reservation book. To keep track of these guests, "NR" (for "no reservation") rather than "WI" (for "walk-in") should be noted. This code may help the staff avoid using the term "walk-ins."

Take the time to look at a party's name. Always look into the guest's eyes; do not stare at the reservation book.

If, when reservations are not necessary, three people walk up to the reservation desk, never assume that they are a party of three. They could be three singles, two separate parties, or even the first half of a party of six. Greet them and ask, "How many in your party?"

It is fine to chat a little with arriving customers if they initiate it, but avoid getting into long conversations that could throw off the timing of their meal and that of the dining room.

HONORING RESERVATIONS

Reservations work both ways. Just as a restaurant expects customers to show up on time for a reserved table, so do guests expect the restaurant to have their table ready on time.

This, unfortunately, is not always possible. The unpredictability of customer flow inevitably leads to occasional logjams, but they should be the exception, not the rule. In general, customers are very understanding about delays if they are treated with respect and straightforwardness.

POLICIES FOR SEATING DELAYS		
Name	**Restaurant**	**Policy**
Priscilla Martel, former owner	Restaurant du Village, Chester, Connecticut	20 minutes, buy drink
Gordon Sinclair, owner	Gordon's, Chicago	20 minutes, bring tidbits; intervene every 5 minutes
Michael de Maria, chef/partner	Lon's at the Hermosa Inn, Phoenix	15 minutes, apology; 20 minutes, complimentary food
Christine Splichal, owner	Patina, Los Angeles	15 minutes, apology and tidbit

The worst thing a restaurant can do is to tell customers half-truths, such as the all-too-familiar "It will just be a minute." It is always better to tell guests that the dining room is backed up, apologize, and offer drinks (where legal) or some sort of snack while they wait. Whereas a lack of information is annoying, candor can do wonders.

How long can a restaurant expect customers to wait for a reserved table before making some sort of amends? Ten minutes? Fifteen minutes? We asked a cross section of owners, managers, and maître d's the following question: "Customers arrive on time for a reserved table at, say, 8 P.M. The table is not ready. How long do you think a customer can wait before management should intervene with an apology, a free drink, or tidbits?" (See table on page 67.)

Seating

Each restaurant should have a predetermined plan for seating guests. The benefits of such a plan are an efficient distribution of guests throughout the dining room and a balanced workload for the wait staff. Management should develop a turn sheet for each station, including the number of tables and covers. By paying attention to the distribution of seated guests in the dining room, the perception is created that the room is nicely filled, while a comfortable amount of physical space is provided for each guest's meal. The wait staff is also able to prepare each table for arriving guests while minimally disturbing nearby guests; the staff have a balanced workload without getting slammed. Seating in bistro and fine-dining restaurants is usually either fixed seating or continuous seating.

FIXED SEATING
Fixed seating is generally used by restaurants that have relatively long seatings, say, two hours or more. Fixed seatings could be at 6 P.M., 8 P.M., and 10 P.M. This is ideal for prix fixe menus because the kitchen is able to calculate the serving time with more precision. The slower-paced meal has less turnover in the dining room but often yields higher check averages. Fixed seatings also allow the kitchen to pace itself better, especially if the menu is extensive or complex.

CONTINUOUS SEATING
Continuous seating tends to work best for fluid, high-volume establishments, such as bistros, where meals are shorter. Reservations might be taken for one table in each station every fifteen minutes. This prevents orders from crashing down on any one

server (or the kitchen) all at once. Continuous seating assumes that guests respect reservation times and orders are taken promptly and accurately. Lower check averages can be compensated for by higher volume.

The continuous-flow system allows restaurants to accept guests without reservations, provided there are empty tables. It is not a good idea to give away a table if the party is only a few minutes late. It is preferable to establish a minimum time after which to give away a reserved table, taking into account weather conditions, traffic, difficulty of finding the restaurant, and how well the guest is known. The time might range from twenty minutes to half an hour or more. For a regular guest, it might be better to lose a table for a night rather than risk losing a valuable customer.

If guests arrive, say, half an hour late for their reservation and their table has been given away, it is best to inform them of the situation and make every effort to seat them as soon as possible. Some guests are content to dine at the bar, especially if that helps them catch a movie or theater curtain. Other situations might call for offering a free cocktail, snacks at the bar, or a bottle of wine with dinner.

ACCOMMODATING THE VIP CUSTOMER

Here are some tips:

- Rita Jammet, co-owner of La Caravelle, Manhattan: "If a good customer calls two hours before service on Saturday, that's just like walking in the door for us. We try to do everything we can to accommodate them, but if we can't, it's best to be honest and not have them come in and wait."

- Dominique Simon, maître d' at Bouley Bakery, Manhattan: "I always keep two tables set aside for circumstances like that. We can do that with a big dining room, and it avoids many problems."

- Henny Santo, owner of Sign of the Dove, Manhattan: "We have 145 seats, so I can usually juggle things around even on a busy night. But you should always tell the customer that there is a possibility there will be a wait. The worst thing you can do is make a promise to a customer that you can't fill."

THE VIP GUEST

Another situation calling for maximum tact and flexibility is when VIP guests—whether regulars, celebrities, or investors—show up unexpectedly without reservations. It is not easy for a maître d' to tell someone such as Bill Cosby or Martha Stewart to wait at the bar until a table frees up. Besides, most restaurateurs want to have celebrities in the dining room—they do wonders for a restaurant's popularity.

THEIR TABLE IS READY, BUT WHERE ARE THEY?

In fine-dining restaurants, employees cannot walk around the bar bellowing, "Schmidt party!" They need to take the time to find out who the guests are and politely inform them that their table is ready. Some large restaurants give beepers to customers so they can be summoned when their table is ready.

When several guests are going to be dining together, they commonly arrive separately. This means that someone will always be left waiting for someone else to arrive. The reservation book can help keep track of these split parties, but what to do with them while they wait?

Some restaurants have found it necessary—especially on busy nights—to ask guests to wait until the party is complete before being seated. Guests often get upset, however, and feel uncomfortable waiting at the bar. Most people prefer to be seated at the table to wait for the rest of the party. This can be costly to the restaurant when, for example, only six members of a party of eight (who must be seated at two four-tops pushed together) arrive at the restaurant. At the last minute, the remaining couple calls to cancel. Now there are only six people, who could easily have been seated at one table for six, saving the restaurant the lost revenue from two covers.

WAITING LINES

What about people who have to stand on line because their tables are not yet ready? The usual practice is to send them to the cocktail lounge, although some places merely leave them standing by the coatroom. Tavern on the Green, in Manhattan, built an elaborate and elegant tent for those "who have to sit and wait." The restaurant tried to make the mere act of waiting a pleasurable experience.

According to Disney precepts, people do not mind waiting on line if they are entertained and kept informed while waiting. Some guests will want to see menus so that they can reduce the time in making decisions once they are seated. Andrea Terry of Lobster Roll, Inc., a casual seafood restaurant on Long Island, New York, has a game plan prepared for whenever guests have to wait more than forty-five minutes. The person responsible for the front door goes to the kitchen to "drop the torpedo." Translated, the order means "Prepare some finger food from the appetizer menu to be passed out to the guests in the waiting line." This approach keeps the guests happy and banishes any thought of abandoning the wait in favor of another, less crowded restaurant. Since Lobster Roll is in a family resort area, Ms. Terry also keeps toys and coloring books on hand to distract the children. She also offers a dog biscuit and a bowl of water to the guests' dogs, back at their cars.

Graycliff in Nassau, the Bahamas, provides menus to guests while they wait in the lounge, and also takes orders there. By the time the guests are seated, their meals are ready, and they are served immediately.

SEATING GUESTS

Assuming that guests have not been kept waiting, the host should ask them if they are ready to be seated—they may want to stop at the bar first. This may not always be desirable, especially if a party is late. The host may politely nudge them toward their table by saying, "We don't want you to be rushed, so maybe you could have your cocktails at the table."

Guests should also be asked if they prefer smoking or nonsmoking areas, if this has not already been ascertained at the time the reservation was made. Different states and municipalities have different laws regarding smoking in restaurants. It is imperative that the restaurant know every nuance of the law; the customers (both smoking and nonsmoking) certainly will.

The host should lead the guests to the table, rather than offering the guests a choice. In the more formal past, men always seated the women in their party by pulling out their chairs. Today the task is usually performed by the maître d' in fine-dining restaurants and by the floor manager in bistros. Actually, who seats the guests is not all that important, so long as there is a host to take care of them from the moment they arrive. Women are generally seated with their backs to the wall, facing the dining room. Men may then face the women, with their backs to the dining room.

If guests bring their coats to the table, the host should repeat the offer to check the coats for them. This is both gracious and practical: Coats draped over the backs of chairs can cause waiters to trip while carrying trays, or risk spilling things on the coats.

If there seems to be a problem with the seating arrangement, ask if the table is satisfactory. Most problems with table arrangements can be worked out by the guests, but the maître d' should remain nearby to help with reseating. If the guests request another table, they should remain at the table where they were seated while the maître d' checks the reservation book to determine if another table is available.

Once the guests are seated, menu presentation can begin. Some restaurants like to get something on the table as soon as possible, either a drink, bread, or a complimentary tidbit, known as an amuse-bouche or amuse-gueule. Other restaurants prefer to take the order before any food is offered in order to sell more.

Conclusion

The front door, including the reservation process, the greeting and the seating, is where guests are welcomed into the restaurant. It is one of the most critical moments for the host-guest relationship. It is where first impressions are made, where the nature of the dining experience is first hinted at, and where the warmth of the guests' relationship with the restaurant is established.

CHAPTER five

Getting Ready
for Service

The first step toward becoming a dining room professional is to pay conscientious attention to mise en place, a French phrase that means literally "put into place." Whether in the kitchen or in the dining room, mise en place means the organization and completion of all the duties and tasks that must be performed ahead of time to carry out the job at hand smoothly and efficiently. In the kitchen, all advance preparation must be done before cooking begins; in the dining room, all flatware and glassware must be on the table or close by before the food or beverage is served.

A restaurant's workday can be very long, so many restaurants schedule opening and closing waiters; this helps to maintain energy levels as well as to avoid the cost of overtime pay. The two-shift system puts even more emphasis than usual on teamwork. The closing or late waiters rely on the work of the opening waiters, and they in turn depend on the work of the closing waiters. The opening dining room crew sets up the dining room and makes sure that everything used for service is clean or polished, readily available and easily accessible, and in ample supply. Once service begins, personnel must be able to devote full attention to the immediate demands of serving the guests. Time cannot be spent preparing equipment and supplies that could have been organized and made ready earlier. Particular tasks to be performed as part of the opening mise en place are:

Maître d'

- Check reservation book.
- Discuss cover count and pattern flow with chef.
- Communicate any special requests to the chef and staff.
- Explain seating requirements to the floor staff.
- Adjust temperature, lighting, and music.

Service Staff

- Arrange tables and chairs according to reservations.
- Maintain proper space between tables.
- Repair any wobbly tables.
- Wipe tables and counters clean.
- Lay tablecloths or set place mats.
- Fold napkins for tables, resetting, and serviettes.
- Polish any serviceware, holloware, flatware, china, and glasses.
- Fill and wipe any condiments, salt and pepper, etc.
- Set the tables.
- Stock side stands.
- Fill wine buckets (just prior to service).
- Prep any underliners.
- Prep decrumbing plates, placing napkin and crumber with appropriate plate.
- Prepare STP (silverware transport plates).
- Prepare the coffee/tea area.
- Stock dupe pads or order-taking forms.
- Stock check printer paper.
- Check supply of staples (for stapling credit card vouchers and so on).

The duties of the closing dining room crew should be coordinated with the responsibilities of the opening crew. The opening crew sets up the dining room and relies upon the closing crew to clean up the dining room and restock it for the next day. Duties of the closing crew might include:

- Return all foodstuffs to the kitchen.
- Clear tables.
- Stack chairs.
- Clean, refill, and refrigerate condiment containers as necessary.
- Replenish china, glassware, and flatware.
- Clean shelves and trays.
- Clean pantry reach-in.
- Adjust lighting and dining room temperature.

Many restaurants use opening and closing checklists for early or late waiters or particular station assignments. Among the items included on such a list are:

- Chairs
- China
- Coffee equipment
- Condiments
- Creamers
- Displays
- Flatware and holloware
- Floor
- Garbage
- Glasses
- Guéridons or side tables
- Linen
- Menus
- Pantry
- Pitchers
- Reach-in
- Refrigerator
- Side stands
- Soup cart
- Tables
- Temperature of dining room
- Trays
- Tray stands
- Trolleys (voitures)

Maîtres d's or dining room managers come from the ranks of the wait staff. In such positions, they often influence purchases that make the dining experience special for guests in several ways. Good servers notice which wares work well in the dining room and which do not, and what they observe can be very useful information. The following are guidelines for the selection of items used in the dining room.

Table linen as we know it is the result of centuries of evolution. Napkins were used as early as Roman times. Guests in ancient Rome brought their own napkins, tying one under the chin and keeping another nearby for wiping fingers. Dining tended to be messy, since forks were not yet used.

By the Middle Ages full tablecloths were common (before that small tablecloths were used, but only to cover the host's place). At large banquets the tablecloth would be changed several times. It was not long before the runner, a long, narrow strip of linen laid along the edge of the table, was introduced. The runner was used by guests to wipe their fingers and mouths. Later came the *touaille*, a roller-type towel affixed to the wall and used by several diners.

In the sixteenth century the individual napkin, not seen since Roman times, came back into fashion. At first the napkin was draped over the left arm, but when large, starched ruff collars came into style, the napkin was tied around the neck to prevent soiling the collar. As an insignia of the station, the maitre d'hôtel carried a napkin rolled under an epaulet on his left shoulder.

The royal forks (when they came into use) and knives were often wrapped in a napkin and carried in a *nef*, or boat. The *serviette*, as the napkin was called, was changed at each course of the meal and was sometimes scented with perfume.

Linen Selection

Until modern times tablecloths and napkins were made of linen, a natural fiber produced from flax. Today manmade fibers are often substituted for or combined with natural ones. Many tablecloths are made of a blend of polyester and cotton. The term *linen*, however, still applies in a general sense to all fabrics used at or on the table (table linen).

Several aspects should be considered in the selection of a fabric for the tabletop. The style and decor of the dining room will dictate the color, pattern, closeness of weave, and texture chosen. The serviceability of the fabric is another important consideration. Can it be easily mended? Will the edges soon become frayed? The fabric should be both attractive and economically suitable. The vendor should be prepared to show a sample that has been laundered several times. Poor-quality cotton napkins can leave lint on the guests. Polyester can pill, is less absorbent, and does not have the high-quality feel of cotton. It also slides off the lap and falls to the floor. But it is less expensive and more durable, and it resists wrinkling.

Colored or patterned cloths are often selected for decorative purposes. While colored cloths generally show less spotting, they are more difficult to launder, repair, and replace than white cloths. In addition, colored cloths may fade and create an uneven look in the dining room. When there is a need for color or contrast, a colored or textured cloth is often used over a white undercloth. Another alternative is to use place mats or colored napkins on top of a white tablecloth. Restaurants that serve fine wines should avoid colored cloths; the color of the wine is best viewed against a white background.

Laundering linens is a serious expense for a restaurant, so it makes sense to take care in the handling and storage of clean linens. A covered shelf, set at chest height, helps prevent linens from becoming soiled before use. Sorting linens carefully by size eliminates the need for unnecessary handling. Common sense dictates that liquids should never be stored above clean linens.

NAPKINS

Paper napkins are usually used only when there is no tablecloth. Paper napkins can be left in a dispenser or at the left of the place setting. For sanitary reasons flatware should be placed upon the paper napkin rather than on the bare surface of the table or counter. If no place mat is used, guests should be provided with additional napkins for their laps, so that flatware need not rest upon a bare surface.

Cloth napkins can be placed in several different places; most often they are in the middle of the place setting, directly in front of the guest, or to the left of the fork and one inch from the edge of the table.

Every restaurant has its own guidelines for the exact placement of napkins and flatware, depending upon the style of service and the complexity of settings. Some may have settings placed as close as a finger, or a crumber's, width from the edge of the table; others allow more space.

Cloth napkins are usually folded in the style of the house. There are countless napkin folds. The choice depends on the ambience and decor of the dining room, compatibility with the other tabletop items, the skill of the staff, labor costs, and the time available to actually do the folding. Generally speaking, the trend is toward simple table settings that do not go with the involved and elaborate folds of the past. Uncomplicated folds take less time and create a mood of simple elegance. Complicated folds involve extra handling and may be perceived as being less sanitary.

Napkins are usually delivered to the restaurant already folded in half or in quarters; the existing creases should be incorporated into the folded design. Doing so saves time and eliminates the need to work around the existing crease. If possible, choose a fold that will avoid exposing the edges of the napkin; after repeated use, the edges of cloth napkins tend to become uneven, and the stitching around the edges can be unsightly.

Napkin folds are also used for ornamentation in the dining room. Napkins can be folded to create a pocket for dinner rolls, bread, or a small bouquet of flowers. This style is known as à la serviette. A common ornamental fold for water pitcher underliners is the artichoke fold.

Silverware Pocket

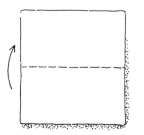

1. Fold the bottom edge up to the top edge.

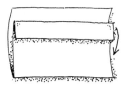

2. Fold the front layer (of the two top layers) down to form a hem.

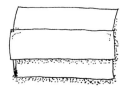

3. Fold the hem down along its bottom edge.

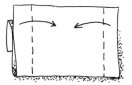

4. Hold the band that runs across the center of the napkin in place, and turn the napkin over to the back side. Fold the side edges of the napkin in to meet at the center.

5. The edges have been folded.

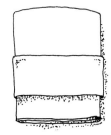

6. Flip the napkin over.

Bird-of-Paradise

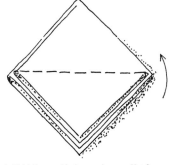

1. Fold the napkin in quarters so the free corners are at the bottom (as shown). Then fold in half to form a triangle with the free corners on top.

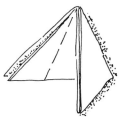

2. Hold your finger in the top corner as you fold first the right side (as shown), then the left side, to the center.

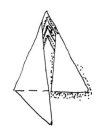

3. Fold the lower points underneath (one side shown here).

4. Fold the triangle in half by bringing the left side under the right side. The center fold will open slightly. Place the napkin so the corner points are on top. Holding the broad end of the napkin with one hand, pull up the four corner points to form petals (as shown).

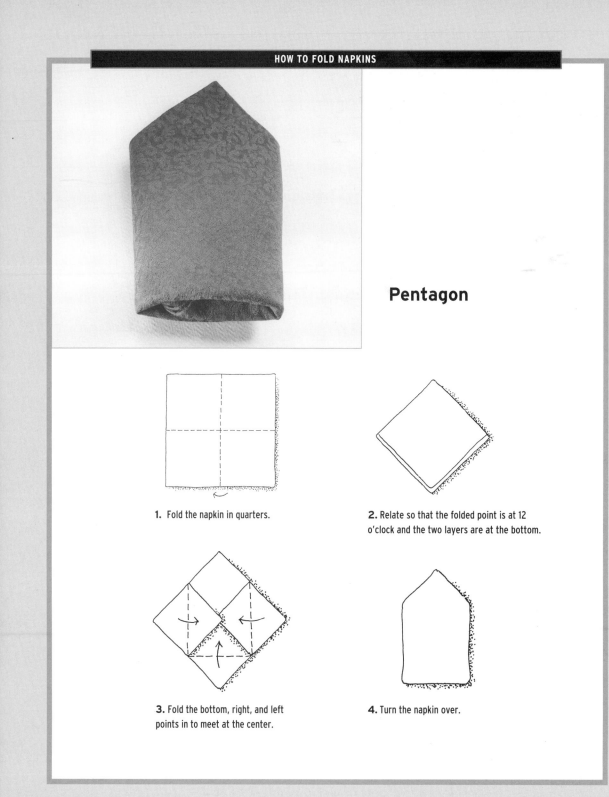

Pentagon

1. Fold the napkin in quarters.

2. Relate so that the folded point is at 12 o'clock and the two layers are at the bottom.

3. Fold the bottom, right, and left points in to meet at the center.

4. Turn the napkin over.

Tuxedo

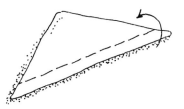

1. Fold the napkin into a triangle. Fold the lower edge up approximately 1 inch.

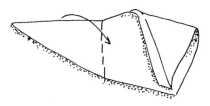

2. Turn then napkin over and then fold the left corner down to the middle.

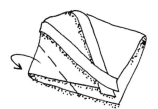

3. Fold the right corner down to the middle, leaving about 3 inches open at the top.

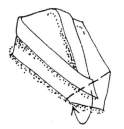

4. Fold both sides back to create the napkin shape shown.

5. Finish by folding the lower portion back.

Artichoke

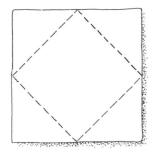

1. Fold the corners of the napkin to the center.

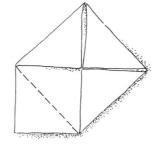

2. Bring the new corners to the center.

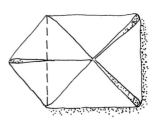

3. Turn the napkin over and fold the corners to the center.

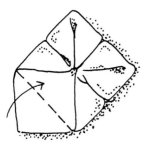

4. Fold corners in to center.

5. Place a glass in the center of the napkin to anchor it. Hold it firmly with one hand as you pull out each of the corners from beneath.

6. Give each corner a slight tug to make it stand up. Pull the small corners of the napkin from underneath to create a leaf effect.

SILENCE CLOTH

A molleton or silence cloth is often used under the tablecloth to cushion the noise of plates and cutlery being placed on the table during service. Some tables have permanent cushioning on the tabletop to serve as a silencer. A second tablecloth or a thin piece of foam rubber or felt can be used as a silence cloth. Some fine-dining restaurants use padding and an underlay or overlay. Besides preventing noise, a silence cloth protects the tabletop, soaks up spills, and prevents the top cloth from sliding. If there are no spills, the silence cloth can be used for several seatings.

TABLECLOTHS

All tablecloths must be inspected before being used in the dining room. Any cloths found to be soiled, stained, frayed, or torn should be delivered to the supervisor, who should contact the supplier for appropriate credit. Before laying a tablecloth, certain preparations have to be made:

- [ ] Set up the dining room. Arrange the tables and chairs in an orderly, symmetric pattern according to the day's reservations. Make sure to leave ample aisle space for service.

- [ ] Clean the tabletops.

- [ ] Level the tables by turning screw glides on the base of adjustable tables, tightening the center bolt of pedestal tables, or inserting pieces of cork or plastic wedges under the legs of nonadjustable tables. Never use matchbooks or wadded napkins; they offer only temporary relief, are unsightly, and give the dining room an unprofessional appearance.

- [ ] Make sure there are no loose nails or splinters that might catch or snag the tablecloth.

- [ ] Spread and secure the silence cloth or undercloth. Smooth any creases and make sure the cloths are centered.

- [ ] Clothe Statler tables—square four-tops that can be opened to round six-to-eight-tops—with this possible conversion in mind; the table should always remain covered, even when opened during service. Select a tablecloth that is appropriate for the fully opened size of the table; the drop (the distance the cloth hangs over the edge of the table) should extend to a point just even with the seat of the chair. Align the tablecloth so that the table can be converted back to a four-top, if needed, without having to re-lay the tablecloth.

The center crease of all tablecloths in the dining room should point up and run in the same direction, generally toward the entrance. This small detail gives an organized look to the room, especially when the tables are not occupied. The linen company should press the tablecloth so that the hem is hidden. When a tablecloth becomes soiled during service, it should be changed. It should never be shaken out in the dining room. This is unsanitary and indicates poor training.

1. Position yourself so that you have seat number one to your right or left side. Pull the fresh, folded tablecloth open, and lay it across the table. The cloth should be opened upward, toward you, with the hems positioned at the bottom.

2. Hold the top piece of the cloth and the center crease between your middle and index fingers, and the first hem between your index finger and thumb.

3. Raise the two layers of the cloth as previously indicated. There should still be one layer of the cloth on the table unattached.

4. Picking up the cloth by the center crease and first hem, flick the wrist away from you. In doing so, you will place the bottom, unattached layer of cloth so that it is hanging over the opposite side of the table from where you are standing.

5. Pull the remaining hem (bottom) toward you while releasing the center crease.

6. The tablecloth will unfold with the center crease pointing upward.

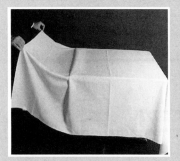

7. Straighten and center the cloth. The cloth should land evenly front to back and side to side; the hem should be rolled under, not exposed.

8. Adjust and straighten to make certain the sides are even.

1. Position yourself at the table so that you have seat number one to your left or right side. Hold a clean, folded tablecloth so that the thick rolled edges are on top (hems are on the bottom).

2. Pull the clean cloth open as you would an accordion.

3. Holding the clean cloth between your fourth and fifth fingers, reach down to pick up the corners of the soiled cloth between your thumb, index, and middle finger.

4. Pull the soiled cloth up and towards you until the far hem (of the soiled cloth) is at the edge of the table.

5. Now lower the partially open clean cloth onto the table. At this point, if the cloths were opened correctly, the hems of the fresh cloth should be on the bottom, center crease on top.

6. Grasp the top layer of cloth (the center crease) with your thumb and index finger; meanwhile, the next layer of cloth is held between your index finger and middle finger.

7. Raise these two layers of clean cloth up and gently flick the bottom layer of the cloth so that it hangs over the far edge of the table. Rest the partially opened cloth on the table so that it covers about one third of the table.

8. Pinch the hem of the clean cloth and soiled cloth together. Pull back both cloths towards you.

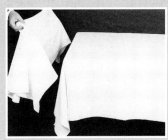

9. When the center crease of the fresh cloth reaches the middle, release it and continue to pull the bottom cloth. The clean cloth should be in place—center crease pointing upward, hems rolled under, all sides hanging evenly. The soiled cloth should be in your hands.

During service, bare tabletops should never be exposed. Some places use an underlay and a silence cloth to avoid completely stripping the table when it is time to replace the tablecloth. However, an underlay and silence cloth make it more difficult to replace the top cloth in a smooth manner.

SKIRTING

Table skirts are used to hide table legs and make a table more presentable. A large dining room that does extensive catering or one that sets up areas for a continental breakfast may have skirting available.

The top edge of table skirts is usually backed with Velcro clips with corresponding Velcro tabs, which are placed on the table edge. When not in use, the clips should be kept in a special container for safekeeping. The skirts should be kept on special hangers that grasp the Velcro edge, to prevent the formation of creases that result from folding.

Since skirt rentals are expensive, as are dry cleaning bills, many restaurants make inexpensive temporary skirts from tablecloths.

STANDARD TABLE AND TABLECLOTH SIZES (ALL SIZES IN INCHES)	
Table Sizes	**Tablecloth Sizes**
30 x 26, 30 x 30, 30 round	42 x 42 minimum, 54 x 54 maximum
36 x 36, 36 round	48 x 48 minimum, 60 x 60 maximum
42 x 42, 42 round	52 x 52 minimum, 64 x 64 maximum
44 x 44	56 x 56 minimum, 66 x 66 maximum
48 round	60 x 60 minimum, 66 x 66 maximum
54 round	66 x 66 minimum, 72 x 72 maximum
60 round	72 x 72 minimum, 76 x 76 maximum
66 round	78 x 78 minimum, 84 x 84 maximum
72 round	84 x 84 minimum, 90 x 90 maximum
72 x 30	90 x 54 minimum, 96 x 54 maximum
72 x 36	114 x 54 minimum, 120 x 54 maximum
96 x 30	90 x 60 minimum, 96 x 60 maximum
96 x 36	114 x 60 minimum, 120 x 60 maximum

Serviceware

Serviceware is a general term for all utensils and wares used in the dining room to serve the guest, in addition to certain kitchen utensils such as carving knives and forks, ladles, and perforated spoons. The main classifications of serviceware follow.

Flatware: Knives, forks, and spoons regardless of style or usage

China: Plates of all sizes, dishes, cups, saucers, underliners

Glassware: Decanters, carafes, pitchers, and all drinking vessels used at a table or at the bar for water, soft drinks, beer, wine, cocktails, and after-dinner drinks

Holloware: Generally, service items of significant depth or volume, such as candlesticks, coffeepots, platters, silver trays, and so on

One of the first things a guest notices, consciously or subconsciously, on entering the dining room is the tabletop design. For this reason, serviceware should fit in with overall design and motif. Serviceware should be selected with an eye to simplicity and completeness of detail, or the total effect in the dining room will be one of confusion and poor taste.

Aside from aesthetic concerns, other qualities to consider when selecting serviceware are:

Washability: Can the item be cleaned using the sanitation capabilities of the restaurant, without requiring excessive time, equipment, and effort?

Durability: Will the item stand up to the wear and tear of daily use?

Economy: Is the item affordable?

FLATWARE

The choice of flatware can vary depending upon a number of factors:

Balance: Size, proportion, and weight should be attractive and comfortable to use.

Design: Flatware design should reflect the ambience of the restaurant.

Durability: Flatware should stand up to daily use and methods of handling and washing.

Handles: Flatware comes in one solid piece or has handles fitted with a bolster or rivets. Materials used may be nylon, stainless steel, hollow plate, or compressed wood.

Stainless steel and silver require distinctly different cleaning methods. To clean stainless flatware, presoak all pieces, especially when stubborn stains occur. Never use an abrasive scrubbing pad, which will mar the finish. Wash pieces in hot water and detergent, then rinse in hot water, at least 181°F.

Cleaning silver does not have to be a long and tedious job; it can be done simply and quickly. Wash all silver in sudsy water as soon as possible after use. Sometimes a few drops of ammonia are added to the soapy water to cut through residue and add to the flatware's brightness, but this is not a recommended practice. Ammonia products should be kept out of the kitchen because so many of the products used there are chlorine-based. When chlorine and ammonia compounds come in contact, toxic gases are released, creating an unsafe workplace.

Silver should be soaked only for a few minutes in the recommended solutions; it should never be soaked for long periods of time. Immediately after washing, rinse thoroughly and wipe dry with a soft clean cloth. To

polish, rub the silver with a high-quality paste or liquid polish, using a soft clean cloth.

For quicker polishing, use a treated silver cloth. Buff with a dry soft cloth. Chemical compounds, such as sodium carbonate, sodium hydroxide, and sodium carboxylates, are also available. Usually one ounce of the compound to a gallon of warm water (containing a piece of aluminum foil) makes a quick-dip solution. Rinse and wipe dry with a polishing cloth.

Detarnishing baths are for fast, easy cleaning of smooth-surfaced silver; they should not be used for silver pieces with designs in high relief.

Clean silver should not be touched by the bare hands, since oils from the skin cause new tarnish spots. Nor should it be bundled with elastic or rubber bands; these contain sulfur and will leave dark marks. To prevent tarnish, wrap silver pieces first in antitarnish cloth and then in clear plastic wrap and store in an airtight place. Never use plastic wrap without completely covering the flatware with antitarnish cloth; if plastic wrap is left in contact with the silver, the flatware can become marked by any wrinkles in the plastic.

These methods for polishing are all chemical (or electrochemical) in nature. That is, they work by converting the silver oxides and sulfides of the tarnish back into metallic silver. Another form of polishing is required to restore the bright finish on silver plate. Burnishing, the principal method used, is mechanical, not chemical. In effect, strong rubbing of the flatware inside a burnishing machine pushes a tiny amount of the silver around, filling the abrasions with a smooth, bright layer of silver. Unfortunately, the use of burnishing machines can cause a gradual loss of the thickness of silver plating on the flatware. The method is appropriate only for wares that possess adequately thick plating, and even then it should be done no more than twice a year.

DETARNISHING BATH

To prepare a detarnishing bath, use a large aluminum pan with enough water to cover the silver. For each quart of water, add one teaspoon of baking soda. Bring the solution to a boil, then turn off the heat.

Add the silver and let stand a few minutes. Remove the silver, wash it in hot sudsy water, rinse, and wipe dry. The aluminum sets up an electrolytic reaction with silver sulfide and removes the tarnish.

Scour the aluminum pan afterward with a soapy steel wool pad, or boil it in a solution of vinegar or cream of tartar and water.

Some wooden handles do not withstand the rigors of commercial dishwashing machines and must be hand-washed, which may be unsanitary.

Knife edge: Knives should retain sharpness of edge, which requires less force in cutting and therefore results in fewer accidental cuts and spills.

Longevity: The pattern chosen should continue to be produced for replacement purposes. Patterns offered at a discount may have been discontinued.

Quality: The quality of the composition and finishing plate should be appropriate to overall standards.

Range: The style chosen should be available in all pieces needed for the restaurant's menu, including cocktail forks, serrated knives, lobster picks, demitasse spoons, and so on.

Stackability: Nesting should be possible with a minimum of scratching.

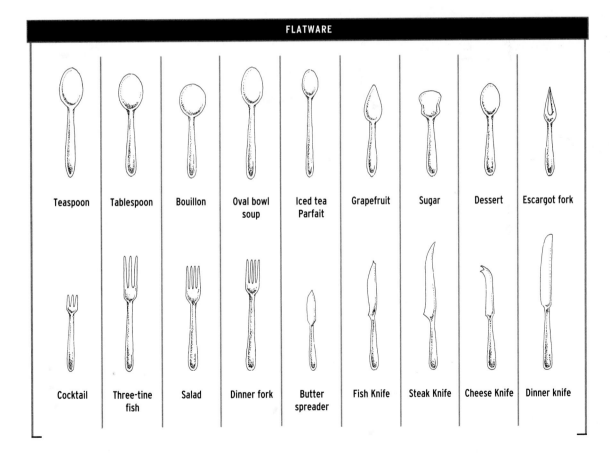

FLATWARE

Teaspoon	Tablespoon	Bouillon	Oval bowl soup	Iced tea Parfait	Grapefruit	Sugar	Dessert	Escargot fork
Cocktail	Three-tine fish	Salad	Dinner fork	Butter spreader	Fish Knife	Steak Knife	Cheese Knife	Dinner knife

Ceramic tureen

Ceramic teapot

Ceramic sauce boat

Ceramic creamer

Ceramic platter

CHINA

Centuries ago man discovered that certain types of clay, when mixed with water and worked with the hands, could be formed into desired shapes. Laid on a rock in the full rays of the sun, these shapes hardened and could hold water; when dried near or in a fire, the resulting vessels lasted longer, absorbed water less readily, and gave fewer off flavors to the contents. Kilns or special ovens were invented to produce different wares. Each district produced a different color, depending on the type of clay available.

In the course of history many types of wares have been developed, each employing a different mixture of clay, feldspar, flint, and sometimes bone, each fired or baked in a kiln at a different temperature. Wares fired at higher temperatures become vitrified. They are glassy, dense, nonporous, practically nonabsorbent. Those fired only enough to harden remain porous, permitting air or liquids to pass through. The characteristics of ceramics, as determined by their composition and firing temperature, are:

Porcelain: Glazed and nonporous with quite a fine texture that gives a ring when tapped. Porcelain is made almost entirely of kaolin, a fine white clay.

Bisque: Unglazed ceramic material that has been fired once, at a low temperature.

Stoneware: Bisque that has been glazed and refired at a higher temperature. Usually white, somewhat porous, frequently with a transparent glaze.

Pottery: Low-fired, with large pores. Generally glazed, so it does not absorb much liquid.

Terra-cotta: Red clay, usually unglazed, and low-fired. Relatively soft and very porous. A familiar example of terra-cotta is a common flowerpot.

Most restaurant china manufactured today has been vitrified. Fired at very high temperatures, this china is durable, easy to clean, and able to withstand relatively high heat and extreme cold. It also can tolerate strong detergents and is thus dishwasher safe.

China that has a patterned design should always have a layer of glaze on top of the pattern; many of these patterns are relatively fragile and would show wear rather quickly if not protected by a vitreous glaze.

Chipped or cracked china should always be discarded, since the more porous interior of the china can harbor bacteria and viruses.

GLASSWARE

Glass is produced by heating silicon dioxide (sand) and other mineral substances to a very high temperature. The molten mass is blown or molded into shapes and then allowed to cool and solidify by careful regulation of its temperature. This process is called annealing. Handles and other parts are attached by welding during this process.

The following factors should be considered when selecting glassware:

Design: Glassware should be coordinated with other dining room equipment.

Manufacture: Glassware should be inspected for clarity, cracks, faults, bubbles, and distortions.

Marketing: Depending on the style of restaurant, the capacity size of the glass could make it look like a short pour when, for example, four to five ounces of wine are poured into a sixteen-ounce glass, even though that may be the appropriate amount.

Range: Multipurpose stock should be ordered when possible so that pieces may be interchanged.

Replacement: Additional supplies should be readily available. Patterns should continue to be produced.

Serviceability: Durable glasses with smooth, simple shapes are preferred. Consider the width of the opening for proper pouring, drinking, washing, draining, drying, and storage.

Glasses can occupy a large surface area, so special consideration should be given to storage requirements and for service needs in the bar and dining areas. Specially designed hanging racks and trays are sometimes used for glasses to facilitate storing and handling. Hanging racks can conflict with health codes in some areas if smoking is allowed at the bar; smoke can get trapped in the inverted glasses. Also, the racks can be perceived as unsanitary if the bartender is not tall enough to remove glasses by their stems.

HOLLOWARE

Holloware pieces used in the dining room are usually specialty items: tea and coffee sets, covered serving dishes, tureens and bowls, ice buckets, oval platters and trays, café diable sets, chafing dishes, punch bowls, suprême sets, and the like. If plate covers are provided, be sure they fit well and, if possible, are interchangeable with other serviceware. Pieces may be sold separately or in sets, for example, a soup tureen with or without a cover. When holloware is used, the appropriate accompanying serving utensils, such as spoons and ladles, should be provided.

Holloware

Stainless diable set

Stainless coffeepot

Stainless creamer

Stainless number holder

Stainless sauce boat

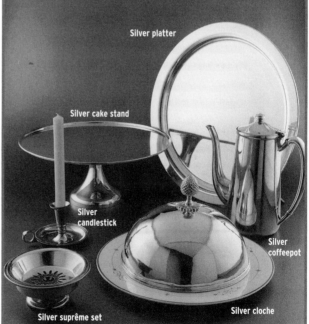

Silver platter

Silver cake stand

Silver candlestick

Silver coffeepot

Silver suprême set

Silver cloche

Holloware is often made from metal, which is stronger than ceramic and better able to withstand the impacts and stress of frequent handling. In addition, a large metalware dish can be appreciably lighter in weight than ceramic, and a greater variety of shapes is available. Metal food containers can create problems, however. Certain metals can taint foods, and strongly acidic (or, less commonly, alkaline) foods can corrode metals. Difficulties also arise in washing, polishing, and maintaining the appearance of metalware.

Setting the Table

Guests' first impression of the dining room—the individual tables and the total effect created together—dramatically influences their dining experience. Proper table setting involves the linens, flatware, glassware, and china. All require the careful attention of the professional server.

THE COVER

The term *cover*, or *couvert*, has several different meanings in the dining room. These include:

- A place setting that is intended for use with a specific type of meal and service. *Cover* here refers to the flatware, glassware and china that are set for the guest.

- The minimum charge for a guest who does not order a full meal. This charge is meant to offset the cost of bread and butter, water, and so on that are not normally included in the bill.

- The number of guests in a dining room or at a table. The use of the term *cover* to mean "guest" should be avoided.

Settings on deuces may be positioned banquette style, at right angles, or with the guests facing each other. Avoid having guests face blank walls.

Table arrangements should be neat and balanced. All tables should be set identically for a uniformly stylish appearance. Whenever possible, place settings should be positioned so that guests face each other. To provide adequate room for each guest, a minimum of eighteen inches should be allowed for each setting.

Settings on deuces may be positioned banquette style, at right angles, or with the guests facing each other. Avoid having guests face blank walls.

On rectangular or square tables, the bottom edge of all flatware, napkins, and cover plates should be in a straight line, usually about one inch from the edge of the table. On round tables, these items should be placed in a straight line, rather than following the rim of the table; the outermost pieces of flatware will be closer to the edge of the table than the plate, which is in the center of the setting.

FLATWARE

Flatware should be checked for spots prior to service and returned to the dish room if soiled. Forks should be placed to the left with the tines facing up or, for a Continental touch, with the tines facing down. Oyster or cocktail forks should be placed on the right side or on the underliner with the food itself. Spoons should be placed on the right, facing up, knives on the right with the cutting edge facing in.

Whenever possible, only those pieces that are required for the food to be served should be set. No more than four pieces of flatware should be set at a time except where a cocktail fork is used. If the menu calls for more, the utensils should be placed just prior to each course. Dessert flatware should be set in after decrumbing and just before the time of dessert service.

Banquet service is an exception to this rule. For a banquet, dessert flatware should be placed above the cover. Flatware positioned above the cover plate should

be moved to the correct position by the server before the appropriate course.

Flatware should be positioned in the order in which it is to be used, from the outside in. To ensure adequate space for the china, the innermost flatware should be positioned so as to leave enough space for the largest plate to be served.

Clean flatware should be carried to the table on a silverware transport plate (STP), pictured at right, a dinner plate covered with a clean linen napkin. In many restaurants a napkin is folded to form a pocket that is placed on a large plate to transport the flatware to the table.

The blades of the knives can be inserted into the pocket with other utensils placed on top of the pocket. Flatware should be placed on the table about three-quarters of an inch to an inch from the show plate or charger and a crumber's width from the edge of the table. These distances are suggestions and vary by restaurant.

CHINA AND GLASSWARE

The bread-and-butter plate should be placed one-half inch to the left of the cover and one inch from the edge of the table. On a round table, there may only be room for the bread-and-butter plate one inch above and to the left of the forks, aligned with the left edge of the outermost fork. The bread-and-butter knife should be placed on the right-hand edge of the plate, with the cutting edge of the knife facing left, toward the center of the plate.

The coffee cup and saucer, whether preset (at breakfast and lunch) or added to the service during the meal, should be placed to the right of the cover. The bottom edge of the saucer should be positioned in line with the top of the adjacent piece of flatware. The handle should point to the right at a slight angle toward the edge of the table (four o'clock position) to allow the guest to grasp the cup handle with ease. The spoon should be placed to the right of the cup.

Coffee mugs are generally used only in restaurants that do not use tablecloths. When mugs are used in place of cups and saucers, the coffee spoon should be placed on a paper napkin or doily (since there is no saucer).

When plates are decorated with emblems, logos, or names, they should be placed facing the guest, in such a way that permits easy readability.

Glassware should be positioned to the right of the cover above the tip of the dinner knife. If more than one glass is to be set—such as a white-wine glass, a red-wine glass, and a Champagne glass—the glasses should be positioned at an angle up from the tip of the dinner knife in order of service from right to left. If the red wine is to be served after the white wine, the red-wine glass should be placed to the left and slightly above the white-wine glass.

Generally, if a water glass accompanies the wineglasses, it should be placed just above the dinner knife with the wineglasses angled slightly above and to the left. In Europe it is common to place the water glass to the left and slightly above the wineglasses, with the Champagne tulip or port glass positioned to the left of the water glass.

STANDARD COVERS

Here are some standard covers used in restaurant service (including plated items brought from the kitchen). These settings may be prepared ahead of time and stored in the side stand. They are referred to as sets or setups. Suggestions for specific menu items follow the main covers.

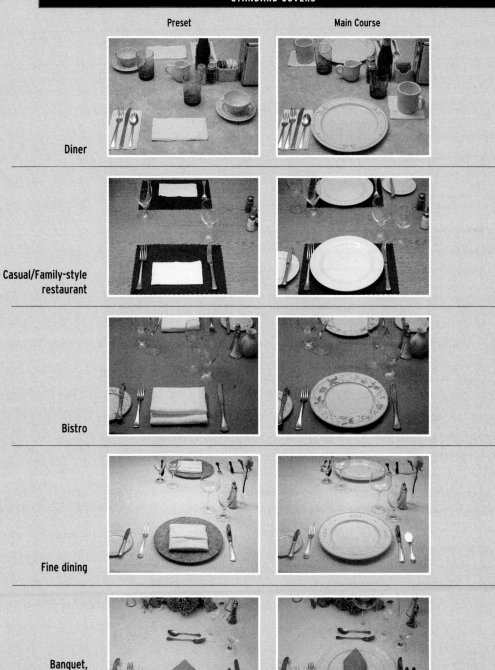

STANDARD COVERS

Preset   Main Course

Diner

Casual/Family-style restaurant

Bistro

Fine dining

Banquet, without charger, set for four courses, including soup

Banquet, with charger, set for four courses

The napkins in the Main Course column for the Casual/Family-style restaurant, Bistro, and Fine Dining categories would already be in the patrons' laps.

À la carte cover: Used for French or Russian service. Serviceware is placed prior to the appropriate course.

Breakfast cover: Fork, knife, spoon, coffee cup and saucer (or mug), napkin.

Dinner cover with service plate: Full cover with a large base plate (also called show plate or charger), which is used to dress the place setting. The base plate may be removed prior to the first course being served, or the amuse-bouche or appetizer course may be served on it. Cocktails may also be served on the base plate, using a cocktail napkin. If the napkin bears the restaurant's logo, it should be facing the guest.

Full dinner cover: Used for American, banquet, butler, and English service. All serviceware (determined by the menu) is placed on the table before the guests arrive.

Dinner cover with escargot appetizer: Full dinner cover plus snail pincers or tongs and a snail fork.

Dinner cover with fish course: Full dinner cover plus a fish fork and knife.

Standard dinner cover with seafood appetizer: Full dinner cover plus flatware for shrimp or seafood cocktail, oysters, or clams on the half shell.

Simple cover: The bare essentials.

Lunch counter cover: The bare essentials, sometimes on a place mat.

Bouillabaisse or fish soup: Large soup plate on a large underliner, soup spoon, small plate for discarded bones or shells.

Caviar: Small chilled plate, small mother-of-pearl, gold, or horn knife, toast basket, butter dish.

Cheese: Small plate, small fork, small knife.

Dessert: Small plate, dessert fork and spoon, soup spoon or knife for cutting pastry.

Finger bowl: Finger bowl filled one-third full with warm water with a slice of lemon in the water, underliner, paper doily between underliner and finger bowl.

Half grapefruit: Small bowl on underliner, citrus spoon, teaspoon, and sugar.

Hors d'oeuvre or amuse-bouche: Large service plate, small fork, and small knife.

Lobster cover: Large plate, large fork, large knife, lobster fork, lobster cracker, finger bowl.

Melon: Small bowl on underliner, dessert spoon or small fork and small knife.

Melon and prosciutto: Small plate, small fork, small knife.

Pâté: Small plate, small fork, small knife.

Spaghetti cover: Simple setting. Pasta can be served in a large bowl or plate. In an Italian setting, a large fork is placed at the right of the setting, so the pasta can be twirled against the side of the bowl. In an American-style restaurant the fork is preset on the left with a pasta spoon on the right.

Side Stand

The side stand is the mise en place station for the dining room. It should be cleaned and well stocked with everything that is necessary for service. Proper use of the side stand minimizes the number of trips to the kitchen for stock items. Because it holds so many different items, a disorganized side stand will hinder rather than facilitate service. Items on a side stand might include:

- Ashtrays
- Bread baskets
- China
- Coffee cups and saucers
- Coffee warmer unit, if using
- Condiments and caddies
- Decrumbing plate
- Doilies
- Flatware
- Flower vases
- Glassware
- Lobster utensils, oyster sets, and escargot utensils, if on menu
- Matches
- Menus
- Napkins
- Place mats, if using
- Silverware transport plate (STP)
- Special menus in large print or Braille or without prices
- Sugar and sweetener refills
- Tablecloths
- Wine buckets
- Wine lists

Edibles, such as oil and vinegar cruets, salt and pepper, ketchup, bottled sauces, mustard, and other condiments, should be handled as follows:

- ☐ Remove storeroom prices.
- ☐ Clean the cover, rim, and body of all jars and containers.
- ☐ Soak lids and wipe dry before service.
- ☐ Refill half-empty containers before service.
- ☐ Refrigerate open bottles overnight.
- ☐ Store on a clean rack or tray.

Some states have sanitation regulations restricting the type of containers in which condiments may be served, to the effect that only containers that are specifically designed for serving condiments may be used for that purpose. Empty bottles should not be cleaned and refilled with a condiment.

Also, marrying ketchup bottles can be a violation of health codes. It is wise to write the date when the bottle was opened on the label. Many places use squirt bottles, which are washed out weekly.

Unused butter and cream must be discarded when the table is cleared; they cannot be given to another guest. Consequently, the table should not be overloaded with these little extras. Replacing them as they are needed is perceived by the guest as caring service—and it is less wasteful of the restaurant's resources.

Tray Stands

Tray stands, or jack stands, are made of wood or metal. They should be cleaned before each shift. Tray stands should be fitted with webbing to make them more secure. Some tray stands are equipped with a small shelf midway between the floor and the top; items should not be placed on that shelf, because they are likely to fall off when the tray stand is moved. Fine-dining restaurants and bistros often cover the tray stands with a sixty-inch tablecloth.

Ambience

FLOWERS

Freshly cut flowers can enliven a dining room, but if they are not maintained, the effect will be exactly the opposite. A few large arrangements in the room may look better than a vase on every table. Deuces often cannot spare the room for flowers, except for a very small vase, possibly containing a single flower.

In selecting flowers for the dining room, consider fragrance as well as appearance. Highly scented flowers will conflict with the aroma of the food and for this reason should not be used. Tall flowers should not be used; they can block the view across the table. The stamens of some lilies can stain linens and should be clipped before being placed on the tables. Peruvian lilies (*Alstroemeria* spp.) look good and last a long time, but they contain a sap that can cause severe skin irritation. Potted plants, which contain soil and sometimes attract insects, should be avoided.

Proper care of cut flowers will extend their beauty and life. Upon delivery, cut flowers should be placed in tepid water in a cool room or refrigerator. Flowers should never be stored near food, especially apples, which give off ethylene gas, a natural ripening agent that causes flowers to fade prematurely. Slightly crushed hard-wooded stems will absorb more water, as will soft stems split about half an inch with a knife or scissors. Soft-leafed flowers (such as poppies) are greatly helped if the tips of the stems are dipped for a few seconds in boiling water. This process also helps revive wilting flowers and wildflowers. Arrangements should be checked daily for water. Nightly refrigeration will also help extend the life of most floral arrangements.

Flowers that last well (ten to fourteen days if chilled nightly), are not overpowering in scent, are relatively inexpensive, and are of a size suitable for use on tables include the following:

- Peruvian lilies (*Alstroemeria* spp.)
- Smaller chrysanthemums (home-grown varieties can have unpleasantly strong scents, but commercial varieties generally do not)
- Miniature carnations
- Dwarf anthurium
- Smaller haliconias (such as Parakeet)

Everlastings (the limoneas, such as statice and heather) can be used in combination with silk flowers, or simply be allowed to dry, in which case they will last up to three weeks.

A great variety of materials may be used in flower arranging, including branches, berries, leaves, colorful fruit, and even decorative products of the vegetable garden. Properly dried materials can also be used. The charm of an arrangement is a result not only of its composition but of the variety of shapes, sizes, colors, and textures of its components.

LIGHTING

Light has a great effect on mood. The desired atmosphere can be achieved in the dining room with the aid of various forms of light (natural sunlight, fluorescent or incandescent lights, gas lamps, or candles). Lighting can be used to:

- Attract attention, as with an inviting entrance light
- Emphasize works of art (or food merchandising displays)
- Expand or reduce the perceived space in a room
- Indicate directions and project information
- Indicate exit and warning notices

- Influence perceptions of food, alter the pace of the meal, and change the atmosphere or ambience of the dining room

- Provide color, animation, and contrast

- Reveal texture and heighten shape and form

- Be more flattering to guests, since skin tones look best in warm-colored light

Bright lights should be out of view in a restaurant. Textures and shapes are best emphasized with lighting directed from the side at an angle, as opposed to lighting from directly overhead or the front, to show the surface in strong relief. Pictures, displays, and other features of interest should be illuminated by directional lighting. When evening dining is in subdued light, illumination should be concentrated over the tables and service area.

For creating mood and intensifying atmosphere, the flicker of candlelight is difficult to reproduce with artificial light. Candle lights are often equipped with removable and washable globes and refillable inserts. Candle lights or small oil lamps require frequent cleaning, at least once a day, for proper maintenance.

Refillable candle lights must be well cleaned before the glass portion is run through the dishwashing machine. This is because high washing temperatures will melt any residual wax, eventually causing the machine to malfunction. A thin layer of oil should be spread inside the container before installing a new candle to make the removal of excess wax easier. Water should not be used for this purpose, since many candleholders are equipped with a small metal base to secure the wick, and water can form unsightly rust on the candleholder. Freezing the candleholder can ease removal of used candles.

Open flames, such as candles or small oil lamps, can pose a risk of fire, especially to menus and napkins, and can create undesirable odors in the dining room. Candles should be lit just as the guests are seated, though many restaurants prefer the look of a dining room with all the candles lit.

MUSIC

Music plays a significant role in setting a restaurant's ambience. It is generally chosen to complement the decor and theme, if any, of the restaurant. The music for a House of Blues franchise is significantly different from that for a Neapolitan-style trattoria or a four-star French restaurant. The type of music selected, the times of day that it is changed, and the volume at which it is played have to be determined for each specific situation. Music should be chosen to enhance the dining experience. The volume should be set to a level just loud enough to prevent one table from hearing every word spoken at the next table.

Server's Personal Mise en Place

All mise en place must be complete before the first guest enters the dining room: tables and chairs in place, napkins folded, clean serviceware set on the tables, side stands stocked, lighting and temperature adjusted. In addition, a server's personal list may include any or all of the following.

- A clean supply of properly folded side towels
- An adequate supply of guest checks in proper number sequence (if a POS system is not in use)
- Corkscrew
- Crumber
- Dupe pad or order forms
- Matches, preferably matches with the restaurant's logo, or lighter
- Miniature flashlight
- Two nondescript pens or pencils in working order

Conclusion

As Brillat-Savarin said, "To entertain a guest is to be answerable for his happiness so long as he is beneath your roof." The professional server can do that successfully only through conscientious attention to mise en place. This means attention to every detail of the dining room, from aesthetics to sanitation, from napkin folding to table setting to the choice of floral arrangements.

The Boy Scout motto applies: "Be prepared." It characterizes all the activities that servers perform behind the scenes to ensure the quality of their guest's dining experiences. It is the only way to be ready for the challenge of actual service.

CHAPTER SIX

Serving Guests:
The Main Event

People go to restaurants to dine in a relaxing, pleasurable, yet stimulating environment. A skilled server, regardless of the type of service offered, must orchestrate the dining experience so that the customer's expectations are not only met but surpassed. If not, the server can expect no return business and below-average gratuities.

Anticipating the customer's needs and wishes is the key to good service; the professional server should always be one step ahead. The ability to remain confidently in control of the guest's dining experience, without being overbearing, is learned gradually, by practicing with each encounter.

The Three R's of Glassware

Monitoring glassware is a good example of anticipating the customer's needs. A server should always remember, and practice, the three R's:

- Refill: If a glass or cup is empty, refill it.
- Replace: If a glass is empty, sell the guest another.
- Remove: If the guest does not want a refill or replacement, remove the glass or cup.

Reading the Table

Skilled servers need to be able to read the table in order to control the pace of the meal, suggest additional items, and occasionally steer the guests away from certain items. A little conversation when the guests are first seated can provide the clues servers need to do their job well.

If done well, everything that happens in the dining room is exactly the same all the time, except for one variable, the guests. Every guest is different and has different needs. Some are in a hurry; some want to enjoy a leisurely dinner. Some want a four-course meal; others would prefer three appetizers; still others are on restricted diets.

In addition to words, servers can make use of nonverbal hints, such as body language, to better serve their guests. When guests peek at their watches, scan the room as if gazing at some distant horizon, pick at their food, or toy with a nearly empty glass, they are sending signals that they are in need of something. If a guest tastes the food, then pushes the plate away, something is wrong. By reading these signs and acting upon them, servers can exceed the expectations of the guests—and make the guests' dining experience favorably memorable.

<table>
<tr><td colspan="2">PRIVACY ZONE</td></tr>
<tr><td>When speaking to guests, remember that people have a zone of privacy, an invisible boundary around them, that can be crossed only by their most intimate friends and relatives. If anyone else (for instance, a server) intrudes into that private space, the</td><td>person will become uncomfortable. The size of the zone varies from culture to culture, but for most Americans, a space of between thirty and thirty-six inches is the minimum.</td></tr>
</table>

Standards of Service

Each restaurant has its own style and establishes its own standards of service. The following guidelines are typical:

- Greet guests within thirty seconds of their being seated.

- Serve women first, then older persons, and then children.

- When serving a table, always look where you are walking. Never walk backward.

- Serve courses in the proper sequence, unless otherwise specified or requested by the guest.

- Serve all food from the guest's right with the right hand. (House policy may dictate that all food be served from the left with the left hand.)

- If guests request water, ask if they would like tap or bottled water. Serve water to everyone at the table. Serve bottled water chilled with no ice. Offer a garnish, such as lemon or lime, but do not assume that the guest wants one.

- Serve beverages from the right with the right hand.

- Remove soiled dishes from the right with the right hand, except bread-and-butter plates, which are picked up from the left. Do not scrape dishes in front of the guests.

- Avoid reaching across in front of a guest. Imagine a line that runs down the middle of the guest's face and chest and plan actions so as to avoid crossing that line. If, because of the seat's location, it is absolutely necessary to reach across the guest, apologize for the breach of protocol.

The Three T's of Service

Viewed broadly, service can be divided into three main areas of concern: technique, timing, and teamwork. Attention to these three T's can guarantee happy customers, which leads to a happy staff and happy management.

TECHNIQUE

Guests try new restaurants for many reasons, but they come back for only one: They liked what they found there, and they want to repeat that experience. Consistency is essential to the creation and maintenance of repeat business. Customers expect the same high level of service every time they visit. The professional server should read the table after each course or beverage is served and again at the end of the meal, to make sure that the dining experience is everything the guest would like it to be and to make sure that the guest knows that the server cares about the guest's needs.

Rather than ask "Is everything all right?" and put guests on the spot while they mentally review the entire meal, the server should ask, "Is there anything else I can get for you?" (Of course, when a guest has a mouthful of food, it is the wrong time to ask anything.)

Servers should treat guests as they themselves would like to be treated, putting themselves in the guest's place and imagining what would be needed at each stage of the meal. Anticipation of need not only impresses the guest, it makes the server's job easier. It allows the server to control the flow of work rather than having to play catch-up.

The server has the advantage of having seen and—ideally—tasted the dishes on the menu and having observed the needs of other diners. Using this knowledge to prevent problems from occurring is vastly preferable to trying to correct problems after the fact. For example, if a guest orders a green salad with blue cheese dressing, to be followed by grilled tuna niçoise, the server could say, "That's served on a bed of greens. Would you prefer some other appetizer?"

TIMING

Timing in the dining room means always having everything in place before it is needed. The flatware for each course should be set before the course is served. The wine that is meant to accompany the main course should be poured before that course leaves the kitchen.

Good timing means food is served when it is at its best—cold foods are delivered cold, hot foods piping hot. It means that the server is able to accomplish these feats in a timely, easy, and comfortable manner, without communicating any sense of haste.

TEAMWORK

The success of a restaurant depends on all the stations running smoothly. In a busy restaurant, there is nothing more frustrating for a waiter than having to wait: for coffee to brew, for more ice, or for something that was supposed to be stocked by another waiter before service. If one person in the restaurant fails to complete his or her job, everyone is affected. Bad service in another waiter's station will impact the restaurant's reputation, diminishing everyone's chances of success. Servers need to help each other out, whether it is assisting in serving a table, starting another pot of coffee if it is getting low, asking the bus person to bring ice before the bin is empty, or pouring water at other servers' tables if necessary.

This consideration for one's colleagues creates a more productive environment. It helps everyone be his or her best, especially when circumstances are most demanding.

The Sequence of Service

All dining room managers establish a sequence of service that makes sense for each meal period in that particular restaurant. For instance, coffee may be offered immediately at breakfast but not at lunch. Of course, if guests request coffee or tea at any time, they must be served immediately, regardless of the house sequence of service.

BREAKFAST AND LUNCH

Breakfast and lunch are faster-paced meals than dinner. Many restaurants present the menu as soon as the guests are seated for these meals. In places where guests seat themselves, menus are often preset. Mugs or cups are normally part of the breakfast cover, along with a juice glass and water glass.

For breakfast service, offer coffee immediately. Offer juice next. Offer refills for coffee and suggest additional orders of juice or tea. After the second refill of coffee or second order of tea, some restaurants provide a fresh cup.

The following sequence of service is meant to address the widest possible range of restaurants. In reality, most restaurants do not offer all of these options. The principle is the same, though, even if the particulars vary.

GREETING AND SEATING

Guests are greeted by the host, the maître d', or the manager within thirty seconds of their arrival. A warm smile with good eye contact will help make the reception a success. A timely and appropriate verbal greeting should accompany the smile. Servers should assist guests with wraps, umbrellas, and parcels, checking these items at the appropriate place.

After the reservation has been verified, guests are seated at their assigned table. Since the person doing the seating can seat only one guest at a time, servers should assist by pulling out additional chairs. It is traditional to seat women first. Extra place settings and chairs should be added or removed prior to seating. This gives guests the impression that the table was set just for them.

Guests place their napkins on their own laps. Napkins should not be replaced unless they become excessively soiled or if they fall to the floor. House policies vary, but generally if guests leave their seats, servers should not refold their napkins: Only unused napkins are folded. Napkins should not be touched by servers unless they have become extremely soiled and are in need of replacement. When guests return, their chairs should be pulled out to seat them.

BREAD

After all the guests have been comfortably seated, but within thirty seconds, it is time to offer water or serve bread. In some restaurants, the house standard of service may specify that bread is to be served only after the order has been taken, so that guests do not fill up on the bread. Since the bread-and-butter plate is to the left of the cover, bread should be served from the left. A fork and spoon are used for serving individual bread portions or rolls.

Sometimes a basket of bread and a dish of butter are placed on the table. For tables with six or more guests, two baskets and two butter plates are more convenient.

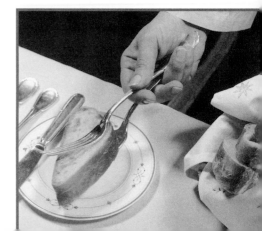

BEVERAGE

No matter which meal of the day, guests generally want something to drink soon after they arrive at their table.

If there is a house specialty beverage or daily special, the server should be sure to mention it. Since many guests prefer to order wine as an aperitif, the server should be prepared with a wine list. Sometimes the host will order for the entire table; otherwise the server should take orders from the women first, beginning with the woman seated to the left of the host and proceeding clockwise around the table, to finish with the host's order. While writing down the cocktail order, the server should repeat the name of each cocktail as it is ordered and write down the standard abbreviation.

The server should excuse himself from the table by saying to the host, "Thank you, I will be right back with your order." It is important for this promise to be kept. The guests should have their beverages before them within two to three minutes from the time that they are seated or have ordered.

When the beverage order is picked up, drinks are placed on the tray in the order in which they will be served, with the position of any similar-looking drinks carefully noted. A gin and tonic and vodka tonic, for example, can be distinguished by placing two stir sticks or two lime wedges in the vodka tonic versus one in the gin and tonic. The tray should be carried on the fingertips of the left hand (much less tiring than carrying with the thumb hooked over the edge). Guests should not remove the drinks from the tray themselves; only the server can feel whether or not the tray is balanced. If guests reach for their own drinks, the tray should be stabilized by grasping the edge with the right hand.

Mentioning the name of each drink as it is served prevents any possible misunderstandings with the order. Drinks should be served from the right and placed to the right of each cover or directly on a cocktail napkin on the show plate. If there is no show plate, the drink should be placed directly in front of the guest. Cocktail napkins should be used only when serving the glass on a table with no tablecloth or on the show plate. If the drink is transferred to the tablecloth, the cocktail napkin should be removed from the table.

MENU PRESENTATION AND ORDER TAKING

The menu should be presented to the guests after the beverages have been served. Since traditional aperitifs are designed to stimulate the appetite, serving the cocktail before the menu is presented can encourage a more adventuresome, and possibly larger, order.

The menu may be presented by the maître d', headwaiter, captain, or waiter. The server should present the menus, right side up, in the most convenient manner for the guest. As with food or beverage, it should be served from the right with the right hand and from the left with the left hand. Before the guests read the menu, they should be informed of any specials that are being offered during the meal period, any unavailable items, or substitutions. This can prevent disappointment. A full explanation should be provided for menu items that might be unclear or foreign to new guests or new items that might be unfamiliar to regular guests.

Often a guest will listen to the listing of the day's specials, then ask, "What was that fish again?" The server should be able to answer without repeating all the specials. This can be done successfully only if the server knows the listing (as opposed to merely memorizing it).

Servers should be honest without being negative in answering direct questions such as "How is the soup today?" Establishing a feeling of trust between guest and server is essential to a comfortable dining experience for the guest, increased sales for the restaurant, and better tips for the server. Sharing information with the guest is the best way to instill trust. Describing an item with specific details, such as "The chives came from our own herb garden" or "Our oysters are flown in daily," can make the meal more memorable and give the guests the kind of information they will be likely to share with potential customers.

All data in the information box at the top of the guest check should be filled in before approaching the table. The table should be observed for cues that the guests might be ready to order, such as closed menus. Or after a reasonable amount of time passes (five to ten minutes) guests should be asked politely, "Would you care to order?" If the guests need more time, the server should withdraw and return in a few minutes.

Generally the order is taken from the right of each guest, but as with all dining room procedures,

---

SOMETIMES GUESTS ARE SO RAPT IN CONVERSATION that they don't notice that the server is ready to take their order. Since it may seem rude to interrupt, the server is presented with a dilemma. Here are some strategies:

- Offer to come back when the guests are ready. Very often this will stimulate an urge to order.

- Try to make eye contact with one of the guests, who may inform the others that it is time to order.

- Seek out one of the guests who is not actively involved in the conversation. Quietly ask the guest if he or she would care to order.

it should be taken in whatever manner will least disturb the guests. When requesting the order for a table of two, it is important to establish eye contact to see who will order first. Traditionally, the man ordered for the woman and then followed with his own order, but today that should not be assumed to be the case. When both guests are of the same sex, the elder is usually first to order. When there are four or more guests in a party, each one usually orders separately. Start with the guest to the left of the host and move clockwise around the table. The host orders last.

The complete order should be taken for each person in the order in which it is to be served: appetizer, soup, salad, and entrée order before moving onto the next person. If salad is to be served after the entrée, however, the salad order should be written after the entrée order. Special requests (using standard abbreviations), such as timing preferences, degree of doneness, and so on, should be indicated on the guest check. It is advisable to repeat the names of dishes as they are recorded, to make sure that the information is being interpreted correctly.

Seat numbers are generally assigned by the house to specific places at the table. Orders taken throughout the meal should be noted with reference to these seat numbers. Regardless of the sequence in which the order was taken, the person seated in chair number 2 remains number 2 on the check. That way, anyone can refer to the check to see who gets what at service time.

COMMON ABBREVIATIONS					
DRINKS		**MEAT**		**EGGS**	
DR	Dry	CX or CHK	Chicken	OE	Over easy
LI	Lime	BLK & BLU	Black and blue/very rare	OM	Over medium
RX or ↓	Rocks	R	Rare	OW	Over well
↑	Up	MR	Medium rare	SCR	Scrambled
OL	Olive	M	Medium		
ON	Onion	MW	Medium well		
TST	Lemon twist	W	Well		
		SOS	Sauce on the side		
		STK	Steak		

BY THE NUMBERS

The system of numbers for tables and chairs in dining rooms has evolved through long experience. The first row of tables begins with numbers in the teens, the second row in the twenties, and so on. The first table in each row ends with a one, not a zero (eleven, twenty-one, and so on). This system makes it easier to count, that is, third row, fourth table is 34, not 33 as it would be if the tables in the row started at 30. Most restaurants have no table 13, because some guests believe it to be an unlucky number, just as many hotels and office buildings have no thirteenth floor.

Seat numbers are usually assigned by the management as follows: Seat number 1 is the one with its back to the door (either the kitchen door or the front door); subsequent chairs are numbered clockwise from that chair. When tables are set at an angle and a chair is not in a direct line with the door, the chair closest to the number 1 position, moving clockwise, is designated seat 1. Seat numbers remain constant, whether the seats are occupied or not. If three people are seated at a four-top, in seats numbers 1, 3, and 4, those numbers are to be used in ordering. This way, if a fourth person joins the group and sits in seat two, there is no need to inform the entire staff of a new numbering system at that table. Should a server need assistance in serving, it is more specific (and more courteous) to ask "Please pour some more water at table 23, seat 3" than to point.

It is important to maintain the established table numbers and seat numbers rather than creating a different system independent of the management's design.

A server should always have a clear idea of the ingredients in the dishes on the menu as well as the manner in which they are prepared. Guests have valid concerns that require clear, unequivocal answers. Among them:

- Nutritional information (calories, fat or salt content, and so on).
- Alternative preparations (involving substitutions for dairy products, for example).
- Allergies. Many people are allergic to dairy products, shellfish, eggs, garlic, nuts, and nut oils. Allergens can cause life-threatening situations and should not be taken lightly.

If there is any uncertainty whatsoever about the answers to questions posed by a guest, the server should consult with the chef.

Not everyone is an expert on cooking terminology, although many diners have become quite sophisticated in recent years. When guests ask about the menu and its preparation, the server should speak clearly, without condescension and without using technical jargon. All servers should resist the temptation to show off their expertise; their job is to make the guest feel comfortable with not humbled by the server's knowledge.

WINE LIST PRESENTATION AND ORDER TAKING

After the food order has been taken, the wine list is presented to the host by the sommelier, maitre d', headwaiter, captain, or server. This is usually done after the food order, because the wine selection depends on the choice of food.

The server records all pertinent information concerning the wine order, such as the name of the wine and the bin number. Finally, the server should ask when the host wants the wine served.

APPETIZER

Before the appetizer is served, all required utensils must be set in place, if they have not been preset. Clean flatware is carried to the table on a clean dinner plate covered with a napkin (STP, silverware transport plate). The appetizer fork is placed to the left of the dinner fork with the left hand, the appetizer knife or spoon to the right of the dinner knife with the right hand. If wine is to accompany the appetizer, it should be served before the food. This is usually done by the person who took the wine order.

After the wine has been poured, the appetizer is served from the right with the right hand. All courses are served according to the standards of service of the house, but generally women are served first. Accompanying sauce may be served from the guest's left. Bread and rolls, water, and wine should be checked and, if necessary, replenished at this time.

SOUP

The soup spoon is set in to the right of the dinner knife, with the right hand. Then the soup is served. As usual, soiled dishes and flatware are removed from the right with the right hand.

MAIN COURSE

The main course is the high point of the meal. It usually takes more time to be consumed, and a leisurely air at the table ensures optimum enjoyment.

By the time guests have reached the main course, their appetite has been appeased and their thirst quenched. Sometimes all that is needed to revive the appetite is a simple but well-designed plate that offers pleasing contrasts in color, texture, and contour and is presented with flair and style. At other times and at other restaurants, special presentations such as sous cloche, en papillote (in parchment paper), flambé (flamed), and other forms of tableside legerdemain help to stimulate the palate. If wine is to accompany the meal, it should be poured before serving the main course.

Since the flatware for the main course was set prior to the guests' arrival, there should be no need to set it now unless it has been used or dropped (though it is wise to double-check before the food comes out from the kitchen). When the main course calls for a special utensil, such as a lobster pick or steak knife, it should be placed in position before the main course is brought into the dining room. Flatware should be handled only by the handle, never by any area that will touch food or the guest's mouth. It should be brought to the table on a STP.

If a guéridon is to be used for preparing, finishing, or plating the main course, it should be checked to see that it is equipped with all needed serviceware.

When serving plated food, china should be handled with the thumb on the rim of the plate, not on any part of it that might contain food. Some restaurants have house rules about the part of the plate that the thumb is to touch, either at the six or three o'clock position. The chef will determine the actual placement of food on the plate; usually the main item is placed at the bottom (six o'clock position). When setting in, the plate should be placed in the alignment chosen by the chef.

When picking up the dishes in the kitchen, the plates should be picked up in reverse order from that in which they will be served. That is, the last plate to be served in each trip should be picked up first. Two or three plates can be carried in the left hand.

In this example, the chef requested that the main item—in this case, duck—be placed slightly off the six o'clock position.

1. Hold a plate between the thumb and the index finger, using the middle fingers for balance. Your thumb should be flat on the rim of the plate, pointing toward the rim, not into the plate.

2. A second plate rests on the inside of the wrist and balances on the ring finger and/or little finger.

3. Hold the first plate between the thumb and index finger. Slide the second plate against the index finger and support it with the other fingers spread beneath.

4. To hold a third plate, rest it on the inside of the wrist and balance on the forearm.

When serving from trays, rather than hand-carrying plates, covered plates should not be stacked more than three plates high. The last plate to be served is the first one to go on the tray. Trays should not be over-stacked, as overstacked trays frequently cause accidents. Servers should always use proper lifting and carrying techniques, for their own safety. See pages 207–208 for details on tray loading, lifting, and carrying.

In Russian service, the main course is presented to the table so that the guests can view the platter arrangement. When plating the food, the server should move swiftly yet gracefully, plating first the main course and then any accompaniments, such as vegetables and potato. The food is placed on the plate so as to facilitate cutting and eating by the guest. The main course should be placed so that the guest does not have to reach over the accompaniments to cut it. Generally the main course is served with the meat or fish in the lower center portion of the plate (six o'clock position). If accompaniments are served on separate dishes, they are placed on the table to the guest's left, after the main course is set.

House policy may dictate that the wait staff ask each table if everything is satisfactory. Ideally the server should be sufficiently alert to notice any problems. As the main course progresses, rolls or bread and butter should be replenished as necessary, and water and wine poured as needed. After the guests have completed the main course, the table is cleared in the same manner as before, with bread-and-butter plates and butter knives left on the table only if they will be used during the next course (salad and/or cheese).

SALAD

According to custom, most American restaurants serve salad before the main course. Americans generally choose soup, salad, or an appetizer—not all three—so, in effect, the salad is a form of appetizer course. After the guests have finished their salads, the table is prepared for the main course. All dishes and flatware that were used with the salad should be removed. Generally the show plate is removed at this time. In many restaurants, especially those using expensive show plates, the show plate is removed even before the appetizer is served, to avoid having the show plate scratched by the underside of the appetizer plate.

CLEARING

When clearing the table after each course, the plates are scraped onto one plate—out of the guests' view and not too close to another table. No more than one tray should be placed on the tray stand; it is very difficult to separate stacked trays when the top one is laden. Some places get around this problem by inverting all trays except the uppermost or laden tray.

Flatware should be piled on one side of the tray. Glassware should be stacked on a separate tray, with the tallest pieces in the center of the tray. No more than four plates should be stacked (and no more than two stacks per tray). Used glassware should always be picked up and carried by the stems, never the rims, for sanitary reasons. Servers should avoid using "the claw," that is, grasping glasses with the fingers inside the glasses. Flatware must never be placed in glasses because it can create invisible hairline fractures that cause the glass to shatter in the heat of the dishwasher. Empty bottles should be laid down to avoid toppling.

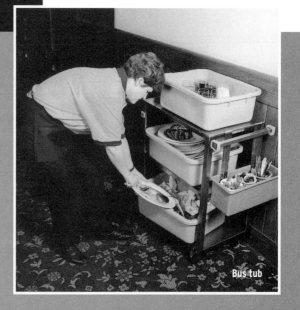

Bus tub

Trays filled with soiled dishes can be quite heavy. Therefore it is especially important to use good lifting techniques to avoid strain injuries and accidents. The server should always bend at the knee as he or she lifts the tray with the left hand above the left shoulder; the tray should not rest upon the shoulder. This position frees the right hand for opening doors and keeps the weight close to the server's center of gravity. The server should squat to set the filled tray onto a tray stand.

A bus tub is easier to use, and there is less chance of breakage, if it is placed on a cart. Separate tubs are assigned for flatware, china, glassware, and waste.

Wrong: Picking up glassware improperly

Correct: Picking up glassware properly

In European meals, salad greens are served after the main course, to allow the guest to better appreciate the main course and to aid digestion. Greens have a lightening and relaxing effect, so eating them after the main course helps to prepare the guest for dessert.

As with appetizer and soup, all necessary tableware should be set in place prior to service of the salad. The salad fork is positioned to the left of the place reserved for the salad plate with the left hand and the salad knife to the right with the right hand. The salad itself is served from the right with the right hand. A pepper mill may be offered or left on the table. When the salad course is finished, the plates should be cleared from the right, the salt and pepper removed, and the table reset for the fruit and cheese course.

FRUIT AND CHEESE

In the United States restaurants that offer fruit and cheese at the end of a meal generally serve them together. In France people generally do not like to mix foods—they prefer to have them *sans mélanger*, or unmixed, one at a time. Normally a cheese board of as few as three or four contrasting cheeses (a total of three to five ounces of cheese) is adequate for even the most discriminating diner. In some restaurants a simple cheese course is offered along with the salad, especially if a Stilton or Roquefort is available. This simplifies the cheese course but does it with style. There should also be variety in the accompanying fruit. Only fresh, ripe fruit should be offered. Because of seasonal variations and fluctuating market availability, it is generally not a good idea to specify on the menu exactly what fruit or cheese will be served, but the server should always know what is available each day.

Before presenting the cheese and fruit arrangement to the table, the server should set a knife and fork in the appropriate places. The arrangement should be checked for knives to portion the cheese, service forks and spoons, plates, and clean napkins. The fruit should be washed beforehand. Each guest makes a selection of fruit and cheese. Carefully slice and plate the desired cheeses. Much food has been consumed by this time, so portions should be kept modest. If after completing their first serving guests desire more, they should be accommodated, of course.

Some restaurants plate the cheese and fruit course in the kitchen instead of at tableside. Although that is less elegant, it is faster, it involves less service, and it allows better portion control.

After the guests have completed the fruit and cheese course, everything that will not be used with dessert should be cleared from the table: bread-and-butter plates and knives, bread baskets, butter dishes, empty wineglasses, and any soiled flatware and dishes.

Before dessert (or whenever necessary), the table should be decrumbed. A special crumber or brush may be used. An alternative approach is to use a folded linen napkin to brush crumbs onto a small plate (six to ten inches), but this method tends to be less effective.

DESSERT

Ending the meal with a superb dessert is as important as beginning it with a quality appetizer. The insatiable sweet tooth of the American public makes dessert a popular course. From a management point of view, the profit margin on most desserts makes this sale quite desirable.

A simple and effective approach to merchandising dessert is to exclude it from the printed dinner menu; dessert on the menu reminds the guest of the amount of food, in terms of both calories and cost, that has just been consumed. A simple dessert card or separate dessert menu arouses guests' interest, and a dessert display or cart, which visually stimulates the guest to order, is even more effective. Merely carrying a tray of available desserts to the table can sometimes be an irresistible presentation.

As with any course, the table should be made ready before dessert is presented and served, and necessary flatware should be set in place. If the original table setting included dessert flatware above the cover (as in a banquet setting), it should be moved down into the appropriate position: The fork is brought down into position from the guest's left; the dessert and coffee spoons from the guest's right. Wine or Champagne to accompany dessert should be served at this time.

All food should be neatly and appetizingly arranged on the dessert cart, if one is used, before presenting it to the guests. The cart should be stocked with all the necessary serving equipment, including serving forks and spoons, napkins, dessert plates, and clean knives for cutting. A container of warm water may prove useful: Dipping a knife into warm water before slicing a cake or pie prevents icing from sticking to the knife.

The dessert cart is presented and the guests are invited to make a selection. Some restaurants offer a sampler plate so that guests can try small portions of several different desserts. Each dessert order is plated, then served from the right side with the right hand.

AFTER-DINNER BEVERAGES

Hot beverages, such as tea or coffee, and after-dinner drinks (Cognac, cordials, or after-dinner wine) are often enjoyed by guests at the conclusion of a satisfying meal. Coffees and teas can be stocked in the pantry or cold-food section of the kitchen. A special house blend of American and French roasts can be created by the coffee purveyor. A selection of herbal and regular teas, easily stored in boxes or tins, can also be offered to the guest.

Hot beverages containing liquor, such as café diable or Irish tea, can be offered in place of a heavy dessert. This type of selection increases the check average and adds style at the conclusion of the meal.

Before serving after-dinner beverages, all necessary flatware, cups, and accompaniments must be delivered to the table. Coffee is poured from the right. Orders for after-dinner drinks are taken in the same manner as before-dinner cocktails. The drinks are served from the right.

TOBACCO

In the past, only men smoked and only at the end of the meal. After a meal, men would gather in a room separate from the women with a waiter stationed in attendance at the door. Then women began to smoke, and both men and women sometimes smoked throughout the meal. Now many health-conscious Americans have protested against public smoking in restaurants. Special smoking sections have been established in the dining room. Some states and municipalities have passed ordinances making separate smoking sections mandatory or have prohibited smoking in restaurants entirely. Even in places where smoking is permitted, air purifiers are recommended to minimize the irritation to nonsmokers.

THE CHECK

After the last course has been served and the meal nears completion, the guests should never be abandoned. A server must be available, for example, to offer additional beverages. Many restaurants instruct their wait staff to present the check only if it is requested by the host. If it is obvious, however, that guests are waiting for their check, the server should approach the table and ask if any further services are required.

The totaled guest check should be presented in a book or in a simply folded napkin on a dinner plate. Friands or mignardises (dainty tidbits) sometimes accompany the check. Like dessert, these lagniappes ("little extra things," in Louisiana) are meant to leave, literally and figuratively, a sweet taste in the patron's mouth at the completion of the meal. At this point the server should tell the guest to whom the check should be paid (to the server at the table or to the cashier).

When picking up the paid check, the server should stand next to the host, write the total amount of cash received from the guest on the check, and excuse himself. The receipt and any change should be returned in the same manner in which the check was presented, either in a book or in a napkin on a plate. The server should never assume that the change is a gratuity or examine or count the tip in front of the guest.

For credit card payments, after the check is presented the server should accept the credit card, process it, and return it to the guest for signature. If the guest has not taken the customer copy of the receipt, it should be given to him.

The wait staff should be prepared to provide any information that might be requested, such as the location of the rest rooms and telephones. Guests may wish to take home their leftovers (doggie bags); sanitation laws vary from location to location and will determine the policy in a particular restaurant.

The wait staff should assist with the departure of the guests, as with their arrival, helping with parcels, wraps, and any personal items left on the table. Bidding the guest farewell should be as engaging as the first hello. Establishing a friendly and lasting impression in a sincere manner encourages guests to return.

RESETTING THE TABLE

Every restaurant has its own policy concerning resetting tables. It is disconcerting for those guests still in the dining room at the end of a meal period to find themselves in a kind of demolition zone. It is generally preferable to reset each table as it is vacated, rather than to reset all the tables at one time. At the end of the evening, glasses can be inverted to avoid gathering dust if the surface is sanitary.

Conclusion

Remarkable Service must be consistent and logical yet flexible. There is no single proper way to serve a meal. Actually, there are three ways: the right way, the wrong way, and the best way.

- The right way is to adhere to the rules as established by management.
- The wrong way is to disregard house policy for no obvious reason.
- The best way is to bend the rules to adjust to unique or unforeseen circumstances.

For example, wait staff are usually instructed to clear soiled dishes from the right: This is the right way. The wrong way would be to remove the dishes from the left. If, on the other hand, two guests are leaning toward each other engaged in conversation, the only way to remove the soiled dishes of one of them without disruption is from the left side.

The prescribed procedures for service are not ironclad. Circumstances will always arise requiring instant decisions that alter the customary way of doing things. At first, these exceptional situations might prove unnerving, but with experience handling them will become second nature.

While individual restaurants develop house rules for service, these are not to be confused with the sequence of events.

Steps of Service

- Greeting
- Seating
- Bread
- Beverage
- Menu/wine list
- Order taking

- Serving
- Clearing
- Check presentation/payment
- Farewell
- Reset table

Sequence of Courses

- Appetizer
- Soup
- First course (May be a combination of the above items. A family restaurant may offer a choice of appetizer, soup, or salad as a starter course rather than as separate courses.)
- Main course

- Salad (Traditionally served after the main course in a European-style meal. American restaurants generally serve salad between the soup and first course.)
- Fruit and cheese (Usually offered only by fine-dining restaurants and some bistros.)
- Dessert
- After-dinner beverages
- Tobacco

seven

Beverage
Service

Our bodies are composed of 90 percent water. We must consume fluids to stay alive, but we drink for several reasons beyond mere survival. We drink for the pleasure of convivial company and for the taste and tactile sensations of a large variety of beverages. Over the centuries, people have devised drinks of all kinds, which we enjoy today in the form of milk and milk-based drinks, fruit juices, infusions (tea and coffee), fermented beverages (wine and beer), and distilled beverages (whiskey, brandy, and other spirits). Even the most basic of libations—water—has been transformed into many subtly different drinks: mineral waters from different parts of the world and sparkling waters, including thousands of variations on flavored sparkling waters, from flavored seltzer to mass-produced soft drinks. Many combinations of these beverage types have been created, such as the mixtures of distilled alcohol, sparkling water, and fruit juices known as cocktails.

Aside from being a source of pleasure in their own right, beverages complement food. Dining room personnel need to be familiar with the patterns of beverage service to orchestrate a pleasurable dining experience for their guests.

STRAWS

While making a curlicue with half the paper wrapper of a straw is attractive, it is difficult to do without touching and contaminating the straw itself. It is best to leave the straw in the paper and set it by the beverage. Using the moisture from the outside of the glass to stick the straw to the side of the glass works well but becomes messy when the straw is removed from the paper. Make sure to retrieve the paper wrapper a few seconds after serving the straw, as part of table maintenance.

Aperitifs

Within thirty seconds after the guests are comfortably seated, they should be offered an aperitif. It should be low in alcohol, so as not to numb the taste buds, and dry, so as to stimulate the appetite. Sweet drinks can cause the guest to have a full feeling before the meal has even begun. There are many kinds of aperitifs: white wines, dry fortified wines (such as vermouth or sherry), aromatized wines, bitters, and cocktails. Sweet fortified wines (such as Madeira) are more appropriate for after the meal, but if a guest requests one as an aperitif, it should be served. The host may ask for a wine list immediately after the party has been seated. While many people will wait until after the food order has been taken in order to choose wines that complement the meal, some will order a bottle of wine as an aperitif. Aperitifs are generally served chilled.

Fortified wines are wines that have been mixed with distilled alcohol (usually brandy) during the wine making process. These include port, sherry, Madeira, Malaga, and Marsala. Since many fortified wines tend to be somewhat sweet, they are generally ordered after dinner, except for sherry. The alcohol content ranges from 16 to 23 percent. Drier sherries, such as Tio Pepe or even Dry Sack, make better aperitifs than Harvey's Bristol Cream. When guests order a sweet sherry before dinner, however, they should not be made to feel uncomfortable. Dry sherry is served slightly chilled at 55° F and sweet sherry at 60° F. Both should be served in a sherry glass.

Sherry glass

Snifter

Aromatized wines are wines to which alcohol and some flavoring, such as herbs, bark, roots, or spices, have been added during the process. Dubonnet is an aromatized wine, usually served as an aperitif. Vermouths, such as Boissière, Cinzano, and Noilly Prat, are also aromatized wines; white vermouth is generally used in making martinis but is sometimes served alone as an aperitif. Vermouth may be red or white, sweet or dry, with an alcohol content between 18 and 20 percent. If requested "up," the vermouth should be chilled over ice, strained, and served in an aperitif glass; it is usually garnished with a lemon twist, orange slice, or wedge of lime.

Herbs and other aromatic plants are added to distilled alcohol to make bitters, such as Cynar, Campari, or Angostura. The exact herbs used are company secrets. Bitters can be served with a mixer, just as with grain alcohol; Campari is often served with soda and a lemon twist, for example.

A popular aperitif is a kir: chilled white wine and a splash of crème de cassis (black currant liqueur), served with a lemon twist. A kir royale is sparkling wine and crème de cassis.

DISTILLED SPIRITS

The process of distilling spirits is simple but delicate. Heating a liquid containing alcohol frees the alcohol from the original liquid in the form of vapor. Ethyl alcohol vaporizes at 176°F. This vapor is collected and condensed into raw alcohol, then the temperature is lowered. This process, when repeated, extracts impurities and increases the proof. One hundred percent alcohol is chemically pure; it is designated 200 proof. Neutral spirits are distilled to a minimum of 190 proof; at this point they are odorless, colorless, and flavorless.

Brandy

The art of distillation, known as early as the tenth century, was not applied commercially until the thirteenth century. Brandy was being produced in the sixteenth century. Dutch shippers contracted with vintners in the Charente region (just north of Bordeaux) to distill their wines, since shipping space was at a premium and the low-alcohol wines of Charente did not always keep well. Condensing wine through distillation seemed like a good solution to both problems. Shippers planned to transport the "spirit" of the wine to Holland, where the water would be replaced. However, after tasting the condensed wine, called *brandywijn* or *brandewyn* (literally "burnt wine"), many people decided that they liked it just as it was.

All brandies are distilled from fruit, grapes being the most popular. Most brandies are between 80 and 84 proof. Cognac is a type of brandy, but not all brandies are Cognacs. Only brandy from the French district of Cognac may bear that district's name. The most distinctive characteristic of a Cognac is that it is double-distilled. Armagnac is a single-distilled brandy from the Armagnac region of France. Calvados is apple brandy from Normandy, France. Grappa is an Italian brandy, similar to marc from France, which is distilled from the pomace of grapes. Brandy is served in a snifter.

Whiskey

Whiskey (also spelled *whisky*) comes from the Celtic word *uisgebaugh*, which means "water of life" (as does the French *eau de vie*). The earliest references to whiskey stills in Scotland date to the mid-fifteenth century. All whiskey is distilled from grain. There are five types of whiskeys:

American: Distilled from sour mash that is made from several grains, including corn. Bourbon must be made from at least 51 percent corn, be aged at least two years in new oak barrels, contain no coloring additives, and come from Bourbon County, Kentucky.

Canadian: Made from several grains, blended with rye.

Irish: Made from barley and corn blended with rye in Ireland. Similar to Scotch but with a less pronounced smokiness and no peaty flavor.

Rye: Made from rye.

Scotch: Made from malted barley that has been dried over peat fires in Scotland; properly spelled *whisky*.

Whiskey can be served "up," on the rocks, with water or soda, or mixed in a cocktail, such as a whiskey sour or Manhattan.

Gin

An unaged neutral spirit, flavored with juniper berries and other aromatic plants. By definition, gin does not have any character before it is flavored with botanicals. Gin first became popular in England during the reign of Queen Anne in the early eighteenth century. Holland gin is low in proof with a clean, malty aroma and flavor. It should not be mixed with other ingredients to make cocktails, as its own taste does not blend well. American dry gin is different in character from Dutch and English gins. Under U.S. regulations, distillers are required to use neutral spirits of 190 proof or more; the gin is generally diluted to 80 proof before bottling. English dry gin is distilled to 180 proof, then diluted to 80 or 97 proof.

Gin is generally served in mixed drinks, such as martinis, gibsons, and gimlets, or simply with tonic and lime.

Vodka

Vodka is a Slavic word for "water." It was originally produced in eastern Europe from the most plentiful and least expensive material available to the distiller—potatoes, for example. Most vodka today is made from grain. Vodka is distilled at or above 190 proof and reduced to between 80 and 110 proof. It must be filtered through or purified with vegetable charcoal for at least eight hours. Like gin, vodka is not aged. Recently some companies have been successfully marketing flavored vodkas (pepper, lemon, and black currant, for example).

Vodka may be served "neat," chilled but without ice, but it is generally served in mixed drinks, such as martinis, gibsons, and gimlets, with orange juice in a screwdriver, with spiced tomato juice in a bloody Mary, or simply with tonic and lime.

Rum

Rum is an alcoholic distillate made from the fermented juices of sugarcane, distilled at 190 proof and then diluted to no less than 80 proof. Some rum is as strong as 151 proof. The four main types of rum are light rum, a very dry type of which Puerto Rican rum is the most noted example; medium-bodied rum; full-bodied rum, of which Jamaican rum is a popular example; and the light-bodied but very aromatic East Indian Batavia arak rum from Java.

Rum may be served "up" or on the rocks, but it is more often served in mixed drinks, such as a Cuba libre (mixed with Coca-Cola and lime) or a piña colada, or simply with tonic and lime.

Tequila

Tequila is distilled from agave (genus *Amaryllis*) from Tequila, Jalisco, Mexico. When produced elsewhere, it is labeled mescal. Tequila is double-distilled to 110 proof, then diluted to 80 proof.

High-quality tequila may be served "up" or in a snifter, like fine brandy. Lesser tequilas are used in cocktails, such as a margarita, which can be served on the rocks or frozen.

Cordials and Liqueurs

Cordials and liqueurs are alcoholic beverages flavored with aromatics and usually sweetened.

Anise: Anesone, anisette, ouzo, Pernod, sambuca

Chocolate: Crème de cacao, Sabra

Coffee: Kahlúa, Tía Maria

Fruits: Cherry (Chéri-Suisse, Cherry Heering, crème de cerise, kirsch, maraschino); banana (crème de banane); black currant (crème de cassis); citrus (Cointreau, curaçao, Grand Marnier, mandarine, Triple Sec); melon (Midori); raspberry (framboise)

Flowers: Roses (crème de rose); violets (crème de violette)

Herbals: Bénédictine, Chartreuse, Drambuie, Galliano, Glayva, Goldwasser, Herbsaint, Izarra, Kümmel, Strega

Miscellaneous: Egg and sugar (Advocaat); honey (Irish Mist); Rock and Rye (orange or lemon essence and rock candy)

Nuts: Almond (amaretto), fruit pits (crème de noyaux), hazelnut (Frangelico)

MIXED DRINKS

Most bartenders will not mix a drink until the waiter prepares the proper glass. It is his or her responsibility to prep the glass and garnish the drink properly. Consequently, servers need to know:

- The primary liquor of the drink (in order to up-sell or offer better-quality liquors)
- Possible variations on the drink that the guest might be considering
- Garnish
- Ways the drink might be served

All drinks taken from the bar must be carried on a bar tray. Here are a few popular cocktails that any good server should know:

Bloody Mary: Vodka with tomato juice, horseradish, Tabasco, and celery salt, garnished with a stalk of celery and sometimes a carrot stick. Served in a highball glass.

Gibson: A martini served with cocktail onions instead of a lemon twist or olives. Served "up" or on the rocks.

Gimlet: Gin (or vodka) with lime juice and a lime garnish. Served "up" or on the rocks.

Manhattan: In the South and Southwest, made with bourbon, sweet vermouth, and a dash of bitters and garnished with a cherry; in the Northeast, rye is used and a twist of orange is added. If ordered "perfect," half of the sweet vermouth is replaced by dry vermouth. Served "up" or on the rocks.

Margarita: Tequila, Triple Sec, and lime juice. Can be served "up," on the rocks, or frozen, with or without salt on the rim of the glass.

Martini: Gin and dry vermouth, unless the guest asks for a vodka martini. Served with a lemon twist or with olives, dry or extra dry (with little or no vermouth). Served "up" or on the rocks.

Rob Roy: Scotch with sweet vermouth. Stirred with ice and strained. If ordered "perfect," half of the sweet vermouth is replaced by dry vermouth. Served in a cocktail glass.

Vodka (or gin) and tonic: Vodka (or gin) with tonic and a wedge of lime. Served on ice in a highball glass.

No restaurant should ever substitute one brand or a different measure for another. If a guest orders a specific brand that is not carried or is out of stock, it should be brought to the guest's attention, asking if he or she would care to make another selection. If the guest doesn't specify a brand, the brand names available for the drink they ordered should be listed.

Some restaurants offer "club service" where the waiter mixes drinks, such as Scotch and soda, in front of the guest at the table. The waiter picks up the proper glass containing ice, a stirrer, an opened split of the appropriate mixer, and the requested brand of liquor poured either into a jigger glass or a two-ounce decanter. At the table the server asks if the guest would like the drink mixed. If the answer is yes, the server pours the liquor into the glass, then pours the mixer until the combined liquid fills half the glass. The drink, along with the remaining soda, is served to the right side of the guest. The same procedure is followed when the drink is ordered with water.

GRADES OF ALCOHOL

There are three main price and quality classifications of alcohol in a restaurant bar. The wait staff should know all brands available in each category in that restaurant. It is also their responsibility to offer a better-quality product if it will enhance the overall dining experience.

- **Well:** Lower-priced house brand. Often kept in the "speed rack" below the bar, out of sight of the guests.
- **Call:** A higher-quality and higher-priced brand that the guest will call for by name.
- **Premium:** Also called top shelf because they are usually kept on the top shelf for more visibility. The highest-quality and highest-priced brands are in this category.

COCKTAIL SERVICE

The proper and safest method of serving a beverage from a cocktail tray is to hold the tray on the fingertips of the left hand, standing with the body's right side to the table. While keeping the tray evenly balanced, one glass is removed from the tray with the right hand. The server steps in toward the table with the right foot, with the right knee bent, and sets the glass in its proper place. The server must be especially careful during this operation, as there is a natural tendency when reaching in toward the table with the right hand to lower the left hand. This can tip the beverage tray and spill the rest of the glasses.

In a fine-dining restaurant, cocktail napkins should be used only when the drink is placed on a hard surface, such as a show plate. The cocktail napkin is intended to absorb moisture, which could drip on the guest, and to cushion the hard surface of the plate from the hard base of the glass. If the paper napkin is imprinted with a restaurant logo, the logo should face the guest. When drinks are served on a tablecloth, paper napkins are not used.

Before serving the first course, the cocktail is moved to the right of the first service glass, and the cocktail napkin and any used garnishes are removed. If the show plate has been soiled by the cocktail service, it should be replaced with a clean show plate if it is to be used as an underliner. The guest may want another cocktail before dinner. The server should be aware of the timing of the meal when serving another beverage. Formally, when wine service begins, cocktail service ends and glasses may be removed. Guests may, however, want to finish their cocktail or have another before ordering wine.

In serving second cocktails before the guests have finished their first, the second is placed to the guest's right, near the top of the knife. The glasses should not be married, as the first glass may contain nothing but melted ice. The guest may indicate that the glass may be removed.

It is more pleasant for all the guests if the children in a restaurant are also served a drink that makes them feel special. Ginger ale or root beer can be viewed as something special. Also, unlike colas, they have no caffeine, which can also mean a more pleasant dining experience for everyone.

Beer

Beer is an alcoholic beverage produced from fermented grain, water, yeast, and hops. The main grain is malted barley, with wheat being the second most often used. Other grains may also be used, such as oats, rice, corn, and rye, but to a much lesser degree. Barley, as well as wheat, oats, and rye, is malted by allowing it to steep in water for a couple of weeks. Just before the grain sprouts, the malting is stopped by drying the sugar-filled germinated grain.

Hops flowers (or cones) contain the aromatic resins, oils, and acids used for bittering the beer; these provide beer's aroma and flavor. Hops also contain tannin, which helps to preserve beer.

Yeast converts the grain sugars into alcohol and carbon dioxide. Yeasts are either top-fermenting or bottom-fermenting; the type of yeast determines the beer type. Top-fermenting yeasts produce ales, while bottom-fermenting yeasts are used to make lagers. There are many kinds of ale and lager yeast, and they can have a profound influence on the beer's taste, sweetness, dryness, fruitiness, and texture. Ales are usually fermented for a shorter time at higher temperatures than lagers.

Lager beers tend to be light, crisp, and effervescent; they should be served at approximately 48°F (8.9°C). European beers are often richer, darker, and more robust than American beers and should be served slightly warmer, at 55°F to 60°F, unless the label recommends a specific serving temperature.

The strength of beer is usually listed as "percentage of alcohol by volume." To compare the strengths of beers with those of wines and spirits, multiply the percentages by two.

TYPES OF BEER

Type		% Alcohol	Type		% Alcohol	Type		% Alcohol
Lagers	American darks	4–5.5	Ales	American brown ales	4.5–6.5	Hybrids	American wheat beer	3.5–5
	American "lites"	2–5		English brown ales	4.5–6.5		Berliner Weisse	2.5–3.5
	American premiums	4–5		English mild ales	2.5–3.6		Dunkel	4.5–6
	Bavarian darks	3.5–6		British bitters	3–6		Weizenbock	6.5–7.5
	Bocks	6–7.5		Classic pale ales	4.5–5.5		Cream ale	4.5–7
	Doppelbocks	7.5–14		India pale ales	5.5–7		California common beer	4–5
	Oktoberfests	4.5–6.5		Imperial stout	7–9		Fruit ales/beers	2.5–12
	Pilsners	4–5.5		Stouts	3–6		Smoked beers	5–5.5
				Lambics	4–6		Specialty ales/beers	Variable
				Porters	4.5–6			
				Scottish Ales	3–8			

Many kinds of beer complement foods. Microbrews—produced by local brewers—are becoming increasingly popular with guests. Offering a good selection of beers will enhance the beverage menu. Beers are especially compatible with lunch but are also quite acceptable as a cocktail or with dinner in lieu of wine.

BEER SERVICE

There is definitely a place for beer in all styles of dining, especially with the beer renaissance that has taken place in America during the last decade or so. Beer enhances the beverage list and creates wonderful combinations with food. For example, pale

ale can be a great companion for spicy Mexican food, while a porter could be appropriate with a rare cut of lamb or porterhouse steak.

Beer must be poured into a perfectly clean glass; if there is any oil or detergent residue on the glass, it will destroy the head and flavor of the beer. There are several theories about the best method for pouring beer. The main difference between them is the resulting head on the beer, which is a personal preference. It is best to start pouring the beer straight down the center to the bottom of the glass, to allow the head to start developing, then tilt the glass and pour the remainder slowly down the side of the glass.

The longer the beer is poured straight down into the center of the glass, the larger the head on the beer. When serving the beer at a table, the server's left hand would still be holding a tray, so the glass cannot be tilted. The beer should be poured down the opposite side of the glass.

If the guest prefers a larger head on the beer, it should be poured more directly into the beer and less on the side of the glass.

According to Peter LeFrance in *Beer Basics*, the correct size of the head is as follows:

Lager   1 inch

Ales $^3/_4$ inch

Stouts $^1/_4$ inch

One type of ale, known as lambic, can be poured much like Champagne, since it is not known for producing the typical foamy head. In fact, it looks like a sparkling wine. Lambic ale is often made with a fruit; classically it contains a raspberry, cherry, or peach taste component. True lambics are aged beers fermented by wild yeast and bacteria that are indigenous only to certain parts of Belgium.

Beers can be matched with certain styles of glassware to heighten the quaffing experience. Steins are sometimes used as well, but in terms of glassware, a footed pilsner glass can be quite attractive for pouring a lager. Other types of glasses that

can be used include snifters, chalice-shaped glasses, and tulips, just to name a few. A framboise (raspberry) lambic looks especially good in a flute typically used for sparkling wines. Each Belgian beer requires a specifically shaped glass for that particular beer, but few restaurants can be expected to carry all the different kinds of glassware.

Some imported beers can deposit sediment at the bottom of the bottle (especially *weisbier*, or wheat beer) and should not be emptied completely. Beer stock should be rotated to ensure freshness and should always be kept out of direct sunlight; beers that are exposed to sunlight develop an undesirable "skunky" flavor.

Responsible Servers

While it is important to serve the guest additional beverages and make more sales, it is more important that the guests leave safely to return another day. Liability laws vary from state to state, but servers have a universal responsibility not to serve minors or anyone who is intoxicated. For more information, contact:

Health Communications, Inc. TIPS Program
(703) 524-1200

Bar Code and Right Mix
National Restaurant Association Educational Foundation
(800) 765-2122

Water Service

Water may be served automatically or on request, according to house standards. If a guest requests water, all the others should be asked if they would like water and if they would like tap or bottled mineral water. If they prefer tap water, glasses are brought on a beverage tray if not already preset, placed above each guest's knife, then filled with ice water from a pitcher. It is also acceptable to serve filled glasses of ice water from a tray. Glasses should be refilled frequently, never letting the mouth of the pitcher touch the glass (the pitcher could pick up germs from the glass, which would then be spread to other glasses). When pouring water, the glass should remain on the table unless there is some risk of spilling. Water glasses should not be removed from the table until the guests leave.

BOTTLED WATER

There are two main types of bottled water:

Sparkling bottled water: Carbonated water in which the carbon dioxide is from the same source as the water or an adjacent source can be labeled "naturally sparkling mineral water" or "naturally carbonated mineral water." If, on the other hand, the label reads "carbonated natural mineral water," then the carbon dioxide is not from the same source as the water.

Still bottled water or nonsparkling water: These noncarbonated waters may or may not be mineral water.

Bottled mineral water can be served at various times throughout the meal. To promote sales, suggest it:

- When water is requested
- When a cocktail is not ordered
- As a mixer with liquor or wine
- During or after dinner to refresh the palate

Every restaurant has its own manner of serving water. Certain aspects of bottled water service, however, remain constant.

- The water should be refrigerated to 38°F.
- Various types and sizes of bottled water should be offered.
- A garnish of lime or lemon wedge should be offered with the water.
- The bottle should be opened at the table.
- Bottled water should be served in a different glass from that used for tap water, preferably a stemmed glass. This will keep another server from accidentally pouring tap water into the guest's glass of bottled water.
- Bottled water should not be served with ice, unless the ice has been made from the same kind of bottled water.
- Large bottles of mineral water should be left on the table or in an ice bucket.

BOTTLED MINERAL WATER

Bottled mineral water is hard water, which some experts regard as being healthier to drink than soft water. This is partly because of the presence of trace elements in hard water, partly because it has not been treated or purified with chlorine or treated with zeolites in water-softening systems. In addition, some pollutants in tap water are causing concern to health officials.

Bottled water is gaining in popularity in the United States. Promoting the sales of bottled mineral water are these factors:

- Bottled water enhances the dining experience.

- It contributes to a sense of style about the operation.

- Bottled water increases the check average (and, consequently, the gratuity).

Iced Tea

Iced tea should be made before service. A strong brew can be prepared daily and allowed to cool to room temperature. An infusion can also be prepared by placing tea bags in cold water and steeping for one to two hours. Either brew will become cloudy if chilled. If that happens, add a bit of hot or boiling water to clear it. Iced tea should never be stored with ice already added.

Iced tea should be served at room temperature in a tall tumbler filled with ice cubes, accompanied by sugar, lemon, and a tall iced-tea spoon. Iced tea is served like any other beverage, from a tray at the guest's right. Refills of iced tea are usually automatic, although guests may need fresh glasses of ice

LEMON WEDGES

To cut lemon wedges:

- Remove the brand name (printed in vegetable dye or on a sticker) and rinse the lemon.

- Cut off both ends of the lemon.

- Quarter the lemon lengthwise, remove the center membrane, and remove the seeds.

- Cut eight wedges per lemon on a sanitized cutting board, not the bottom of a beverage tray, which is unsanitary and will be marred with cut marks.

or additional lemon wedges. As with water glasses, iced-tea glasses should be left on the table and the emptiest glass filled first, then proceeding with the pitcher, clockwise around the table.

Conclusion

Beverages, with or without alcohol, constitute an important part of the dining experience. Responsible beverage service is essential to the survival and success of any restaurant today. Although all aspects of service require the wait staff to be knowledgeable, it is especially important for servers to be well versed in the fine points of beverage service. Knowing the nature of the items served is key to assisting the customer, and essential in selection and proper presentation.

eight

Wine Service

Since wine holds a unique and very important place in dining, it is essential for the dining room professional to acquire a basic working knowledge of it. This chapter should provide that basic knowledge, although the study of wine can easily become a lifelong pursuit for those who become interested in the subject.

The Wine Itself

Vines are cultivated throughout the year. A vine may take three to five years before producing fruit that can be used to make wine. These vines may continue being productive for another seventy years or, in some cases, as long as a century.

Grape juice becomes wine through the process of fermentation. Fermentation occurs naturally when sugar and yeast meet under the proper conditions. In the process of wine fermentation, yeast, a living organism found on the outside of the skin of ripe grapes, transforms sugar, naturally present in grape juice, into alcohol and carbon dioxide.

Specific wines obtain their distinctive characteristics partly from the control of the fermentation process and partly from a combination of other influences, including the climate and soil in which the grapes were grown, the variety of grape, the condition of the grapes when picked, the age of the vines themselves, and the storage techniques used after fermentation.

Vintage

The date on a bottle of wine signifies the vintage year, the year in which the grapes were picked. Certain regions, notably for Champagne and port, date only the wines of exceptional years. These wines are known as vintage wines.

A vintage chart, which lists the relative quality of the years of harvest of various wines, can be helpful, but it is important to remember that table wines are living things: They are constantly changing. No two wines, even of the same district or grape type, are going to develop at the same rate. Furthermore, not all the wines made in a great year are great, and not all wines made in a relatively poor year are poor. Sweeping generalities cannot be applied, especially when the thousands of vineyards involved are considered. Vintage charts can be used as a guide only to the probable quality of the wine of a given year.

For low- to mid-priced wines, wine distributors generally ship the next vintage when the previous one has been depleted. This may not be noticed in time to update the printed wine list. It is the server's responsibility to make the guest aware of any vintage change, as well as any change in price. When presenting the bottle, the server may say something like, "The vintage you ordered is out of stock, and we were unable to update the wine list for tonight's service. Is this vintage acceptable?" Most of the time the new vintage will be fine, but it is much better to make the guest aware of it rather than have the guest discover it, initiating a feeling of distrust. For better wines and older vintages, the exact vintage is crucial. The wine must be tasted by the manager or sommelier before the wine is accepted and the wine list changed.

Types of Wines

TABLE OR STILL WINE

Table or still wine is simply grape juice that has been fermented. Some people assume that the term "table wine" means that the wine is somehow inferior to other wines, but that is not necessarily true.

SPARKLING WINE

When grapes are crushed and begin to ferment, carbon dioxide is produced as a by-product. If this carbon dioxide is captured sometime during the fermentation process, the result is a sparkling wine. The three ways to produce sparkling wine are:

1 *Méthode champenoise:* Fermentation begins in vats, just like other wines; however, from the time the wine is bottled for the second fermentation, the wine remains in the same bottle until it is consumed. Sugar and yeast (the first dosage, or *liqueur de tirage*) are added to the bottle, producing new carbon dioxide. While the wine sits in contact with this yeast, additional flavors develop. The spent yeast is gradually moved to the neck of the bottle by riddling, or gradually rotating the bottle, which is stored with its neck sloping downward. When all of the yeast sediment has moved to the cork, stopper, or cap, the neck is frozen and the cap or cork removed briefly. This expels the sediment. At this point, a second dosage, consisting of sugar and wine, the *liqueur d'expédition*, is added, the amount varying according to the style of wine being produced. These wines are labeled "fermented in this bottle."

2 *Charmat or bulk method*: The *charmat* method is used to produce inexpensive sparkling wines. Still wine is inoculated with a dosage in large tanks, under pressure. The resulting sparkling wine is then filtered and bottled.

SPARKLING WINE STYLES		
Category	Dosage	Sweetness
Extra-Brut	Little or none	Driest
Brut	Small amount	Dry
Extra-Dry	More than Brut	Medium dry, with some sweetness
Sec	More than Extra-Dry	Medium sweet
Demi-Sec	More than Sec	Sweet
Doux	Largest amount	Very sweet

3 *Transfer method:* Similar to the *méthode champenoise*, with the wine transferred to a special pressurized machine after the second fermentation. This machine removes sediment more quickly than traditional methods. The wine then receives its dosage and is rebottled. These wines are labeled "fermented in the bottle."

FORTIFIED AND AROMATIZED WINES

Fortified wines are those wines that have alcohol added, such as brandy, either to increase the alcohol content of the original wine or to stop the fermentation process. Many dessert wines are fortified wines.

Aromatized wines are those wines to which herbs, flowers, bark, or other flavorings have been added. Aromatized wines may be dry or sweet. Vermouth is a popular type of aromatized wine.

Wine Labels

The wine label gives essential information about each specific wine. Every wine bottle has at least one main label, and some feature neck and back labels with additional information concerning the locale or the company that produces (or bottles) the wine. Servers should familiarize themselves with the label before approaching the table. The label will indicate the four main items of information required by the guest: the type or name of the wine, the vintage, the region, and the producer.

While each wine-producing country has its own set of regulations governing the labeling of wines, all wines brought into the United States must list the alcoholic content of the wine. The label also indicates if the wine is a sparkling or still table wine. Most labels state the region, and often the vineyard or commune, in which the wines were produced. If there is no neck label, the vintage (if there is one) will appear on the main label, together with the name of the producer and/or shipper of the wine, as well as the importer. Any designation or special quality will also be shown.

Finally, all wines sold in the United States are required by the Bureau of Alcohol, Tobacco and Firearms (BATF) to bear a warning label about certain dangers inherent in the consumption of alcohol.

Tasting Wine

The tasting of wine calls upon more than the taste buds. To fully appreciate the character of a wine the senses of sight and smell as well as taste must be used.

Color and clarity: To determine the color and clarity of a wine, the glass is tipped and the edge of the wine is examined against a white background. Red wines lose color with age and fade from red-purple to ruby to red, red-brown, mahogany, tawny, and finally to amber-brown. White wines develop color with age and change from pale greenish yellow to straw yellow to gold, old gold, yellow-brown, amber-brown, and finally to brown. Rosé wines age from pink to orange to amber.

Body: To judge the body of a wine, some experts suggest swirling the wine in the glass. The "legs," or drippings running down the side of the glass from the rim, reveal the body of the wine. Dry, light wines have thin legs that flow quickly; full-bodied wines have slower, thicker legs. Other experts say that only by tasting the wine can the body be judged.

Aroma: Two-thirds of the judgments made about a wine are based upon its aroma. To release the aroma, the wine is swirled, allowing it to evaporate against the side of the glass. With more of the wine's surface in contact with the air, the aroma is intensified. The big red wines need five to ten minutes in a glass to fully develop their aroma. The wine term *bouquet* refers to those aromas, which are created during the lengthy aging of fine wines.

Taste: Taking a little wine in the mouth, the taster inhales through the mouth and "whistles" in the wine, actually chewing the wine to expose it to all the taste buds. All parts of the tongue can taste all four tastes (sweet, sour, salty, and bitter), but different parts have different degrees of sensitivity to the basic tastes. The front of the tongue is most sensitive to sweetness, the back to bitterness, the sides to sourness and the center to saltiness. The wine is judged for its degree of sweetness, acidity, and tannin. Too much acidity is unpleasantly tart, too little is dull, but balanced acidity gives a pleasant, lively sensation. In a young red wine tannin shows up in a puckering quality that will diminish as the wine gains balance with age. Tannin is essential for proper development of any good red wine.

Not only do dining room personnel serve wine, they also sell wine. The customer's impression of a wine, as well as other parts of the meal, is influenced both by how the wine tastes and by the manner in which the wine is presented, opened, and served.

Servers should try to taste wines to develop their judgment and range of experience. Keeping a notebook helps to remember wines previously tasted. It is necessary to record the name, vintage year, producer, cost, and brief personal comments. Many restaurants will make provisions for dining room personnel to taste the wines being offered on the wine list.

Wine Storage

Wine behaves like a living organism. It has a life cycle: It is born; it matures; it may get sick and recover; or it may die.

For a wine to be at its best when opened, it must be stored properly. The serious enemies of wine are prolonged contact with air, extreme heat or cold, fluctuations in temperature, vibration, sunlight, and strong odors (never store wines with foods).

Wine is best stored in a dark, well-ventilated, insulated, and temperature-controlled room. Many sources suggest that the proper storage temperature for all wine is between 55° and 60°F; others recommend a slightly lower temperature. All agree, however, that wine should be stored at a constant temperature, as excessive fluctuations in the temperature can result in the early demise of the wine.

Wine bins must be sturdy and wine bottles secured against rolling and vibration. This is especially important with robust red wines (where the deposition of sediment is inevitable with age). Wines should be stored horizontally. This will keep the cork moist and prevent it from shrinking. A shrunken cork allows air into the bottle, which may spoil the wine.

Wine labels should face up toward the ceiling, so that the wine can be identified without moving the bottle. The bins should be identified with numbers and/or labels. Some restaurants use small numbered labels on top of the bottles corresponding to numbers designated for the wine on the wine list. This allows for fast identification without disturbing the bottles. The server should remove these numbered tags before presenting the wine to the guests.

Convenient access to the wine storage area from the dining area is essential; otherwise, keeping a par stock (a supply equal to the amount normally needed) in the dining room is advisable.

Wine Serving Aids

For the guest to fully enjoy and appreciate wine as part of the dining experience, all wine service equipment must be handled properly. For service to proceed smoothly, corkscrews, wine buckets, decanters, napkins, baskets, and candles must be ready for use at all times. As always, mise en place is extremely important.

CORKSCREWS

Of the many varieties of corkscrews on the market, most professional wine waiters prefer the lever T-type corkscrew, which folds to a convenient pocket size. This is also known as a waiter's tool. The best corkscrew must have a spiral worm with the point in a direct line with the spiral. The worm should have at least five curves, the outside of which should be grooved; this gives a stronger grip on the cork. The spiral should be long enough to penetrate to the bottom of a two-inch cork. Avoid the use of worms that have small openings on the inside; they can cut corks (especially the old corks on expensive wines), causing them to break during extraction.

AH-SO

This cork removal tool supposedly got its name because it is "ah, so easy" to use. The way to use it is to insert the longer prong of the ah-so between the cork and the bottle and, while applying slight downward pressure, rock the prong back and forth until the shorter prong can also be inserted between the cork and bottle. Once both prongs are inserted, rock the handle from prong to prong, applying downward pressure. When the ah-so is fully inserted, simultaneously pull the handle upward and twist it to release the cork.

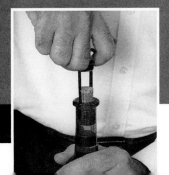

Most people who drink wine have broken a cork at one time or another. Corks usually break because the worm of the corkscrew was not far enough into the cork, because the worm was inserted at an improper angle and the cork is bent during the process, and/or because the cork was in poor condition. What to do?

Simply remove and discard the broken piece from the worm. Carefully insert the worm into the remaining portion of cork, trying to let it catch part of the cork without applying too much downward pressure. Turn the worm as far as possible, connect the lever, and lift. Present what is left of the cork as if it were a whole cork.

Careful: If pressure is applied, the cork could be pushed into the bottle of wine. There is a tenden-cy for wine to spurt out during this operation; also, the first glass of wine poured is likely to gush out of the bottle the instant the cork floats free of the neck—not particularly elegant, but not cause for a career change. There are even cork retrieval tools.

If no retrieval tool is available, the server can retrieve it with a piece of string. While it is generally improper to remove a bottle from the guest's view once it has been opened, in this case it is better to take the bottle away from the dining area, since the procedure might appear to be unsanitary. To retrieve the cork:

- Tie a figure-eight knot in the end of a clean piece of butcher's twine or heavy string. With the cleaned handle of a bar spoon, shove the knotted end of the string into the neck of the bottle, just past the floating cork. Ease the string and cork toward the neck of the bottle with the spoon handle.

- Once the knot is wedged between the cork and the neck of the bottle, give a steady pull on the string to pull the cork up and out of the bottle. This piece of the cork may, but preferably should not, be presented to the guest.

- Wipe the inside of the mouth of the bottle with a clean napkin to remove any pieces of cork. If a little piece of cork happens to go into a guest's glass (usually the host's, since the tasting portion is the first poured), continue pouring the wine for everyone. Replace the affected glass.

House policy may dictate that another bottle be brought to the guest rather than making the customer wait while the broken cork is being retrieved.

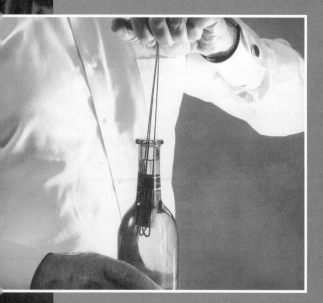

WINE BUCKETS

Wine buckets come in several styles, but whatever the style, a wine bucket has but two purposes: to lower and/or to maintain the temperature of the wine to the guest's liking. The wine bucket or cooler should not hinder service or the diners' enjoyment of the meal. The bucket should be filled three-quarters full with a mixture of two parts ice to one part water. The water makes it easier to place the bottle deep into the ice for quick, thorough chilling. A serviette or cloth napkin should be draped on the wine bucket for service. The guest should be asked if the wine is chilled to his or her liking. If the answer is yes, the wine bucket should be removed. Chilled bottles of wine are sometimes placed on the table in wine holders in order to maintain their cool temperature.

WINE BASKETS

Wine baskets are used only with red wines. Their primary function is to facilitate gentle transferring of a mature red wine from cellar to table or guéridon, for decanting. Some restaurants serve all red wines from baskets; most simply stand a young red on the table, though a more elegant presentation might call for a silver or china wine coaster.

Glassware for Wine Service

Almost as many types of wineglass exist as there are wine regions. A large restaurant or hotel may have a half dozen or more different sizes and shapes of glasses, but a moderate-size restaurant can get along very well with one all-purpose style of wineglass plus flutes for sparkling wines. The basic wineglass can be a clear, tulip-shaped glass with a capacity of about eight ounces. It should never be more than half full, to leave room for swirling the wine and allowing its bouquet to be released but collected in the air space above the wine. For large glasses, two general rules of thumb apply: white wine, half full (or four ounces); red wine, one-third full.

A typical all-purpose wineglass

If more than one all-purpose glass is desired, both the size and the shape must be considered when making a selection. The size of the glass must be compatible with the table setting, yet large enough to allow for a generous serving of wine to be swirled. Aperitif and dessert-wine glasses generally have a four- or five-ounce capacity, and only two to three ounces should be poured in. Red-wine glasses have a capacity of nine to sixteen ounces, although only four to five ounces should be poured. White-wine glasses are generally smaller than red-wine glasses, with a capacity of seven to nine ounces. Since white wine is served chilled, a smaller serving (about four ounces) is poured, allowing the remainder to stay in the chilled bottle.

GLASSWARE DESIGN

The best design for a wineglass is a stable-based, stemmed, bowl-shaped glass with the rim turned in slightly. The white-wine glass is tall and the bowl has a smaller opening to capture and hold the aroma and bouquet; the red-wine glass has a wider opening to promote aeration and to release acidity. The stem of the glass must be long enough to permit grasping the glass comfortably without touching the bowl, which would cause the temperature of the wine to rise. A stable base reduces the possibility of tipping the glass. The traditional saucer-shaped sparkling wine glass (according to legend, it was originally fashioned after Marie-Antoinette's breast) has lost favor. It has been replaced by a tall, narrow, fluted or tulip-shaped glass with a six- to eight-ounce capacity. This glass is filled about three-quarters full. The tulip shape lets the Champagne stay cooler longer, allows for appreciation of the color, and preserves the effervescence. Coupes and hollow-stemmed saucer glasses tend to warm the Champagne quickly, and their large surface areas cause it to lose its effervescence too swiftly. For this reason the saucer glasses are no longer recommended for sparkling wine, though they are commonly used for sorbet as an intermezzo.

The sight, smell, body, and flavor of a wine are ideally displayed and enhanced in a classic crystal wineglass, as thin as is affordable.

CLEANING GLASSWARE

Because the aroma and taste of wine are easily affected by foreign elements, special care must be taken in the washing and storage of glasses. The most effective method for preparing glasses for the table—after they have been washed and double-rinsed—is steaming and polishing, then drying with a clean dry cloth. Strong detergents and improper rinsing in industrial machines may leave a residue that can mask the quality of the wine and discourage the effervescence in a sparkling wine. Steaming involves no foreign elements (such as soap) that might affect the taste.

STORING GLASSWARE

All efforts to clean the glasses will be in vain if the storage method soils them afterward. For short periods of service, glasses can be stored upright on side stands. If they are placed upside down, they may acquire the smell of whatever they are resting on or become contaminated. If hung from overhead racks, oily smoke and odors can collect on the glass and impair the flavor of the wine. (State and local health codes may vary on the

STEAMING GLASSES

Steaming glasses is a simple procedure.

- Fill a hotel pan or similar container two-thirds full of hot water and cover the pan with aluminum foil. Make a small hole in the foil to allow steam to escape. Keep the pan hot by placing it over a lit can of Sterno like a chafing dish or bain marie. Hold the wineglass by the stem with the bowl directly over the hole, thus allowing the steam to fill the bowl of the glass.

- Or hold the glass over a clean pot filled with hot water. Or steam an entire rack of glasses over an uncovered hotel pan.

- Finish by wiping with a clean lint-free cloth. Local health codes may mandate the use of rubber gloves during polishing—or not permit steaming or polishing at all.

use of overhead racks.) To keep dust or dirt out of upright glasses, they should be covered with paper towels or a clean cloth. For longer periods of storage, glasses should be kept base up in a rack of the correct size. If glasses are stacked in a rack that is not deep enough, the stems of the glasses may be broken.

HANDLING GLASSWARE

Wineglasses are fragile and expensive, and so in addition to proper cleaning and storage, they must be handled and carried correctly. Servers should never "claw" glasses, or put their fingers inside of the bowls of the glasses. Skin oils can be

1. Turn left hand palm upward, keeping hand relaxed. Place a glass upside down between index finger and middle finger. Add a second glass between middle finger and ring finger.

2. Add another (third) glass by placing it between thumb and index finger.

3. Place a fourth glass between fourth and fifth fingers.

4. When adding a fifth glass between the thumb and index finger, be sure the originally placed glass is as far into the space between the thumb and index finger as possible. The fifth glass can be additionally secured by sliding the base under the other one.

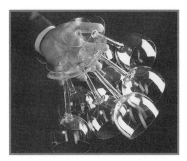

5. Add a sixth glass between index finger and middle finger; a seventh glass between middle finger and fourth finger, and an eighth glass between fourth finger and fifth finger. As you are adding these final glasses, nestle the bases between the originally placed glasses. Curl thumb and index finger upward, applying pressure against the bases of the glasses. This helps to lock the glasses to one another.

removed only with detergents, which are far from ideal for glasses. Soiled glasses should be handled by the stem or with two fingers around the base of the bowl. Contact with the bowl of the glass should be avoided at all times.

If a number of glasses must be carried by hand, management may allow them to be held upside down by placing the glasses between the fingers and locking the bases together with the thumb.

Carrying glasses in the manner shown eliminates the need for use of a tray and thus the need to dispose of the tray after placing glasses before the guests. This skill supports speed while maintaining safety and hygiene. The number of glasses one can carry may be adjusted according to hand size.

Clean glasses should be handled individually, using two fingers and the thumb to hold the stem of the glass. Wineglasses should be placed on the table prior to service as part of the table setting, to expedite service. If not included in the table setting, they should be stored at side stands or the bar, conveniently accessible to the table. Once a glass has been polished, the less it is handled, the more attractive it will remain. Like other glasses, wineglasses are transported on trays.

WINE DECANTERS

Wine decanters are cleaned and maintained in the same manner as wineglasses. Since decanters are generally used for older, more delicate, and more expensive wines, particular care in cleaning, storing, and handling is essential.

Taking the Wine Order

The position of sommelier, or wine steward, has become rare in today's restaurants. The sommelier's expertise, nevertheless, represents a branch of the culinary arts that should not be too casually set aside. People everywhere are becoming more aware of wine and how it complements food. The fine service of wine may add to the guests' knowledge and enhance the occasion, as well as encourage return business.

Whether by a sommelier, maître d', or other server, the wine order should be taken with elegance and grace. The server should check the type of wine, the vintage, and producer before leaving the wine storage area. Many restaurants offer a wide selection of wines by the glass, in which case many people at the table may need to see the wine list. The server should address everyone at the table: "Would you care to see our wine list?" or "Will you be having wine this evening?" The server should not assume that only one person, man or woman, will ask for the wine list. While any one of the guests might make the ultimate decision, the wine list should always be presented to the host or hostess of the party, from the right. Then the server quietly excuses him- or herself and tends to other duties for a few minutes, being watchful for any sign that the host or hostess is ready to order or wishes assistance.

When the server returns, he or she should ask, "May I be of any assistance with the wine list?" The server should not make any suggestions while the guest makes a selection but should be prepared to answer any questions and take the order. If the guest desires some assistance in selecting the wine, however, a knowledgeable server can make an intelligent suggestion based on what foods the guests have ordered and the preferences of the guests, such as "not too dry." The server can also ask, "What do you normally enjoy?" Using the response, the server can suggest similar styles of wine from the house wine list.

Wine charts are used in some restaurants to inform the service staff of which wines are available and what foods they best accompany. These charts allow the staff to make intelligent suggestions. A typical chart includes the list number (from the wine list), name, phonetic pronunciation, year, bottle size, price, type (red, white, sparkling), origin, serving temperature, characteristics, and recommended accompanying dishes. The more involved charts also deal with the body, flavor, and bouquet. Wine charts are usually posted in the wine distribution center in the restaurant for easy access and convenience to wine servers.

If the guest asks how much wine to order, the standard guidelines are: a half bottle for two persons; a full bottle for two to six persons; a magnum or two full bottles for seven to twelve persons. The order is then left to the discretion of the host.

When taking the wine order, the server should write everything down—the size of the bottle, the year, type, name, and location code or bin number. The wine list should then be removed from the table and the host asked when the wine is to be served. Precise instructions are necessary. If the guest asks that the wine be served with the meal, the server should inquire further to determine which course. Finally, the guest should be thanked for the order, and the server should withdraw.

Customers Who Want to Bring Their Own Wine

In restaurants where alcohol is served, as much as 35 percent of revenues may be based upon the sale of alcoholic beverages. It is important to balance the establishment's needs with those of clients who want to bring in special wines.

A policy might be established that guests may bring in a special bottle of their own wine only if that particular wine is not on the restaurant's wine list. This does not address the question of lost revenue every time a customer does it.

The only establishments that routinely allow bring-your-own are those without liquor licenses, but the practice may be restricted by local laws. Some cities prohibit this practice. A customer who wants to bring a special bottle of wine from his or her cellar for a special occasion should not be offended by being refused. It should be made clear that this is an exception to the rule, and the corkage fee should be stated if there is one. The corkage fee may be waived for special customers.

Corkage fees reimburse the restaurant for the cost of handling the wine, washing the glasses, cleaning napery, and so on. Corkage fees generally run from $10 to $20 per bottle. An alternative is to charge the client the equivalent of an average-priced wine on the list. Since a percentage of the corkage fee will be added to the gratuity, the server does not lose out.

Serving Wine

Once the wine has been ordered, a decision must be made as to when it will be opened and served. If the host has given no instruction in this regard, these guidelines should be followed: White and rosé wines should be opened and served with the first course; red wines should be opened and held at room temperature, on the table, immediately following the presentation to the host.

There are, of course, exceptions. Some guests may prefer no white wine at all and have red throughout their meal. Or white or rosé wine may be requested with the main course, for example, when all the guests at the table are ordering poultry or fish as a main course. Some (but not all) red wines should be decanted or poured into glasses as soon as possible. This aerates the wine, allowing it to breathe. In addition, some very tannic young red wines are softened by this exposure to air. After aeration, the red wine should be served just before serving the main course. Many older reds would be damaged by sitting in a glass or decanter for a long period and should be poured very close to the time of the main course.

If separate wines are to be served for different courses, and if the glasses are to be set for each service, the glasses should be carried to the table on a hand tray or on a wine cart. Some houses allow carrying the glasses by hand, holding them by the stem. The new glass should be placed on the table from the right side of the guest, using the right hand, to the left of the previous glass. The next wine should be poured before the previous glass is removed. If wine still remains in the old glass and the guest wishes to keep it, the glass should not be removed, but glasses should be removed as soon as the previous wine is finished, unless a guest indicates otherwise. Depending

CORRECT WINE TEMPERATURES		
		Ideal
Dry white and rosé	44° to 54°F	48°F
Light-bodied red	50° to 55°F	53°F
Medium- to full-bodied red	55° to 65°F	60°F
Sparkling	41° to 47°F	44°F
Sweet (but not fortified)	41° to 47°F	44°F
Port	Room temperature	

on the style of service, the house rules may allow the server to ask the guest if he or she may remove the glass. This can prevent embarrassing situations caused by assuming the guest is finished. In some cases, as at the end of a course or when a wine change has been ordered, it is proper to ask for permission before removing the old glasses, regardless of whether or not there is wine remaining.

The server must be certain that the wine is at the proper temperature before serving.

These temperature suggestions can be further refined within the following ranges: For reds, generally, the younger the wine, the lower the temperature; the older the wine, the higher the temperature. Delicate light wines and sweet wines are served cooler than full-bodied white wines. Beaujolais and Sancerre Rouge—like their Italian relative, Dolcetto—are sometimes served cool or slightly chilled. Allow the wine to arrive at the desired temperature naturally.

WHITE AND ROSÉ WINES

White and rosé wines must be chilled before serving. The temperature range for serving these wines is from 44° to 54°F. Overchilling will diminish the bouquet of the wine.

The wine bucket should be filled three-quarters full with a mixture of two parts ice to one part water. Fifteen minutes in a wine bucket will sufficiently chill a white or rosé wine.

After opening a chilled wine, the server should be sure to wipe the water from the outside of the chilled bottle with a napkin each time it is removed from the wine bucket and before the wine is poured. This avoids dripping very cold water on the guests.

The following procedure involves the use of a waiter's corkscrew. Some establishments may use variations on the method described or may use a different style of corkscrew, but whatever method is used, it is important that the style of service be the same for all servers.

If a wine bucket is needed, place the wine bucket to the right of the person ordering the wine before the bottle is brought to the table. When serving white or rosé wines, ask the taster if the wine is chilled to his or her liking or if it should continue to chill in the wine bucket. If the wine needs no further chilling, place the bottle on the table or on an underliner. If the wine needs further chilling, or if the guests may order additional wines that may require chilling later in the meal, the wine bucket may stay beside the table. If neither of these conditions applies, remove the bucket at this time.

Show the bottle to the person who ordered the wine, from the guest's right side, while quietly indicating the vintage, the producer, and name of the wine for the guest's approval. Present the bottle on a serviette so the entire label can be read (photo 1).

If approved, proceed to pour; if not approved, make the necessary corrections at this time.

Preferably place the bottle on a surface to open it: in a wine bucket for white, rosé, and sparkling wines; on the table, guéridon, or side stand—in that order of preference—for red. Some restaurants allow bottles of still wines and sparkling wines to be opened in the air (if servers are confident and proficient). Never brace the bottle against the thigh or between the legs.

Cut the capsule (the covering over the cork) just below the second lip of the bottle, to prevent any contact of wine with the foil, plastic, or wax, although some establishments prefer the capsule to be cut just above the lip (photo 2).

Place the neck of the bottle between the thumb and the blade and draw the blade around the bottle. Avoid rotating the bottle, as this may disturb any sediment in the bottle. After the first cut, turn the hand palm up and draw the blade around the bottle to complete the cut (photo 3).

To remove the capsule, hold the waiter's corkscrew with four fingers of the right hand, with the edge of the blade toward the thumb. Steady the bottle with the left hand. Place the right thumb on top of the capsule and the edge of the blade firmly against the neck of the bottle at or just above the cut line. While pressing down with the thumb, slide the blade up and over the top of the bottle, freeing the capsule (photo 4).

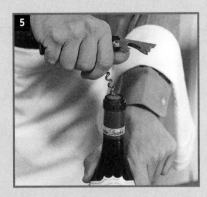

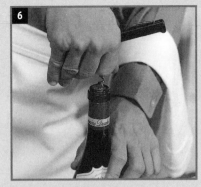

The cut capsule should be put in the server's pocket, not in the wine bucket.

Insert the corkscrew slightly off center at a slight angle and straighten it up with one or two turns (photo 5).

The corkscrew is turned until only one notch of the spiral is left above the cork, about five and a half turns (photo 6).

Tilt the handle of the corkscrew so that the shorter leg can rest on the lip of the bottle, held in place with the forefinger (photos 7 and 8).

Pull the corkscrew straight up, pushing down with the base of the index finger while pulling up with the pinky while being careful not to bend the cork and not to touch the mouth of the bottle with the hands. When withdrawing longer corks, it may be necessary for the elbow to rise as well (photo 9).

After releasing the lever, turn the corkscrew a final notch. Rock the cork slowly back and forth while pulling the cork toward the ceiling (pull gently, to avoid making the cork pop).

Wrap an index finger around the cork (without touching the end of the cork that was inside the bottle) and untwist the corkscrew from the cork (photo 10).

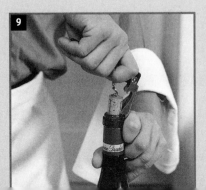

Place the cork to the right of the host's glass or on a small dish, if desired. Corks from red wine may be placed on end, with the moist end up (to avoid staining the tablecloth), allowing it to be seen by the host. The purpose of presenting the cork is to identify the producer, whose name or logo usually appears on the cork, and to make sure that the cork is in good condition and that only one end is moist. This indicates proper storage. Tartrate crystals, which may appear on the cork, are a natural by-product of wine and do not mean the wine is bad (photo 11).

Wipe the lip and mouth of bottle using a clean serviette (see the note on decanting red wine on page 156). A third of a portion, about one ounce, is poured for the person who ordered the wine (photo 12).

The label always faces out when pouring, to facilitate guests' viewing the label. Lift and twist the mouth of the bottle at the conclusion of pouring, to prevent wine from dripping down the side of the bottle onto the table. Wipe the mouth of the bottle again with the serviette. All wine is tasted in the same glass that will be used to drink it from. As the guest tastes, the bottle is presented on the serviette again (photo 13).

If the wine is accepted, pour for the women, then for the men, pouring for the person who ordered the wine last. (House protocol may vary for larger parties.) A 750 ml bottle contains 25.6 ounces, so the server must portion accordingly. A portion is between four and five ounces regardless of the glass size. Some Burgundy glasses may hold sixteen to twenty ounces, so a proper portion of four ounces is one-fourth to one-fifth of a glass. If the party is larger than six people, a five-ounce pour per person will result in the host receiving no wine. The server should pour four ounces in each glass, or it could be suggested (for parties of this size) that two bottles be ordered. Reading the table is very important, however. For example, the party may desire one bottle of each of several types of wine in smaller portions rather than several bottles of one type of wine.

Remove the cork at this point unless the guest wants to keep it. It has served its purpose and should be discarded (but never in the wine bucket).

Refill glasses as needed, filling the emptier glasses first, at close to the level of the fullest glass, then evenly dividing the rest. If a guest's glass is sufficiently full, skip that guest in the protocol of pouring. Since some guests may not want more wine, discreetly offer the wine rather than automatically pouring it.

If a second bottle of the same wine is ordered, present a new glass to everyone at the table. Since this requires more glasses and hence more storage space and more time spent washing and polishing glasses, some establishments offer a new glass only to the taster. Present new glasses to all guests, however, whenever a different wine is ordered or when a second bottle of a rare, older, red wine is ordered (since there may be significant variation from bottle to bottle).

Always replace glasses when they are no longer presentable, are smudged, or contain sediment.

RED WINE

When serving red wine, remember these procedures.

- Red wines are not usually chilled, so no wine bucket is needed.

- Wine should be decanted to aerate or if the wine contains sediment. Wine should always be handled carefully to avoid disturbing the sediment. Bottles of red wine should be stored and carried with the labels facing the ceiling.

- Wine may be opened and decanted some time prior to pouring and placed in the center of the table to aerate.

- During decanting, never completely empty a bottle of an older vintage red wine, for fear of pouring out sediment.

SEDIMENT AND DECANTING

All red wines may develop sediment in the normal process of aging.

Any sediment occurring in a white wine is usually colorless and does not affect the taste or quality of the wine. The sediment, which is not due to aging, may derive from pectins or tartars and usually disappears in a warm room. If not, stand the bottle upright to allow the sediment to fall to the bottom of the bottle. Decanting is not necessary, unless requested by the guest.

The sediment in red wine comes from tannins and color pigments. Because this sediment has an unpleasant and bitter taste, it should never be allowed into a guest's glass. Decanting is done to draw off the clear wine and to leave any sediment in the bottle. Ideally, the wine should be decanted as early as is appropriate for the particular wine before it is to be served. This allows the wine to breathe. Contact with air may expand the bouquet and enhance the flavor of a wine. Decant as soon as the bottle has been opened.

All wines should be stored and transported with the label up. However, if a wine with sediment has been rested with the label on one side, it should be placed it in the basket the same way to avoid stirring the sediment. Wine connoisseurs will appreciate your explanation.

WHEN IN DOUBT, DON'T PUNT!

The server should never pour sparkling wine by inserting the thumb into the "punt" or inverted dimple in the bottom of the sparkling wine bottle and supporting the bottle underneath with the four fingers.

In decanting, the wine server should follow these procedures:

Use only a perfectly clean and dry decanter.

Transport the bottle gently and carefully, preferably in a wine basket (photo 1).

Be sure to cut the capsule by turning the blade of the waiter's corkscrew, not the bottle (photo 1). Remove the entire capsule from the neck of the bottle. Remove the cork (photo 2).

Clean the lip of any residue (photo 3).

Hold the clear shoulder of the bottle in front of a lit candle and pour a few drops of wine into the decanter. Swirl and pour off this bit of wine into an extra glass. This ensures that nothing in the decanter contaminates the taste of the wine. Meanwhile, hold the bottle of wine steadily in front of the candle, so the flame can be seen through the shoulder of the bottle (photo 4).

Continue to pour the wine into the decanter, closely observing the shoulder of the bottle. Stop pouring the moment sediment appears.

Allow the host to taste the wine and, upon approval, ask when the wine is to be served.

Serve as usual. Leave the empty bottle on the table along with the decanted wine.

To serve sparkling wine properly, follow these procedures. (Directions are for right-handed servers; left-handed servers should reverse the positions to achieve comfortable and smooth service.)

Chill the bottle in a wine bucket, if necessary, before serving. More time is required to chill sparkling wine than white wine because the glass of the bottle is thicker.

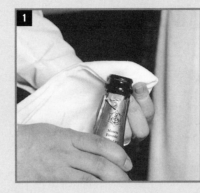

Leave the bottle in the wine bucket, at a 45-degree angle; place a serviette over the top of the bottle. Loosen the foil capsule.

Holding a thumb on top of the cork, carefully untwist the wire cage with the other hand.

If the cork starts to rise, hold it in with the thumb and allow pressure to escape slowly. This may occur with shaken or insufficiently chilled bottles.

With the cork held with one hand and the bottle kept at a 45-degree angle in the wine bucket, directed away from the guests, turn the bottle with the other hand. Hold the cork, resisting its pressure while allowing the gas to escape slowly.

Never allow the cork to pop or escape all at once. Remove the cork completely. Keeping the bottle at a 45-degree angle for a few seconds after the cork is removed will prevent overflow.

Once the cork is removed, present it to the host. Wipe the mouth of the bottle (photo 1).

Use a serviette to wipe excess water from the bottle. As with still wines, expose the label when pouring.

Pour slowly, about one ounce, for the host's approval (photo 2). While the host tastes the wine, again present the bottle on a serviette, so that the guests can see the label. Once approved, pour one to two ounces for the next guest, let the foam subside (photo 3), and pour another two to three ounces (photo 4). Follow the same procedure for each guest.

Pouring a little sparkling wine first, then pouring again after the foam subsides, is referred to as "priming" the glass or "pouring in two motions."

Return the sparkling wine to the bucket.

SAKE SERVICE

Sake is a brewed rice beverage with an alcohol content between 15 and 20 percent. It is a light yet hearty beverage, in some ways similar to beer but without the carbonation. With the increasing popularity of Japanese-style restaurants, today's servers need to know how to serve sake.

Each brand of sake has a distinctive flavor. Most (but not all) sakes are not, generally, improved with age, and there is a lively competition in Japan to be among the first to taste the new sake of a fresh harvest.

The Japanese never pour sake for themselves—it would be considered rude. The host and guests pour for each other. Sake cups are customarily filled to the rim when poured by the host, as a sign of the host's hospitality or generosity. The recipient always holds the cup out to receive the sake, never places the cup on the table to be filled. When the guest has had enough, the cup is left full.

Sake is often, but not always, served warm. When it is mulled to about 100°F, or slightly above body temperature, the warmth releases sake's subtle flavors and aromas. The very best sakes, however, are usually served chilled, to prevent the premature loss of their delicate flavors and aromas.

Conclusion

Wine represents a very large portion of the total check—and consequently the gratuity. In some fine-dining restaurants, the wine may exceed 50 percent of the bill. In addition, the markup on wine makes it one of the most profitable items a restaurant can sell.

The ability to speak knowledgeably about wine with guests increases their confidence in the server and the restaurant. Opening a bottle of wine with grace and confidence is one of the hallmarks of a professional server. Wine knowledge and serving skills are clearly important areas for any server to develop.

There are an incredible number and variety of wines to taste and contemplate. While wine knowledge is essential in fine-dining establishments and in many bistros, the study of wine must be limited in a book of this size. A number of excellent books and periodicals on the subject are listed in the Bibliography (see pages 264–275), for those who wish to continue their study of wines.

nine

Farewells

The last things a guest experiences at a restaurant are often what is remembered most. Consequently, how the server handles the end of the meal greatly influences the way guests perceive the entire dining experience and therefore affects the likelihood that they will become repeat customers. Since this is when guests pay the check, the quality of service provided near the end of the meal can also affect the gratuity.

After-Dinner Beverages

Providing information on what a restaurant has to offer in the way of after-dinner drinks is not pushy salesmanship. This information can be provided in detail on a printed list with the desserts or verbally toward the conclusion of the dessert course. Drinks such as Cognac, Armagnac, cordials, or port can make the dinner a more complete experience. It is crucial that the professional server know the brand names and characteristics of cordials and brandies that are available and the vintages of dessert wines or ports. With the exception of dessert wines, these drinks are traditionally served with coffee after dessert, but guests may want them served with dessert.

Coffee

Coffee is an international sign of hospitality and can be the perfect conclusion to any dining experience—if certain guidelines are followed. To fully appreciate coffee, it is important to understand a little of its culture and history.

The word *coffee* is derived from the Arabic *gahwah* or from Kaffa, a province in southwest Ethiopia believed to be where coffee was first used as a beverage. Coffee is a tropical evergreen shrub that produces a cherrylike fruit. The seeds inside that fruit are the coffee beans. The shrub produces ripe cherries three or four times a year.

There are two common types of coffee beans, robusta and arabica. Robusta beans are higher in caffeine but also higher in chlorogenic acid, which produces an inferior taste. Arabica has about a third of the caffeine, and it produces a superior cup of coffee. It is also more expensive.

THAT EXHILARATING FEELING

Arab legend has it that Kaldi, an Abyssinian goat herder, observed his goats eating the berries and noticed the uncommon frivolity that followed. Then Kaldi tasted the berries and also experienced an exhilarating feeling. Eventually, as word spread, monks in the mid-ninth century brewed the bean in hot water, and coffee the beverage was discovered. The plant, however, was not cultivated until the fifteenth century.

CAFFEINE

Many people today are concerned about caffeine in their diet. To eliminate some of the confusion about the amount of this stimulant in various products, consider these figures, based upon a seven-ounce serving (except as noted):

Brewed coffee	80–135 mg
Drip coffee	115–175 mg
Espresso (1.5 ounces)	100 mg
Instant coffee	65–100 mg
Brewed decaffeinated coffee	3–4 mg
Drip decaffeinated coffee	4–5 mg
Instant decaffeinated coffee	2–3 mg
Brewed tea	40–60 mg
Iced tea (12 ounces)	70 mg
Instant tea	30 mg

By comparison, an eight-ounce bar of milk chocolate contains about 8 mg of caffeine, while a twelve-ounce can of Coca-Cola contains 45.6 mg of caffeine. Regional variations affect caffeine levels. In the South, where large amounts of iced tea are consumed, a weaker brew of tea is served than elsewhere. The total amount of caffeine consumed may therefore be the same for northern and southern drinkers of iced tea. Espresso drinkers, on the other hand, get a more concentrated dose of caffeine than drinkers of American-style coffee, but their portion size is much smaller.

(Source: Bunker and Williams, *Journal of the American Diet* 74 [1979]: 28–32.)

In order to bring out the flavor and quality of the coffee bean, coffee must be properly roasted. Too light a roast results in a thin and characterless product. The darker the roast, the more robust and less bitter the flavor. The longer or darker the roast, the less caffeine. Any bean from any country can be roasted to any level, but some beans lend themselves to a lighter or darker roast. American (full city roast) is the lightest roast. French and Italian are darker roasts, depending on the individual roaster. There are many variations in between, such as Vienna and New Orleans. Again, depending on the roaster, Vienna and Italian may be darker than French, or vice versa.

DECAFFEINATED COFFEE

Early in the 1900s Dr. Ludwiz Roelius Agerman developed a process of steaming unroasted coffee beans with the chemical solvent benzene. This process extracted the caffeine from the beans, which, when roasted, he called *sans caféine*, from the French for "without caffeine."

Although several methods are available, today there are two basic systems for decaffeinating coffee. Both use water for extracting the water-soluble caffeine from beans.

Swiss water process: In this method, the beans are simply soaked until most of the caffeine is extracted. The water is poured off, and the beans are then dried and roasted. While many people prefer this method because of its purity, some of the flavor is inevitably lost to the water along with the caffeine.

Chemical process: In this process, the beans are soaked in water to which methylene chloride has been added. This gas, which extracts the caffeine from the water, is released into storage tanks to be used again. The water is then poured back onto the beans, replacing some of the flavors. The beans are dried, then roasted. The use of methylene chloride is prohibited in some countries.

Decaffeinated coffee can be purchased in the form of beans for grinding, already ground in portion packets, or as powdered instant. Ideally, freshly brewed decaf should be served. If hot beverages are controlled in the pantry, this is easy to do. Great care must be taken to identify and serve the correct type of coffee, since many people cannot tolerate caffeine. If packets of powdered instant are used, they should be emptied into a preheated individual coffeepot.

COFFEE SERVICE

As with food, the table should be set before the service of the coffee with appropriate flatware, sugar, cream, and cups or mugs. It is preferable to preheat the empty creamers so the cream is warmed slightly and does not cool down the coffee. Coffee

STORING COFFEE

A number of points to be observed when storing and holding ground coffee or whole beans:

- Store coffee in a well-ventilated storeroom away from strong-smelling foods.
- Use an airtight, opaque container or vacuum packaging to ensure that coffee oils do not evaporate or become rancid, which could result in poor coffee.
- Keep the coffee container in the refrigerator but, preferably, not in the freezer.
- Rotate stock and check the date of grinding on bags.
- When possible, grind coffee to order. Coffee beans, like peppercorns, lose much of their flavor and aroma soon after grinding and are always best when freshly ground.

BREWING COFFEE

For the best possible preparation of coffee, follow these steps:

- Use freshly roasted and freshly ground high-quality coffee beans. If using preground, prepackaged coffee, open the bags only as needed. Ground coffee becomes stale with exposure to air. Opening several bags and stacking the filters can create stale coffee and produce grounds in the pot from the bottoms of filters.

- Use the correct grind for the particular coffee machine.

- Make sure all the equipment and pots are clean and free of residual oils. Oils become rancid and absorb room odors.

- Use filtered water that is free of any unpleasant smells or flavors.

- Use the recommended proportion of coffee to water.

- Coffee is best brewed at 205° to 208°F and held at 185°F. Boiling water will "burn" the grounds. Once brewed, never boil coffee, or it will develop a bitter flavor.

- Equipment should have sufficient capacity to meet the needs of the dining room.

- Preparing coffee by the pot is recommended for most situations. Large urns are best left for banquets and institutional uses. The fresher the brew, the better the product.

- Coffee should be held on a burner no longer than twenty to twenty-five minutes. Coffee can be held warm in thermal units for much longer periods.

- The flavor components of coffee have different densities. If allowed to stand in a thermal carafe, they can separate into layers. The flavor layers can be remixed by pouring off one or two cups of coffee and pouring them back into the carafe just before serving.

- Avoid marrying, or combining, pots of coffee. If a pot has been held for twenty-five minutes or longer, it will reduce the quality of the fresh pot when added.

- Use only orange- or green-handled pots for decaffeinated coffee.

can be served from the glass brewing carafe or from a preheated pot made of metal or ceramic, depending upon the style of service. A metal or ceramic pot should be carried on an underliner plate with a napkin, with the underliner held as a splashguard while the coffee is being poured. Good service techniques and well-designed pots should eliminate the need for splashguards. Coffeepots with a long, low spout minimize the possibility of splashing.

The cup should be left on the table when pouring and filled fairly close to the top, leaving enough room to add cream and to stir without spilling. By filling the cups adequately, the server will need to make fewer return trips to the table for refills. For the same reason, it makes sense when pouring for one guest to ask the other guests at the table if they would like coffee, and thus eliminate unnecessary extra trips.

Today there are dozens of popular dessert drinks made with coffee, from Irish coffee to flaming extravaganzas that show off the tableside artistry of a restaurant's

CREAMERS

Most creamers contain half-and-half rather than whole cream, but many people prefer milk or nondairy creamer. Regardless of its contents, the creamer should be small. It is unsanitary to offer a reused, possibly contaminated, creamer to another guest. In addition, large creamers are often overfilled, which is wasteful. Warm the creamer or keep it at room temperature until needed, then partially fill it just before serving to the guest. Creamers that have been filled and refrigerated will reveal an unsightly ring of fat and milk solids once some of the contents have been poured.

If individual disposable creamers are used, serve them in a small dish of ice so that the unused containers stay chilled and can be used later. When these are brought to room temperature and rechilled over and over, they can spoil. This spoiled cream will curdle in the guest's cup of coffee. Although the cup can be replaced, the guest may suspect that other products are less than fresh.

staff. Coffee drinks are high-profit—but only if the server remembers to include them on the check. Coffee is among the most frequently forgotten items.

ESPRESSO

The term *espresso* refers to an Italian process of roasting, grinding, and brewing coffee as well as to the finished beverage itself. The coffee must be dark-roasted and finely ground. Espresso should preferably be made from arabica beans, although many good espressos contain a blend of arabica and robusta beans.

Machines used for espresso prepare individual portions of coffee in seconds. Steam is forced through the grounds, infusing the coffee under pressure. The great advantage is that each cup is freshly prepared. While the dark-roasted beans used in espresso contain slightly less caffeine than lighter-roasted beans, the caffeine is more efficiently extracted than in other brewing methods. That's why espresso is served in small cups.

Taken black, espresso (known simply as *caffè* in Italy) is served in a demitasse cup with a demitasse spoon. The exact proportion of water to grains varies with the coarseness of the grounds and the pressure and temperature of each machine, but the general ratio is 0.25 ounces of grounds to 1.5 ounces of water. The grinders used for espresso are designed to dispense the correct amount of ground coffee.

Sugar is provided for espresso and cappuccino, which is espresso with foamed milk. Espresso is served in a demitasse cup with a demitasse spoon. Creamers are not served with either of these coffee drinks. Sugar should be preset on the table.

Americans often request lemon peel with espresso. *Caffè* served this way is called *espresso romano*. It is not generally served in Italy. A lemon twist, including the sour pulp, is not recommended because the citric acid overwhelms the delicate acids that give the coffee its bright taste. Needless to say, if a guest requests either lemon peel or twist, it should be delivered without comment.

For the best possible preparation of espresso, follow these steps:

- Check the temperature and pressure gauge of the machine.

- Add the proper amount of coffee to the filter. Tamp or press down the grounds into the filter.

- Insert the filter into the machine. Press the button to start the steam infusion (about twenty-five to thirty seconds). About five seconds of infusion time should pass before the espresso comes out of the filter.

- Serve in a warmed demitasse cup. Immediately after the coffee has brewed, tap out the grounds into a receptacle.

Cappuccino is named after the Capuchin monks, who wore robes of a color similar to cappuccino. A cappuccino is one-third espresso, one-third steamed milk, and one-third foamed milk (although some experts prefer one-third espresso and two-thirds foamed milk). Ideally it is served in a straight-sided cup as opposed to a curved one, to better measure the equal thirds of espresso, steamed milk, and foam. French café au lait is coffee with warm milk; café crème is similar to cappuccino. The popularity of these specialty coffees in the United States is increasing thanks to the availability of superior products and methods of preparation.

For the best possible preparation of cappuccino, follow these steps:

- Start as for espresso, through inserting the filter into the machine. Steam the milk. (Steaming the milk before brewing the espresso makes the beverage warmer.)
  This takes practice.

- Place the cappuccino cup under the spigot. Press the button to start the steam infusion.

- Wipe off spout after immediately after steaming.

- Add steamed milk to the coffee, while holding back the foam. Spoon on some foamed milk. Sprinkle cinnamon, cocoa, or chocolate shavings on top of the foamed milk if requested.

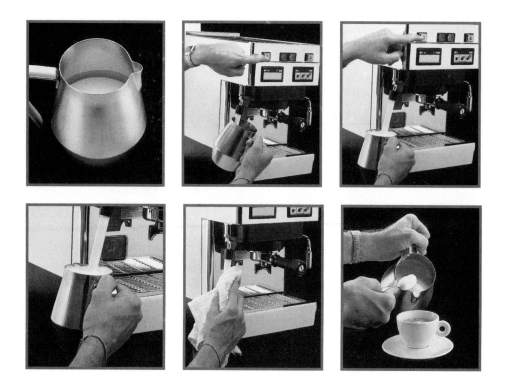

ITALIAN COFFEE TERMS

Many Italian coffee terms have passed into English. These include:

Doppio: A double, or two portions of regular-strength espresso in one cup

Ristretto: Espresso made with less water—about one ounce of water with the same amount of grounds—and therefore having a much stronger flavor.

Lungo: Espresso made by letting more water run through the grounds—about two ounces of water for the same amount of grounds. Sometimes called caffè americano.

Corretto: Espresso with alcohol, traditionally anisette, Cognac, grappa, or sambuca.

Caffè freddo: Iced, sweetened espresso, generally served in a tall glass.

Cappuccino: Espresso with foamed milk, sometimes garnished with a sprinkling of cocoa or cinnamon.

Cappuccino chiaro: Light cappuccino, made with more milk than regular cappuccino.

Cappuccino scuro: Dark cappuccino, made with less milk than regular cappuccino.

Cappuccino freddo: Cappuccino served in a tall glass, over ice.

Caffè latte: Espresso with more steamed milk than a cappuccino, generally without froth.

Macchiato: Espresso with a little steamed milk on top.

Latte macchiato: Steamed milk, usually served in a tall glass, with a little espresso on top.

Con panna: Like macchiato, but with whipped cream instead of steamed milk.

Tea

All tea comes from the leaves of the tea shrub (*Camellia sinensis*), cultivated in the East Indies, Africa, Australia, South America, China, Japan, and other places in Asia. The leaves, leaf buds, and internodes of the tea plant are cut and cured and classified according to the method of manufacture, for example, green tea, black tea, or oolong. Tea is graded according to the location of the leaf on the plant and leaf size, for example, orange pekoe (the smallest), pekoe (slightly larger), souchong (large), and congou teas. Tea also refers to an infusion made from tea leaves.

Tea is prepared by infusing tea leaves with fresh hot water; for convenience, a tea bag or tea ball may be used.

Infusions can also be brewed from herbs, bark, and grasses, singly or in combination. All types of tea can be further flavored and scented with dried flowers such as rose, chrysanthemum, or jasmine. Jasmine-scented black tea is low in caf-

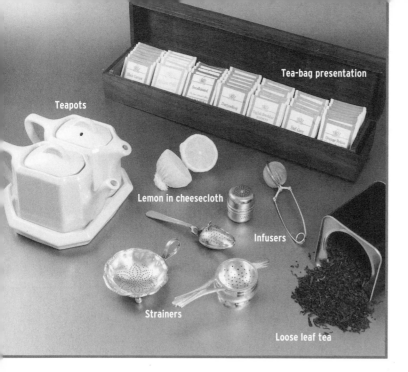

Teapots

Tea-bag presentation

Lemon in cheesecloth

Infusers

Strainers

Loose leaf tea

feine. Herbal infusions, technically tisanes, made from dried flowers, leaves, or fruits, are naturally caffeine free. These include chamomile, peppermint, spearmint, rose hips, and hibiscus. Restaurants are only beginning to explore the rich choice of quality teas available.

TEA SERVICE

Water contains dissolved oxygen that is essential to a lively cup of tea. When water is boiled, that dissolved oxygen is driven off. Most green teas are best brewed at water temperatures between 160° and 180°F. Most black teas are best brewed between 190° and 210°F.

In a formal, classic manner, tea is served with two preheated ceramic teapots with a capacity of about twelve ounces. Preheating takes the chill off the pot, ensuring a better infusion and helping the tea stay hot longer. One pot is used for the infusion (black tea should steep for a maximum of five minutes and green tea for a maximum of three minutes) and the other for additional hot water. This pot should be served at the end of the infusion time. Both pots are presented on underliners with a lemon wedge garnish. Sometimes the lemon is wrapped in cheesecloth to prevent seeds from falling into the cup or juice from squirting in unwanted places.

A heated cup is served on a saucer. The guest always pours. The guest first pours some brewed tea into the cup, then adds hot water to the desired strength. Herbal teas should also be served in this fashion. Since the richness of cream would mask the delicate flavor of tea, a choice of milk or lemon should be offered. In proper tea service, sugar cubes are served with tea, though honey may be preferred

with herbals. If only one pot is served, the hot water should be poured over the tea bag to begin steeping before the pot is served to the guest. An extra underliner should be served for the used tea bag, which should be removed from the table immediately after use.

Tobacco

Tobacco service, as practiced in some fine-dining restaurants, deserves special attention. When cigarettes or cigars are offered and served, an ashtray and a package of matches should be placed to the right of each cover, or one ashtray set so as to be conveniently shared by two guests.

CIGARS

Service for cigars is normally performed in a room separate from the dining room, unless it is part of a special cigar dinner. Cigar service is usually provided from a cart or guéridon equipped with cigars, cedar strips (from the box of cigars), a cigar clipper, an ashtray, and nonsulfur matches.

For proper cigar service, the server should:

- Present the cigars and allow the guest to make a selection.
- Unwrap the cigar and present the cigar to the guest.
- Clip the cigar.
- Warm the cigar if requested.
- Light the cedar strip or nonsulfur match and light the cigar with it, allowing the flame to be drawn to the cigar as the guest turns it to ensure that it is evenly lit. Some guests prefer to do this themselves.

CHANGING A SOILED ASHTRAY

When changing a soiled ashtray, care must be taken to prevent ashes from spotting the tablecloth. The following is an effective method:

- Take two clean ashtrays to the table.
- With an inverted ashtray, reach for the soiled ashtray, cap it with the clean ashtray, and remove both the soiled ashtray and its covering clean ashtray.
- Place the second clean ashtray on the table.
- Keep the soiled ashtray capped until reaching the bus/dishwashing area, to prevent ashes from flying through the air.

Check Presentation and Payment

The timing of the presentation of the check depends on the type of dining establishment and specific house policies. In more casual restaurants, the check is presented after the dessert and coffee are served. In some fine dining restaurants, policy may dictate that the check is not presented until the guest requests it. Whatever the timing of the delivery of the check, the presentation should not make the guest feel pushed or rushed out the door.

After the meal is over and everyone appears to be finished, it is permissible to ask, "Would you care for another drink, or may I refresh your coffee?" If the response is negative, a waiter may ask, "May I bring you your check?" or "Would you care for the check?" The check should never be tallied before asking permission, lest the server appear to be anxious to get rid of the guests.

The guest check may be presented in a special check presentation wallet, or turned facedown on a simply folded napkin or a plate, or folded in half on a cash tray. If no one at the table has specifically requested the check (or is clearly hosting the party), it is best to place the check in a neutral zone not too close to anyone. If there is an argument about who is going to pay, it definitely should be placed in a neutral zone. In some restaurants guests are expected to take their checks to the front desk or register. If that is the house policy, the server should so inform the guests. The server should not leave the table immediately after delivering the check. If guests are ready to leave, they may wish to pay immediately. If they do not indicate that they are ready to pay the check, the server should withdraw a short distance and wait for a sign that they are ready.

The server should be prompt but not overly hasty in retrieving payment once it is placed with the check. If it is in cash, the money should be discreetly counted before leaving the table; the plate is taken to the cashier, then returned to the table with the change and receipt. If the payment is not in cash, the server should take the credit card for processing, then return the voucher and the credit card to the guest, along with a plain pen, not capped and containing no advertising, with the possible exception of

---

CHECK PLEASE!

No matter the type of restaurant, most guests find having to wait for their check especially frustrating. Some of the nonverbal clues a guest might use to ask for the check include

- Looking around the room, as if searching for something
- Making a check mark in the air
- Writing with an imaginary pen in the air
- Placing a credit card on the table
- Reaching for the wallet or placing it on the table
- Returning napkins to the table
- Fidgeting
- Part of the group getting up to leave (likely a sign that the guests feel the server has been tardy in presenting the check)

the restaurant's name or logo. A good server does not ignore the table after the check has been paid. The guests may still want more coffee or water.

"ARE THEY EVER GOING TO LEAVE?"

How to deal with those diners who never seem to leave? Usually these are people who are having such a good time that after the meal they sit and sip endlessly, as if they were in their own living room. Meanwhile, the party waiting for that table is fuming at the bar. What is a server to do, especially in a fine-dining or bistro/trattoria restaurant, where clients are not very forgiving about waiting?

The Farewell

The late Joseph Baum, the well-known creator of such landmark restaurants as Windows on the World and the Rainbow Room, used to say, "The two most important things in a restaurant are the greeting and the dessert"—that is, the customer's first and last impressions. The absolute last impression is the good-bye. Restaurateurs who take the time to say "Good-bye" and "Thank you" to every customer engender goodwill. It shows that they care about clients even after the bill has been paid. When customers walk out the door unnoticed, they may be left with an uneasy feeling—certainly not a warm one.

It is not hospitable to ask, "Was everything all right?" If it wasn't, the server should have recognized it before then. Besides, there is not much that can be done at that point. It is best to say simply, "Thank you for coming. I hope you'll join us again. Good night."

PLATE OF MIGNARDISES

Some restaurants offer a plate of mignardises, such as petit fours or chocolate truffles, with the check. Something as simple as wrapped mints or special cookies will give the guest a "little sweet with the sour."

JEAN-CLAUDE BAKER, OF CHEZ JOSEPHINE, SHARES SOME THOUGHTS ABOUT DEALING WITH CUSTOMERS WHO NEVER LEAVE.

"A lot has to do with the price of the restaurant. If you are at Le Cirque in New York or maybe Valentino in Los Angeles, where dinner could be $100 or more per person, customers should be able to linger as long as they like. In a more casual place, such as Chez Josephine, with a lower average check and only seventy seats, you have to rotate the tables to survive. We have a payroll of twenty, and we'd starve if we didn't.

"Early diners are usually no problem. But the eight-to-ten-P.M. seating is where people often come late, order late, and sit over coffee or after-dinner drinks. Waiters are not usually aware of the timing problem, but managers and owners are, and they start to panic. They have to do something!

"If I know the customers, I might say, 'Please, you have to save my life! This table was booked at 10 P.M. and I have some people waiting at the bar for twenty minutes. Could I buy you a Cognac at the bar so you could save me?' I don't offer cheap dessert wine that comes in tankers; Cognac may cost me money, but it keeps the customer happy. When I share my problem with customers, they become part of the solution. People tend to be very nice about it. Most have no idea such problems exist.

"If I don't know the people, I might have to be more firm and professional. I might say, 'I'm sorry, but sometimes we have people waiting for tables that they have reserved at a certain time.' I might offer them something at the bar. It is a double-edged sword, really. If you approach people in the wrong way, you could destroy the good relationship that you have had for the past two or three hours."

Conclusion

In many sports, what matters most is the way the end of the game is played. While food service is not a game, many diners will remember only what happened at the end of the meal: the equivalent of the last plays and the final score. There is a major difference, however: Unlike in competitive sports, where someone has to lose, if servers pay close attention to the details at the end of a meal, there is victory for everyone. Guests will be happy, servers will get better tips, and management will make a profit—and, perhaps, turn first-time visitors into regular customers. Practicing the methods we've discussed so far will lead to success…most of the time.

Special Service Challenges

If all has gone well, guests have departed the restaurant feeling that they have been treated well and looking forward to a return visit. Unfortunately, things do not always go well. Let's take a look at some of the things that could go wrong—and what to do about them. As Duke Ellington once said, "A problem is a chance for you to do your best."

When something goes wrong in the dining room, the professional server really has two problems to solve. First, of course, is to remedy the immediate problem. More important is the guest's perception of the way the problem was remedied. If either is not handled well, the restaurant can lose a future customer, not to mention all the potential customers that will never visit because of complaints made by the original customer. Fortunately, the best way to handle one problem also solves the other.

What if a Customer Has a Complaint?

Anticipating guests' complaints is as important as anticipating their needs. After serving any food or beverage, servers should stay long enough to observe the guests' behavior and reactions, not disappear. If a guest seems dissatisfied with the food, beverage, or service, or if the server perceives any potential problem with a guest, it is wise to notify the dining room supervisor or manager after immediately handling the problem.

When a food item is returned because it is overcooked, undercooked, served at the wrong temperature, or unacceptable in any way, the guest is usually not charged for a fresh item if the kitchen or dining room is at fault. However, an additional charge may be made if the guest ordered incorrectly in the first place, as when a customer asks that a fresh steak be prepared rare, even though he ordered one well done. In some cases it may be better to appease the guest—even if the restaurant was not at fault—in order to keep, or develop, a regular customer.

If a guest is uncomfortable with the lighting or the temperature at the table, the waiter should first check to see that the prescribed settings have been maintained. If there is still a problem, the table should be changed to accommodate the guest.

THERE'S A FLY IN MY SOUP

If a foreign object is discovered in a guest's food or beverage, apologize immediately and replace the item. Most people understand that such things can happen, even in the most fastidious of places, but the mere glimpse of a hair or insect can spoil the appetite of even the most reasonable person. A guest may wish to order something different.

Always give the guest whatever replacement is requested, and make sure the offending item is removed from the bill. If the server handles this quickly and calmly, the guest will usually be forgiving. As soon as the problem has been resolved to the guest's satisfaction, be sure to inform the chef and manager.

The following six-step method for remedying an unfortunate situation should sound familiar, since it reflects at least three of the Nine Basic Principles of Hospitality and Service: Remarkable Service instills trust, depends on effective communication, and calls for flexibility.

None of these steps requires much more than common courtesy and an honest desire to please the customer, yet many restaurants miss this opportunity to secure repeat customers.

- Say you're sorry. In most cases, guests are willing to be understanding about a mix-up as long as they receive a genuine apology. Guests need to know that the server realizes that something is wrong and honestly wants to do something about it.

- Pay attention. If you listen carefully to what the guests are saying, there is a better chance of fixing the problem to their satisfaction. It's also the only way to get the information that's needed. It shows guests that the restaurant cares. Anything less than absolute sincerity will add insult to injury. Making and maintaining eye contact is essential. (This requires a special effort on the part of servers, because their job normally requires them to be scanning the dining room.) Guests with a complaint could perceive looking away as rudeness or inattention. To give the guests your complete attention, you should focus your eyes on the guests and their table only. Summarize the complaint or ask questions to make sure that it has been understood correctly.

- Make things right. Sometimes all that is needed is to give the guests what they wanted in the first place. Very often the problem was caused by miscommunication, either by the guests, who may not have really known what they wanted when they ordered, or by the server or the kitchen. It does not matter to the guests where the problem originated; in fact, they may be most upset by something that they themselves caused. What matters is that they feel they will be treated fairly in the resolution of the problem.

- Make it up to them. Even when things have been made right, the guests may still feel uneasy, if only because the order wasn't right the first time. To remedy that, you must do more than correct the error, by providing a little something extra. This might be a complimentary dish or drink (depending upon house policy), some special service, or some special attention. Different situations require different solutions.

- A promise is a promise. Never promise anything that you cannot deliver. If you say, "I'll be right back with your steak, just the way you like it," you must deliver on that promise. "Right back" may not mean the same thing to the guests that it does to the server. It is better to give an actual, realistic measure of time—five minutes, for example—and avoid any additional disappointment. This is an ideal time to provide a small snack, compliments of the house, to distract guests during their wait. Remember, the guests have already seen that things can go wrong; the server must go the extra mile to win back their trust. Likewise, if an offer to "comp" an item is made, make sure that it does not appear on the check at the end of their meal.

- Check back. While the guests are still at their table, find out if they are satisfied with the way the problem was handled. Additionally, management policy should require a call to the guests within a week to find out if they were pleased with the reparations that were made. If the phone number is not available from the information taken during the reservation process, the manager should ask the guest for it. The guests will be pleased with this concern for their happiness. It also gives the restaurant a chance to do its best, to find out how effective the recovery efforts were, and to let the guests know that the management values their opinions and patronage.

What if a Customer Tastes a Wine and Refuses It?

This problem can be resolved by suggesting a similar wine, from a different vintner or supplier, as a replacement. There are two reasons for offering a substitute:

1 The wine is bad. Since there is a good possibility that other bottles from the same case are also spoiled, the guest should not be served another potentially bad bottle.

2 The wine is not bad, but for some other reason it is not to the guest's liking. The guest therefore would not be happy with a new bottle of the same wine.

Some restaurants prefer the server to leave the wine and glasses on the table, excuse himself or herself, and bring the matter to the attention of the manager or maître d'. The manager can approach the table with an extra glass (or the sommelier with a tastevin) and ask how he or she may be able to assist the guests. The manager (or sommelier) can determine if the wine is in fact spoiled. In either case, future business is enhanced by trying to accommodate the customer and offering to help choose a different wine. For this reason, most restaurants replace the bottle immediately, with no questions asked. Admittedly, this generous approach can be painful when the wine in question is very expensive.

Even if house rules permit the server to make such decisions, the replacement must still be brought to the attention of the manager or maître d' immediately. Different restaurants have their own house rules that apply to this situation, and they should be followed, although even then the maître d' may make exceptions for valued customers.

The unused portion of an open bottle of wine that is not spoiled can always be sold as a wine-by-the-glass special or used for a staff tasting. Spoiled bottles of wine can be returned to the supplier for credit.

What if an Accident Happens?

If a minor spill occurs, the items on the table should be moved to one side for a moment, a clean napkin laid over the spill, then all the items returned to their proper place. With the assistance of a partner, this maneuver can be performed almost instantaneously. The guest isn't embarrassed by the spill and the table looks as if nothing had ever happened.

If something is spilled on a guest, the server should first assist the guest and clean up the spill. Of course, an apology is in order. An offer to pay the dry cleaning bill may be appropriate. The guest should be given a business card (to be returned with the dry cleaning receipt) with a notation of the date and the article of clothing and the manager's signature. The incident should be entered in the logbook for later reference.

If a serious accident occurs, the dining room manager should evaluate the situation immediately and decide if medical attention is required. In the event of any mishap, tending to the guest is of first and foremost importance. Once this has been done, house policy generally dictates the use of an accident report. This report should include all pertinent information concerning the accident:

- Name of guest
- Date and time of accident
- Name of server
- A complete description of the accident (including photographs of the area, if possible)

It is better to act than to react to a situation, always staying in control, no matter how trying the circumstances. The server or manager should:

- Listen carefully to the problem
- Apologize for any inconvenience
- Never argue or raise the tone of the conversation

The degree of finesse demonstrated in handling problems will encourage or discourage the future patronage of every guest present in the dining room.

What if the Unthinkable Occurs?

A reservationist's nightmare is getting a call from a customer who claims to have suffered from food poisoning as a result of a meal at the restaurant.

Every restaurant should develop a plan before a guest reports an illness that is believed to have resulted from dining there (see page 178). The receptionist's manual should include incident report forms and detailed procedures to follow. In many states, restaurants are required to notify the health department within twenty-four hours of such a phone call. Ideally, this is a situation that will never occur, but it could mean the closing of a business if it does and if it is not handled professionally.

FOOD SERVICE INCIDENT REPORT

If a guest calls suspecting a case of food poisoning, the employee should not become defensive, but should record facts that will enable the restaurant to investigate the problem. If the manager is not available, the employee should explain to the caller that a representative will try to call back within an hour or at the beginning of the next working day.

The person receiving the phone call should fill out the form and immediately hand-deliver it to the manager, who should:

Procedure Checklist

☐ Contact the manager/owner.

☐ Speak with the maître d' and chef.

☐ Speak with the person who received the call, if necessary.

☐ Collect, bag, and refrigerate any food in question.

☐ Reproduce the guest check.

☐ Obtain a menu abstract to determine the quantity of item in question served and to which tables it was served.

The manager should contact the health department and the insurance company after information is gathered and then call the complainant back.

DO	DON'T
Be sympathetic	Be apologetic or deny it
Tell them you're sorry they are ill	Say you're sorry the food made them ill
Get the form to the manager immediately	Suggest symptoms
Get all the information you can	Offer medical advice

SEE PAGES 261–262

What if a Table Gets Rowdy?

In a sense, rowdiness is in the eye of the beholder. What would be unacceptable behavior in a formal, fine-dining environment might be normal in a free-spirited bistro or family restaurant. If, however, a party is generating more noise and disturbance than is appropriate for a given establishment, that is, annoying other guests or even creating a dangerous situation, the situation must be controlled, firmly but diplomatically.

The server should immediately contact the manager or maître d', who must speak to the head of the party. If the guests cannot be controlled, they will have to be asked to leave. While this may deter that party from returning to the restaurant, failing to control the situation in a calm manner will discourage guests at nearby tables from returning, guests who would be more desirable as repeat customers.

What if a Guest Gets Drunk?

In most cases, the problem of rowdiness is really one of inebriation. Excessive use of alcohol must be controlled in the dining room and bar, not only because of its effect on the smooth management of the room and the comfort of other guests but because there are laws that make the establishment liable for any problems that result from the overconsumption of alcohol by guests while in its care. (These laws should be posted in the restaurant.) Even if guests have been drinking before their arrival, the restaurant is responsible for their leaving in a safe condition.

When guests have overimbibed, it is sometimes difficult to reason with them. As in the case of rowdiness, the situation calls for the calm experience of a manager or maître d'. One of the keys to success in dealing with drunks is to avoid any appearance of confrontation; they are often susceptible to arguments and fights.

DEALING WITH A DRUNK

Obviously, a guest should never be touched or embarrassed; the observance of these rules is even more important when a guest's normal judgment is impaired by overconsumption of alcohol. The following guidelines may be useful in dealing with the situation:

- Try to get the inebriated person on your side. Telling a guest "We want you to come back and we're very concerned about your driving home tonight. Let me get you something else to eat" can sidestep a confrontation. This tactic helps by changing the ratio of alcohol to food in the guest, and it also uses up some time, which is the only effective way to metabolize alcohol that is already in a person's system. Also try to get the guest to drink plenty of water.

- An intoxicated guest sometimes behaves badly because of the presence of friends. If this appears to be the case, try to get the inebriated person to step away from the table—so nearby guests can be spared the disruption of their dinners—where there is a better chance of discussing the situation calmly.

- If the guest refuses to listen to reason, offer the extra food on the house. Explain that if he or she insists on leaving while intoxicated, the restaurant is legally required to notify the police. Say something like "We would really like to avoid that. Please sit down and have some food and water."

- If there is someone else in the party—a spouse, a friend, or a relative—who can be used as an ally, there is a better chance of success in negotiating with an intoxicated guest.

- A report of any incident of this kind should be filed in the logbook.

What if Guests Bring Cellular Phones, Pagers, or Other Annoying Electronic Devices into the Dining Room?

Normally people answer their cell phones fairly quickly and (in all but the quietest of dining rooms) their conversations do not annoy guests at nearby tables. If someone is constantly receiving and making calls, however, he or she could be asked to take calls in the lounge.

Doctors, firefighters, and others who depend upon the use of pagers (or scanners) for notification of emergencies clearly need to be able to get their messages, but they can be asked to keep the volume turned down to a level that is acceptable in the dining room.

Children these days are almost never without some sort of electronic game or toy, and sound effects are simultaneously the essence of the game's charm (for the children) and one of the curses of modern life (for nearby adults). Asking a child to turn down (or off) the sound will probably provide only a temporary respite. It is better to distract him or her with some other amusement. Many restaurants keep a supply of coloring books and other quiet toys on hand for this purpose.

These items are also effective for reducing tension in the waiting area of busy restaurants. It is often helpful to have a number of different kinds of toys and games available: It gives the child more choices, and a second toy can improve the mood of a table when a child becomes bored with the first toy.

DROP THE SPOON

A baby's favorite (and endlessly repeated) game might be called Oops, I Dropped the Spoon. Get It and Wash It Off Again. Here's an easy way to avoid becoming trapped in this game, forever: Tie a piece of string onto the high chair, cut the other end two spoon lengths above the floor, then tie the spoon to the free end. When the baby tosses the spoon, it can't hit the floor. Mom or Dad pulls up the string and continues eating (without constantly asking the server for a clean spoon) in relative peace. Baby still has fun. The parents will not only appreciate the suggestion, they'll probably adopt this technique at home. They may even mention to their friends where they learned it.

What if the Guests Are Famous?

Some celebrity guests want nothing more than an opportunity to dine in peace, without being gawked at and fussed over. A maître d', sensing this to be the situation, will try to find a table that is somewhat out of the way and will assign an experienced server who is unlikely to be flustered by the presence of the celebrity. On the other hand, there are restaurants that are visited by celebrities precisely because they want to be seen. The staff of such places is accustomed to dealing with the special needs of their well-known guests.

Well-known guests and regular customers tend to be treated better than first-time visitors to a restaurant. This seems natural, but consider how it appears to the first-timer at the next table. It is important that all guests feel that they are receiving the best possible service. After all, those first-timers may become VIPs and regular customers in the future.

What About Guests Bringing Pets into the Dining Room?

According to most health departments, the only live animals allowed in restaurants are seeing-eye dogs or other assistive dogs. Guests with pets sometimes sit in outdoor café areas where available. If an outdoor café area is not available, the guest should be told of the health department regulations and politely told where the pet could stay during the meal. Some restaurants keep a supply of plastic bowls, marked for pets, on hand. Offering a bowl of water and a biscuit for a guest's dog is a gesture of hospitality that will be remembered by the dog and its owner.

What About Privacy?

Guests, being human, have all sorts of personal and business concerns that they would prefer to keep private. It is very important for servers not to accidentally violate their privacy. If, for example, there is a telephone call for a guest, the server should simply say, "You have a call, sir [madam]." It is neither necessary nor proper to announce the name of the caller.

While addressing a male guest by name is courteous, assuming that his female companion has the same name is not.

Conclusion

While customers are not always right, they are never wrong, so the professional server must behave as if they are right.

At some point in any server's career or in the life of an establishment, something out of the ordinary will occur. Remarkable servers can make use of their tact, flexibility, and good sense to get through the situation, no matter what it may be. Aside from minimizing the disruption to the workflow and (in some cases) protecting the establishment from potential lawsuits, the calm and reassuring presence of a good server or manager can forge an excellent long-term relationship with valued customers.

CHAPTER eleven

Special Functions

A banquet is an elaborate, often ceremonial meal for many people, frequently in honor of a person, persons, or an occasion. Regardless of the nature of the occasion, a banquet is a special meal, one that requires a great deal of planning. All of the factors involved—lighting, linen, wine selection, menu composition, and pace—must be planned in advance. With proper planning, the affair can be executed to perfection. Planning and execution are usually the functions of the catering department, but in smaller establishments they often become the responsibility of the dining room staff. The service staff should provide a high level of professional hospitality, making these special occasions memorable.

There are, essentially, four types of catering businesses:

- An establishment that does on-premises and off-premises catering
- An establishment that does off-premises catering exclusively
- A restaurant with full catering facilities
- A restaurant with limited catering facilities

Throughout this chapter we will refer to catering and banquets mainly as they pertain to restaurants, even though many professional servers have made a career of catering service.

Advantages of Catering

In catering, all sales are booked in advance. Consequently, the number of guests and the amount of food to be served are all known beforehand. This can offer some distinct advantages. For the server, a catered affair means the prospect of a guaranteed gratuity and the possibility of additional tips for special service. For the restaurant, there are other benefits:

- Cash deposits, which ensure an adequate supply of working capital
- Efficient portion and cost control
- Controlled labor costs, with a set number of hours and employees required for a function
- Reduced inventory costs (specialty items can be rented, and costs passed on to the client)
- Accurately forecasted sales and profits

- Use of facilities and equipment during normally unproductive hours or days when the restaurant is closed

- Revenue that can be used for upgrading facilities and equipment or for additional advertising—without having to raise menu prices

- Introduction of the restaurant to new, potentially regular, customers

Banquet Service

Banquets use several table service styles: American, platter, butler, or buffet service. Some events may use a combination of service styles, such as butler service for hors d'oeuvres and buffet service during dinner. To ensure success, careful planning is required, no matter which service style is employed. If established service procedures are to be altered, these changes or variations must be organized and all service personnel briefed on the changes well before the event. The demands put upon catering personnel require a mastery of a variety of service styles and a total understanding of all the details of a function and its timing.

To ensure that all duties are covered and that all servers are aware of their responsibilities, a meeting is usually held prior to the catered affair. The headwaiter uses this time to remind personnel that although a banquet is a routine function for them, it is a rare event for the guests, and every effort should be made to make it special for them.

While the servers, understandably, concentrate their efforts on serving at their own tables, it is important that they realize that the flow of the entire banquet is of paramount concern. For example, a sequence of service for all tables should be established ahead of time, and servers must follow it—the event is not, after all, a competition to see which waiter can serve his or her tables fastest.

Particular points to be covered prior to the function are:

- Menu and floor plan

- Number of tables and covers per waiter and per captain, if applicable

- Sequence of events, food and beverage service, and entertainment

- Mise en place, with attention to special equipment

- Specific points to remember, such as specialty presentations, styles of service, or special requests

Staffing and Setting up for a Banquet

The number of service personnel needed for a banquet depends on the total number of guests and the style of service. If American service is used at the banquet, one server should be allowed for every twenty guests; for Russian service, two servers for every thirty guests; for a buffet, one server for every thirty guests. For cocktail receptions or for butler service of hors d'oeuvres, one server should be scheduled for every thirty to forty guests.

When setting up the dining room, the head table should be positioned for optimal visibility by all guests. A dais, or raised platform, can be used if necessary, to allow viewing of the head table. The rest of the table plan depends on the type of function, the size and shape of the room, the number of guests to be seated, and the preferences of the organizer.

Round tables are ideal for banquets, since they allow for easy conversation among guests. Square footage allotments for banquets vary, depending on the specific service details (such as size of dance floor, placement of cake table or gift table, and so on). For sit-down affairs, from twelve to fifteen square feet per person should be allowed. Buffet service requires a little less space, ten to twelve square feet per person.

All tables, with the exception of the head table, should be numbered. Table numbers can be mounted on stands and should be visible to guests as they enter the room. Guests can obtain their table numbers from either a master seating chart or a special table set up to supply table numbers. The seating chart should be drawn prior to the affair. The organizer refers to the seating chart for checking all necessary arrangements and for stationing servers. The host consults the seating chart in developing a guest-seating plan. Any seating plan should allow for extra guests. Allowing for a minimum of 5 to 10 percent of the total number of guests should be adequate, but it is best to discuss this with the host.

As always, first impressions are very important. Tablecloths should be laid in an organized and systematic manner. Any overlap of cloths on a table should face away from the main entrance so that it will be less visible to guests viewing the room on arrival. Selection of tableware is based upon the menu. All tableware should be laid according to the style and sequence of service.

DECORATION

Consulting with the florist is part of the planning process. Servers need to know how to set the tables in conjunction with the decorations on the table. Generally, the florist is scheduled to arrive just after the tablecloths are laid but before covers are in place (so the centerpieces can be set). The florist may require assistance or may drop the centerpieces off earlier in the day for the servers to place them.

Servers should be careful to avoid spilling the water in the vases or disturbing the floral arrangements. Centerpieces should be below or on a stand above eye level so that the guests can see each other across the table.

Garland runners, often used with centerpieces, need to be placed prior to any condiments, such as salt and pepper shakers or candles. Runners should stop before the end place settings so that plates do not rest on the runners. The centerpiece is usually taken home by one of the guests at the table.

CANDLES

The florist may also supply candleholders. Candles should be lit before the guests arrive at the banquet. In an à la carte setting, candles should be lit as the guests are seated. Whenever candles are used, servers need to be especially watchful: Guests often toss their napkins or programs too near the candles when they rise from the table to dance or speak with friends.

Bar

There are two kinds of bar service, open bar and cash bar.

An open bar means that guests may have as much to drink as they like during a specified time period. Guests are not charged for drinks, but the host pays in a prearranged fashion. At a cash bar, guests pay for their drinks when they are ordered. Generally one bartender is assigned for every fifty people at either an open or cash bar.

Very often bar service is discontinued during dinner, when wine is normally served. The bar may reopen when dessert is served, so guests may order cordials or other after-dinner drinks during the dancing phase of the event.

When a facility has no physical bar, two clothed and skirted eight-foot tables can serve as front and back bars. The bartender must be especially careful to handle all bar items in a sanitary manner under such conditions. An ice scoop, for example, is mandatory.

Platter Service

The main goal of platter service is to serve fully cooked food while it is still hot and to serve it in an elegant manner. It is particularly useful at banquets or wherever large groups of people must be quickly served. Platter service can be an addition to preplated American-style service—for example, when offering extra main-course helpings.

All food is fully cooked, and placed on silver or porcelain platters or in soup tureens. Servers bring the platters to the dining room, present them to the head of the table, and show them to the guests before beginning to serve. The server stands with feet together, to the left of the guest. The platter rests on the palm of the left hand, which is protected by a folded side towel. The server bends at the waist, advancing the left foot slightly, and brings the platter close to the rim of the guest's dinner plate. Food is plated with the aid of a serving spoon and fork with the server's right hand.

Considerable skill, strength, and dexterity are required to perform proper platter service. Trays can be heavy and hot and must be held firmly in the left hand while the food is being served with the right hand from the guest's left. Practice is required to prevent dropping or breaking the food or spilling the sauce. Precise timing and organization are essential if the food is to reach the guests at its peak. The personnel in the kitchen must calculate the exact moment to platter the food so that it is presented to the guest without any change in flavor. Carving must be done in a minimal amount of time. Coordination for plating and serving throughout the meal can be achieved only if there are open and free-flowing lines of communication between the kitchen and the dining room.

While speed of service is essential, the food must still be arranged attractively and correctly. This is especially true when the dishes are accompanied by different garnishes, which must blend perfectly with the principal ingredient. The protein is placed on the portion of the plate closest to the guest, using the appropriate utensils, and the accompaniments placed neatly above the protein. They should be

RULES FOR PLATTER SERVICE

A few basic rules for platter service should be observed. The suggestions that follow will make it run smoother.

- Serve foods from platters from the guest's left; move counterclockwise around the table.

- Set in clean plates from the guest's right; move clockwise around the table.

- Remove soiled plates from the guest's right; move clockwise around the table.

- Serve beverages or soup from the guest's right; move clockwise around the table.

arranged on the guest's plate in the same form and shape as they appear on the platter. The food should be handled as little as possible to avoid breaking and changing its appearance. Teams of servers are sometimes used in platter service, since plattered foods or soups usually require a separate garnish, accompaniment, or sauce. The back waiter follows the front waiter in the same direction around the table, serving the accompaniment.

Additional suggestions for successful platter service:

- Know the number of portions expected from each platter.
- Use a clean serving spoon and fork for each dish.
- Avoid dripping food such as soup on the table or, worse, a guest. Dripping from the bottom of a ladle can be prevented by touching the bottom of the ladle onto the surface of the soup in the tureen after filling the ladle. Any soup that is clinging to the bottom of the ladle will fall back into the tureen.
- Lift and place the food gracefully. Never slide it onto the guest's plate.
- Become adept at the proper use of fork and spoon before attempting to serve the guests.

Buffet Service

Some buffets incorporate elements of various styles of service.

Guests may serve themselves at the salad station, be helped by a carver at the carving station, or watch a cook preparing pasta at the pasta station. Servers are responsible for cold and hot beverage service, clearing, setting coffee cups, sugars, creamers, and so on. When using a coffee station, extra care should be taken to keep the station free of debris. Sugar packets, disposable creamers, stir sticks, and the like tend to accumulate quickly. While it's wise to have a small basket on the table for discards, guests sometimes ignore it. Servers should monitor the cleanliness of the station at all times. Milk and cream can be served from insulated, and clearly labeled, containers. Individual milk or cream packets should be kept on ice.

Even with buffet-style meals, though, pouring coffee at the table is the preferred form of service.

After the dinner plates have been cleared, the creamers and sugars should be placed on the table; two of each would be sufficient for large rounds of ten. A table of twelve will need three sugars and three creamers. If the cups are not preset, part of the preparation for the event should be to stack ten saucers in the center of a

Particular concerns of buffet service include the following:

  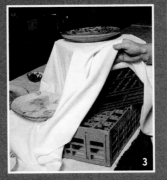 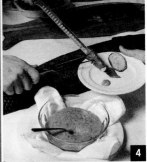

- If space for the length of the buffet line is limited, create wider tables by setting additional 8-foot tables on 4-inch-square blocks behind and overlapping the other 8-foot tables. The blocks should have small notched holes for the feet. The holes prevent the legs of the table from sliding off the blocks, which could cause the entire table to collapse. Using holes of different depths, deeper in the front than the rear, can provide a slight sloping of the table toward the guests (photo 1).

- If skirting is not available for the table, use table-cloths. A seventy-two-inch cloth will cover the tabletop and drape to the floor on one side of an eight-foot table. Another cloth of the same size will cover the other side of the table to the floor and the tabletop. This economical way of skirting can be disguised by using colored forty-five-inch squares placed on an angle, creating a bent diamond over the edge of the table (photo 2).

- To add height and create more visual interest, place items on the table on a variety of improvised platforms, including inverted empty glass racks or inverted empty milk crates covered with a cloth (photo 3).

- During a buffet, be sure to keep the table well stocked and presentable for the guests.

- Sometimes a buffet cannot be replenished from the back. When bringing in fresh food, remember that the guests have the right of way.

- Keep the buffet table and surrounding area clean, as guests frequently drop or spill food on the table or floor.

- Use underliners beneath sauces and dips to catch any drips. A soiled underliner can be replaced more quickly and easily than the entire cloth. Keep sauces and dips close to the table edge so that guests won't have to reach very far for them; this will result in less spillage (photo 4).

- Hand-wipe plates for the buffet line before service. Dishwashing machines do not always get all the food off the plates. It is very unappetizing for a guest to pick up a plate and find dried food adhering to it.

- Either place flatware at the buffet line (preferably at the end rather than the beginning so that the guests do not have to carry it through the line with them) or preset it at the tables. Extra china and flatware should always be available.

beverage tray and set ten cups around the edge of the tray. At coffee time, the server can simply place a cup on the top saucer, then place the saucer on the table with the handle of the cup in the four o'clock position. The server should proceed around the table clockwise, while another server follows with pots of regular coffee and decaffeinated coffee.

If the client requests it, an espresso cart may be rented to offer espresso and cappuccino. Orders can be taken by the server on a table-by-table basis or the guests can go to the espresso cart themselves. Although the word *espresso* means "fast," it can take a long time to serve a large quantity of these hot beverages. As china espresso cups are not usually available as rentals, the client should be informed in advance that paper cups may have to be used.

Timing of a Banquet

The importance of constant communication between the dining room and the kitchen during a banquet cannot be emphasized enough. The timing of courses may need to be coordinated with the band (or DJ) and certain traditional ceremonies. The banquet manager's and the client's planned schedule of events (Champagne toast, blessing, welcome speech, cake cutting ceremony, and so on) should be fully understood by the banquet headwaiter, the chef, the band, the photographer, and the videographer. Last-minute changes to the schedule on the day of the event must also be communicated to all concerned.

Although it is proper to set all food and beverage after the guests are seated, at casual banquets some may be preset on the table. This may be acceptable only if a cocktail/hors d'oeuvre hour is held in a separate room from the dinner and if it has been fully discussed with the client during the planning of the event. Preset items may include ice-water glasses, bread and butter, and a cold appetizer.

Preset items can save service time and allow more time later for dancing or other planned events. If a toast is planned upon seating, Champagne can be poured as well, though it is better to pour as guests are seated. (Not pouring for unoccupied place settings or for guests who do not consume alcohol can help to reduce costs). Since many people do not drink Champagne, the client may choose to have Champagne and sparkling cider offered, butler style, as the guests enter the dining room.

If the band is to receive a meal (often contracted at half price), it is advisable to feed them first. When the band stops to eat, the guests can be seated before the main course is served. The band returns when the guests have completed their main course so that the dancing can begin.

Conclusion

The service of banquets is much like professional service at other times. All the same skills are required, but in addition to the server's normal duties a greater awareness is required. Even more than usual, the server must be part of a smoothly coordinated team.

Because of the scale of these events, very careful attention to money is crucial to the success of the restaurant or caterer. It makes sense that these large affairs be handled with contracts and deposits.

CHAPTER twelve

Money Handling:
Taking Care of Business

No matter how impressive the food and service, a restaurant cannot stay in business if the servers do not properly collect the money for the checks. If the establishment does not use a computerized point-of-sale (POS) system, the handwritten guest check is the most important business form used in a restaurant for controlling food and beverages. It serves three specific purposes:

- Ordering food from the kitchen and/or drinks from the bar
- Obtaining payment from the guest
- Accounting, to the cost control department, for items sold

All information concerning a sales transaction between server and guest must be recorded on the guest check. To organize this data, most guest checks are made up of three distinct parts: an information box, the body of the guest check, and the customer's receipt stub.

The information box contains statistically valuable data, such as the date, table number, and server. It might also include the number of guests at the table, the location of the table (if there is more than one dining area), the time the order was taken and served, and the sequential number of the guest check. This number appears on the customer's receipt as well. The details recorded in the information box are used by the server at the time of service to ensure that tables receive their proper orders. Management also uses this information to determine how many tables or covers were served on a given day, how many meals, as well as how many tables and meals were served by each server. Recorded ordering and serving times allow management to identify busy periods and to adjust service or kitchen staff to meet demand and to improve upon the timing of service. The sequential guest check numbers provide a control system for management to account for every order.

The body of the guest check includes what is ordered, how it is to be prepared, special or specific requests for each item, the total charged for all items, taxes charged, and the service charge (if applicable).

The receipt stub is offered to the guest at the completion of the meal. It includes the name of the operation, the logo (if there is one), the date of the transaction, the total amount of the bill, and the sequential guest check number.

The layout of guest checks varies considerably, the nature and style of the restaurant dictating the type of guest check used. Casual restaurants may have the name and price of dishes and drinks already printed on the guest check to simplify order taking (only quantities need be added). Some guest checks include an area for tallying the orders by courses.

WAITER'S CHECK REPORT				
Check	Waiter	Signature	Unused Checks Returned	Sequence

Guest checks are issued by management to the designated cashier, who is responsible for signing them out to the servers at the beginning of each shift and for collecting all unused checks at the end of each shift. A lost check might indicate theft or carelessness. Before and after each meal period, the sequential numbers should be inspected to make certain that all checks that have been signed out are in the properly numbered sequence. A form should be designed for the waiters to sign out and be responsible for a sequence of checks.

Writing an Order

The check should be clearly and legibly written so that it can be understood by:

- The person taking the order
- The person entering the order into the POS system
- The kitchen staff
- Another waiter who might have to take over the table or replace someone at the end of the shift
- The guest
- The cashier
- The manager
- The bookkeeper

Symbols and abbreviations for food and beverage items can vary. All staff should use the same set of abbreviations to avoid confusion. Management often adopts standard abbreviations to be used by all service staff. Servers should be given a list of these abbreviations during their orientation and training. If a POS system is used, the abbreviations should match the names on the computer. To avoid confusion, no two abbreviations should be similar.

Generally, one check is written for an entire table, unless separate checks are requested when the order is taken. To facilitate writing and interpreting the guest check, a chair numbering system is developed by management and used by all members of the serving staff (see page 112).

After leaving the table, the waiter tallies the order in the space provided on the guest check or on a separate copy of the check known as a dupe (for *duplicate*). Tallies are usually done by course. Separate dupes may be required for the appetizer and salad courses if these items are picked up from separate stations in the kitchen. A POS system can be programmed to send the items to appropriate stations as well as to use two- or three-ply paper in the printers so that duplicate copies will be printed. The design of the guest check may include the necessary dupes in the form of tear-away carbon copies of the original guest check. Dupes are often color coded, with a different color assigned to each kitchen station.

Depending on the type of control system, guest checks can have any number of dupes, usually a minimum of three: one for the kitchen, one for the server, and one for the guest. The kitchen uses its dupe to fill food orders. The servers use their copies to know to whom each order belongs. The guest's copy is used as the bill and is later turned over to the cashier.

Sometimes dollar amounts are rung up on the register before a dupe goes into the kitchen. This pre-check system guarantees that all food ordered from the kitchen is charged to the guest. Should an error be made when an item is rung up, there is usually a pre-scribed house policy for the handling of a void or misring.

If an entire check has been filled and a second check is required, the first one should be subtotaled and added to the second. When presenting the check to the guest for payment, both checks should be included.

Check Presentation and Payment

While the techniques and timing of presenting the check were previously covered, there are still some fine points that need to be addressed.

Before the final tally of a handwritten check, any questionable prices should be checked against the menu or wine list. The subtotal should be checked twice. If it does not add up to the same amount, it should be checked again. Next the sales tax must be computed. The percent of tax varies from state to state, county to county, and city to city. For accuracy and consistency, a tax chart should be consulted whenever possible. Compute and record the service charge if applicable. Finally, calculate the grand total.

Any POS system will total the bill and calculate the taxes, but the server should carefully review it before presenting it to the guest. The server still has two responsibilities: one, to make sure that the restaurant collects what it is owed; and two, to make sure that the guest is not overcharged.

Whether a wallet or a plate is used to present the check, it must be clean and presentable. It shouldn't have any rips or chips. In restaurants where candles are used, guests often hold the check presenter wallet up over the candle to read the total, sometimes scorching (or even burning a hole in) the cover. Such damaged check presenter wallets should be discarded

Any questions guests may have concerning the bill should be answered politely. Guests have the right to understand what all charges represent. If an error has been made, the check should be recalculated and presented again. If a guest becomes difficult, the problem should be turned over the manager or maître d'.

HOW TO HANDLE VOIDS

- Circle the dollar amount and draw a line to a blank space in the body of the check. Never erase or black out an incorrect item.

- Write a brief explanation of why the item was voided.

- Record the new amount on the check (on a new line).

- Have the cashier or manager (whoever has been designated to handle voids) initial the transaction. A tally sheet for all voids is often used to simplify the reconciliation of voids on all checks. This tally also helps identify any server in need of additional training.

- If, for any reason, the whole check is voided, draw a line through the entire check, indicate that it was voided, and note the reason or reasons for the void.

- On POS systems the manager must void the item from the check. The typical procedure is to print the check, circle the item that needs to be voided, write the explanation, and give the check to the manager. These voids are often collected at the end of each shift to correlate with the voids report from the day's sales.

Personal Checks

If the management accepts personal checks, there should be a standardized procedure to follow. It usually includes, but is not be limited to, the following steps:

1   Checking the date written on the check.

2   Comparing the numerical figure with the written dollar amount.

3   Making sure the check is made payable directly to the restaurant (it is not advisable to accept second-party checks).

4   Requesting and recording identification of some sort; a current driver's license, a valid credit card, or a check-cashing card will usually suffice. If the dollar amount is above a maximum limit established by management, two pieces of identification and approval are normally required.

5   Initialing the check and presenting it with the guest check to the cashier.

Traveler's Checks

In most cases, traveler's checks are as good as cash. Certain precautions should be taken, however, when accepting traveler's checks as payment:

1   Checking that the traveler's checks are made payable to the restaurant.

2   Remembering that the second signature must be written in the presence of the server or cashier.

3   Comparing the countersignature with the original. If it is the same, the payment should be handled like a cash transaction. If the countersignature is not clearly the same as the original, the guest should be asked to write the name again on the back of the check.

4   If the traveler's check is from a foreign bank, the guest should be asked to show a passport for identification.

Credit Card Transactions

Credit cards and debit cards are widely used. Most restaurants subscribe to one or two major credit card companies, such as American Express or MasterCard/Visa, for the convenience of their patrons. The seals of the credit cards honored are usually displayed near the front door, by the cashier, and sometimes on the menu. All service employees, especially those answering the telephone, should know which credit cards are accepted.

MANUAL MACHINES

If the restaurant uses a manual machine, the following steps are followed to complete the transaction:

- Take the credit card and the guest check to the cashier, who imprints the card and the date on a charge-record form. In some smaller places, the server carries out these procedures.

- Before leaving the table, ask the guest to sign the back of the check. This is for the guest's protection, verifying that his or her signature matches the one on the credit card.

- Swipe the credit card through the authorization machine.

- Key in the dollar amount, including the estimated gratuity.

- Insert the credit card in the machine.

- Insert the correct bank credit card slip into the machine.

- Slide the arm across the machine and back to its original position.

- Check to make sure the credit card number, the date, and the restaurant information and number have been imprinted clearly and legibly.

- Fill in the charges, tax, and authorization number. (Registering the authorization number protects the restaurant from loss due to fraudulent use of the credit card by the patron.)

- Present the form, the guest's credit card, and a plain black pen to the guest. The guest adds the gratuity (or leaves cash), calculates the total charges, and signs the charge slip.

- Say "Thank you," using the guest's name.

- Show the guest which part of the voucher is the customer copy.

AUTOMATIC MACHINES

Many POS systems are connected to credit card authorization centers. Instructions vary according to the system, but the electronic transfer is basically the same whether it is connected to the POS system or not. The amount (total of the check plus estimated tip) is entered into the authorization machine, and a slip is printed that includes the authorization number. This slip should be presented to the guest in the same manner as a manually prepared voucher. Since various systems print vouchers in different forms, it is thoughtful to tell the guest which copy is the customer copy. There are no carbons to destroy with this method. After the guest signs the voucher, the server must reenter the exact amount (including gratuity) into the payment system. At the end of the shift or at a specified time, the funds are electronically transferred into the restaurant's bank account.

Certain circumstances may warrant calling for authorization. A manager should be called to resolve these problems:

- Charges are above the floor limit for the restaurant that has been established by the credit card company.

- The signature on the card and the charge record do not compare properly.

- The card appears to have been physically altered.

The credit card voucher slip is equivalent to cash for the restaurant. It must be given to the cashier. If the voucher is lost, the restaurant will not be paid and the server may be held responsible. The carbons (if any) from the voucher should be destroyed, since some unscrupulous people have taken the credit card numbers from these and made fraudulent charges. The vouchers must be manually totaled, bound, and sent to the bank for processing and payment.

The two basic methods used to process credit and debit card transactions are manual transfer and electronic transfer. Each method uses a different machine. Accuracy with either of these methods is crucial for both parties to be treated fairly, without the slightest suggestion that there is any intent to cheat.

Problem Areas

Sometimes the credit card authorization machine will decline the charge. In that case:

1   Try the card again, just in case the machine read the number incorrectly. It's possible but unlikely.

2   If the card is declined again, the guest must find another form of payment. This situation can be handled two ways:

- Ask the host if there is another credit card that can be used, saying, "The machine won't take this one." Usually guests know they are over the limit or that their payment was a little late and will quickly produce another card.

- To prevent embarrassment in front of the host's guests, quietly tell the host that he or she has a phone call at the front desk. When away from the table, explain that the credit card was declined and ask for another one. Some managers feel that this is too phony, that honesty is best. This decision is best made by the management.

3   If the guest argues that the card "must be good" and insists on talking to the bank, the bank's number is on the back of the credit card.

Occasionally the credit card company will request that the cardholder call the credit card company. In some cases an additional line of credit can be extended at that time. If this occurs, the server or cashier simply processes the card again and authorization is provided.

If the authorization machine displays the message "Call issuer," the server or the manager must call the number, which should be listed by the authorization machine. The issuer may say to keep the card, cut it in half, and send it back to the issuer. This, needless to say, can be somewhat distressing for the guest. But once the card has been run through the authorization machine, the credit card company knows the card has been in the possession of the restaurant, and it cannot be returned to the client. The card could be stolen; the account could be severely past due or canceled; or someone may have made fraudulent charges on the card and the guest may be totally innocent. It is not the server's place to judge, just to get the money for the meal.

Vouchers

Complimentary meals or vouchers are usually handled with a special letter or a form called a chit. The chit or letter should be filled out and verified. It should be signed and turned in with the guest check. A notation should be made on the guest check that a voucher was used. If the dollar amount of the charges exceeds the allotted figure, the difference must be paid. Management should include detailed information on the original voucher to explain what is included, any expiration date, and instructions to present the voucher upon arrival.

The server should be aware of all methods of payment and how they should be processed. In addition to house accounts, where certain guests are allowed to simply sign the check and pay at the end of the month, these might include promotional discounts, coupons and gift certificates; and prepaid or promotional complimentary meals.

Gratuities

Tipping is said to have originated from the practice of giving an innkeeper a gratuity in return for keeping one's stay a secret. It evolved into the custom of paying a little extra for proper and prompt service. The word *tip* is believed to have originated as an acronym for the expression "to insure promptness" and *tips* from "to insure proper service." The practice of tipping restaurant service personnel has developed to the point where gratuities are expected and may form the largest part of a server's wage. Self-service restaurants have become popular, not only because they provide quick service and standardized foods but also because tipping is not required.

The act of tipping can be awkward for the guest as well as for the server. Often guests do not know how much to tip and feel inept figuring out a percentage of the bill to arrive at an appropriate figure. The server is often anxious about the gratuity, fearing that it will be inadequate or even nonexistent.

Money awareness is extremely important at all times. Unfortunately, not everyone is honest. The best safeguard against dishonesty is to pay attention. Anyone handling money must be careful to execute each step of a transaction separately.

Cash Transactions

1 Count the cash received from the guest and mark the amount on the guest check.

2 Count the change before it is returned to the guest. When checking the change, do not add or subtract. Rather, count from the amount owed to the amount paid.

3 To avoid confusion, handle one transaction at a time, so that there is never a question about the moneys owed and returned. A "short-change artist" might ask for larger bills such as a $50 bill and then a $100 bill in the middle of the transaction to cause confusion and then take advantage of the situation. The best defense against these practices is to make the change first, then take care of any other transactions the guest wishes to make—always using only the guest's money.

What if a Guest Leaves Without Paying?

A "walk-out" is a guest who leaves the restaurant without paying the bill. If a guest is noticed leaving, it is best to assume that he or she has forgotten. Tactfully remind him or her (out of earshot of the other guests) about the check. The management should be notified immediately if a guest leaves the premises without paying. The manager will decide if the police need to be called. The server should not try to apprehend the guest alone; this could be dangerous.

What if a Guest Cannot Pay?

If a guest is without money, checks, or credit cards and has no obvious means of paying the tab, notify the manager or supervisor immediately. Most establishments have prescribed techniques for handling such situations that do not involve the server. The decision to call the police should be made by the manager.

What if the Restaurant Is Robbed?

The most important thing to remember during a robbery is to stay calm and to avoid direct eye contact, which can anger a robber. Heroic or dramatic actions can endanger the lives of innocent people, both guests and employees. It is important to try to remember any physical details about the thief that will help to identify him or her later. Management should have a policy in place that covers such situations, and all personnel should be acquainted with it.

Sometimes guests ask the server to calculate the tip. If the guest doesn't mention a percentage, the server should ask, "Is 15 percent appropriate?" The server should be able to make the calculations at the table.

If no tip is left, the server needs to assess the situation to determine if the service was unsatisfactory. If this is suspected, the guest should not be approached, but the manager should be notified. Since the gratuity is included in the price in many other countries (*service compris*), foreign visitors to the United States may make the assumption that this is also done in America, or they may not know the customary percentage. The manager, once notified, may speak with the guest to determine whether the service was unsatisfactory or if there has been a misunderstanding. The manager must decide, in each case, if it is appropriate to help the guest understand the custom of tipping.

To help prevent this uncomfortable situation from occurring, many operations add a service charge directly to the guest check. Usually an addition of 15 to 20 percent of the price of food and beverage is imposed by the house to ensure the incomes of the service staff and make it easier for the guests to tip. This can be done only if the management is confident that service is of consistently high quality. Recent trends suggest that this practice may eventually be the norm, rather than the exception to the rule, as service standards in this country improve.

To successfully implement the service charge, it must first be properly presented to the public. The guests must be informed, via the menu or a table tent, that a service charge will be added to the final bill, so that there are no surprises when checks are received. A service charge does not necessarily mean a waiter will lose his or her competitive spirit and provide lackluster service: Cash tips are often left along with the service charge if the service is remarkable.

Another contemporary approach to tipping is for the restaurant operator to establish proper salaries for professional service personnel, building the added expense into the sale price of the meal. In this way the operator assumes financial responsibility for the service staff.

It is the server's responsibility to keep records of all tips. The servers must provide copies of these records to the employer, who in turn passes the information on to the Internal Revenue Service. Cash tips must be reported to the employer on a monthly basis, on or before the tenth of the month following that in which the tips were received. To facilitate this procedure, tips can be recorded daily and calculated on a monthly basis, using a Daily Record of Tips Form (IRS Form 4070A) or similar worksheet. Monthly reports of tips to the employer can be made by using an Employee's Report of Tips Form (IRS Form 4070). Servers who receive more

SEE PAGE 263

than $20 in tips in any given month are required to report their tips using the IRS forms. Willful neglect by an employee to report tip income to an employer can result in a penalty of 50 percent of the tax due on unreported tips.

In addition, if a restaurant's reported tips are less than 8 percent of the restaurant's total sales, it may have to report allocated tip income. The restaurant allocates the same amount to all of its servers, who are, in turn, responsible for taxes on that allocated amount.

A complete explanation of the tax responsibilities of servers is available in IRS Publication 531, "Reporting Tip Income."

Conclusion

A restaurant is many things to many people, but it is always a business. It must make money to survive, prosper, and fulfill its obligations to its investors, its creditors, and its payroll. Clearly the handling of money by the service staff is essential to the existence of the business.

Safety and
Sanitation

A conscientious effort must be made to ensure the personal safety of everyone in a restaurant, guests and fellow workers alike. Accidents do not just happen. More appropriately called incidents, they are usually caused by neglect, carelessness, thoughtlessness, and ignorance. Most can be avoided.

Falls

Falls account for most accidents in restaurants. People can easily fall over furniture, cords, equipment, even handbags. For this reason, nothing should be left in the path of traffic. Never leave anything in stairwells or near doors. To minimize the chance of tripping, electrical cords should be kept off the floor. Furniture, if temporarily moved, must be put back where it belongs as soon as possible, and equipment put away immediately after use. Chairs must be kept out of dining room traffic aisles. All servers should be aware of women's purses under chairs or tables, since the handles may trip someone in the aisle. If a bag or its strap is discovered protruding into or obstructing a walkway, the server should not move the bag but ask its owner to move it to a safer place. Some additional causes of falls are:

Loose carpet threads or other faulty part of the stairs or railings: Such disrepair should be reported to the manager at once.

Wet or oily floors or spills that have not been wiped up: Spills are often caused by someone whose hands are already too full. Therefore when a spill occurs, it should be wiped up by the first available employee (rather than waiting for the person who caused the spill).

Unsuitable shoes: Shoes that are perfect in the dining room are not necessarily safe in the kitchen. Safe, nonskid rubber soles can be applied to any shoe.

Unsafe ladders, chairs, and windowsills: A safe ladder is one that is tall enough to permit working comfortably while standing at least one step from the top. Standing on chairs or windowsills is very dangerous.

THE TEN RULES OF RESTAURANT SAFETY

1 Safety is everyone's business. Consider yourself a member of the safety committee. Report unsafe conditions immediately.

2 When you see anything on the floor that does not belong there, be it a spill or an object such as a handbag, remove it or ask the guest to remove it.

3 Report all injuries, no matter how slight, and get immediate first aid.

4 Walk, do not run, especially in halls or on stairs. Always keep to the right, and be particularly watchful at corridor intersections.

5 Be especially careful with swinging doors. If there is a window panel, look before opening; if not, open the door slowly, using the handle or push plate. Use the appropriate in or out door.

6 Avoid horseplay and practical jokes. Harmless fun can result in injury.

7 Report all defective equipment. Obey safety rules when you are working with any equipment.

8 Avoid backing up or making sudden jerky movements.

9 Always wear shoes with nonskid soles.

10 Always store cleaning chemicals far away from any food products or service ware.

- If the tray does not have a cork or nonskid surface, place a damp napkin on the tray to prevent items from slipping.

- Place heavy items in the center of the tray and slightly toward the carrier.

- Place flatware and smaller items toward the outer edge of the tray.

- Never stack cold food on top of hot food when plate covers are used. Heat travels upward and could warm the cold plate to possibly unhealthy temperatures.

- Place liquid carriers (coffeepots, water pitchers) toward the center of the tray.

- Let nothing project over the edge of the tray, where it can be easily jarred.

- Keep open plates containing food well away from the hair.

- Do not overstack or overfill trays. Get help or make additional trips. A tray should contain no more than six to eight covered plates or two stacks of four dirty plates with flatware placed around the edges of the tray.

Loading, Lifting, and Carrying Food Trays

Many restaurant incidents can be prevented through the correct handling of trays in the dining room. Proper balance, with equal distribution of items, is essential for transporting food and related items. Certain guidelines should be followed in loading a tray to ensure safe and sanitary handling.

When carrying stacked dishes without using a tray, servers should not carry more than they can handle. Resting a stack of plates in the bend of the arm should be avoided, as the stack may collapse. A stack of clean plates should be covered with a clean napkin and carried directly in front of, and slightly away from, the body.

Practice is essential in developing tray and dish handling skills.

Some servers prefer to rest the tray on their spread fingertips instead of their flattened palm. They feel it gives more balance and maneuverability. Only experience can tell what works best for a particular person. Try both methods and decide

- Carrying heavy trays or awkward loads should not be attempted until the server has practiced enough to do so confidently.

- When lifting a tray, let six inches of the tray project over the edge of the tray stand, side table, shelf, or counter it is resting on. Placing your flattened palm under the edge of the tray, toward the middle of its broad side, grip the edge of the tray with your free hand. (See photo, page 207.) If the tray is heavy, the hand should be kept there.

- Bending carefully at the knees and lifting with the legs and back (not the arms), slide the tray out and onto the flattened palm or fingertips.

- When carrying a tray at shoulder level (known as a high carry), hold your upper arm close to the body and the elbow against the body.

- The tray can be rested on the shoulder for additional support only if absolutely necessary, but this should be avoided—the tray can easily become unbalanced, allowing items to fall. The high carry is particularly effective when a tray must be carried through a crowd.

- When carrying a tray at waist level (such as a cocktail tray), keep your shoulders back. Slouching shoulders will cause the tray to be unstable. The weight of the tray should rest on the hand. While the tray may touch the forearm, the load should not rest there, or it may tip. In maneuvering through a crowd, the server should guard the tray with the unoccupied hand.

- Do not allow guests to remove drinks from a cocktail tray unless you are supporting the tray with both hands. If supported by only one hand, the tray will become unbalanced and tip.

for yourself, practicing first with an empty tray, then, when that feels comfortable, with a loaded tray.

If the doors you must pass through are hinged on the right, carry the tray on the left hand; if they are hinged on the left, carry it on the right hand. This way the free hand can open the door and protect or balance the tray. If either the right or left hand is not strong enough to support a loaded tray, however, use the stronger hand.

Never serve the guest directly from— nor clear the table directly to—a large tray held in the hand. In French service, always clear china and flatware from the table by hand, without the use of a tray; clear glassware directly to a handheld beverage tray. Never set the tray on the table.

Busing Dishes, Glasses, and Flatware

Bus boxes or bus tubs are often used in operations with high turnover, where speed is important. When loading a bus box, rest it on either a rolling cart or a tray stand. The seat of a nearby chair is commonly used; however, the bottoms of tubs are often wet, resulting in wet or stained chair seats. Bus boxes, like trays, should never be set on tables.

LOADING BUS BOXES

- Place refuse into one corner of the bus box.
- Load the largest dishes first, placing heavy items in the center. Cups and bowls may be nested. Place glasses upright to one side; do not put anything into glasses that might cause them to chip, crack, or tip over. Flatware should go on the opposite side from the refuse (so that flatware is not accidentally tossed in the trash). Load butter dishes, creamers, or other food receptacles last.
- If a rolling cart is not used, carry the bus tub over the shoulder or in front of the body, ideally with a clean cloth covering the soiled wares.

- See that ashtrays and receptacles are provided and used in all appropriate areas of the dining room.

- If candles or oil lamps are in use, watch to be sure that napkins or menus do not catch fire.

- Be careful cleaning ashtrays. They should never be emptied directly into wastebaskets or other rubbish containers.

- Do not use defective electrical outlets. Report them immediately to the manager.

- Report all frayed cords and loose connections to the manager.

- Never use an improper extension cord (too long or rated too low for intended use) or adapters. Plugs have three prongs because the ground is important; do not attempt to defeat the purpose through the use of two-pronged adapters.

- Never overload a circuit.

- Exercise extreme caution when flambéing food in the dining room. Take special care when lighting gas jets or alcohol burners. Always remove the pan from the flame before pouring the alcohol. Keep guéridons at a safe distance from the guests, draperies, sprinklers, or heat sensors. Extinguish all flames before moving a guéridon in the dining room.

Fire Safety

Fires present two clear classes of danger: the injuries and destruction caused by the actual fire, and the panic that overcomes people and prevents them from thinking and acting rationally. Fire safety encompasses both preventing fires and doing the right thing if a fire breaks out.

The best way to fight fire is to prevent it. As with accident prevention, fire prevention depends on the application of common sense by everyone in the operation.

Every restaurant must have a fire plan in effect. This is an orderly sequence of steps that is coordinated with the local fire department, in compliance with local building codes.

If a fire does break out, the emergency action taken in the first five minutes is extremely important. To be prepared in the event of a

WHAT TO DO IF A FIRE BREAKS OUT

- Do not panic.
- Pull the nearest fire alarm box.
- Notify the main switchboard and fire company as to the exact location and nature of the fire.
- Take the logbook from the front desk (it contains information about the number and locations of people inside the building).
- Assist guests to safety.
- Send someone to explain any special concerns to the fire-fighters when they arrive.

fire, the staff should be trained to know the floor plan of the area and the entire building, to be familiar with exit routes and alternatives, and to know the exact location of fire extinguishers and how to use them. Every member of the staff should be trained in assisting guests to leave the building safely in the event of an emergency.

Burns

Some dining room equipment and utensils can cause severe burns.

Hot plates and platters should always be moved or positioned with the aid of a serviette. Guests and other service staff should always be told whenever any service ware is hot. A side towel should be draped over the cover or at the edge of any hot service items.

Hot beverages are another potential hazard. Service should never be rushed. Care must be taken in transporting hot liquids, especially when moving through a crowded dining room.

All serious burn injuries should receive medical treatment at once.

Choking

Choking on food is one of the leading causes of accidental death. Unless treated, a choking victim will die in four minutes. Choking victims may exhibit some of these symptoms:

- Panic
- Inability to breathe
- Inability to speak
- Clutching the throat
- Blue skin
- Collapse

Very often other guests do not notice that someone is choking, because they tend to pay the most attention to someone who is speaking.

The Heimlich maneuver is generally considered the best first aid for choking. Caution is recommended, however. Any administrator of first aid must, according to law, exercise "reasonable care and skill" or else be liable for negligence.

- Do not panic.

- Call or send for help immediately and give explicit details as to the location and nature of the accident. If calling emergency services, do not hang up until they do. More information may be required, or they may be able to offer some advice over the phone about temporary assistance to be administered until professional help arrives.

- Do what needs to be done in a logical order.

- When giving first aid, do not attempt more than you are qualified to do.

- Things can be replaced; people cannot. Do not endanger yourself or anyone else.

- As soon as the emergency has been handled, write a report covering the details, the location, and the severity of the accident.

Posters are available that detail first aid for choking, but it is recommended that dining room personnel be certified in the use of the Heimlich maneuver and in CPR. Additionally, staff should be aware of the location of other safety features such as the fire extinguisher, the first-aid kit, and the phone with easy-to-read emergency phone numbers.

Emergency Procedures

In order to be prepared for any kind of accident or emergency, every restaurant must have a specific course of action. These procedures should be reviewed with the staff periodically. Since there is seldom time to consult a book when faced with an emergency, everyone must be aware beforehand of what to do and how to do it.

Sanitation and Hygiene

No matter how well designed a restaurant is, the impression instantly conveyed by such things as a stained tablecloth, soiled or water-spotted silverware, dirty glasses, or a slovenly employee will undermine guests' confidence in the operation. In addition, unsound sanitary practices can threaten the health and well-being of the patrons and workers. Every place should have at least one employee who is knowledgeable about specific local and state health codes. An awareness program for all employees should be developed and upheld.

PERSONAL HYGIENE GUIDELINES

Regardless of local laws, strict observance of the following rules is essential:

- Have physical and dental examinations at least once a year.

- Take a bath or shower daily.

- Use deodorants but refrain from perfumes and colognes, which can conflict with the aromas from the food.

- Keep hair clean, neat, and under control.

- Wear clean, suitable clothing at all times.

- Wash hands frequently with germicidal soap and hot water before starting work, after using the toilet, after smoking, and before preparing food.

- Keep fingernails clean.

- Always keep clean rubberized finger bandages on cuts or sores. Rubber finger cots are particularly effective in guarding finger cuts.

- Avoid touching the scalp, face, eyes, and arms.

- Never use a serviette to wipe the face or arms.

- Do not wear jewelry or hair ornaments that may drop into food.

- To prevent pencils and pens from falling into food when bending over, keep them in pockets below waist level. Never put pencils and pens in the mouth or behind the ears.

- Never smoke, spit, chew gum, or whistle on the job. (It is considered bad luck to whistle in a kitchen. This superstition may have originated among sailors. It has been said that mutineers often signaled each other with whistles. Since whistles were used for legitimate shipboard communications as well, it is more likely that indiscriminate whistling was dangerous because of the risk of miscommunication.)

- Cover the face when sneezing or coughing.

- Always use an ice scoop for handling ice cubes, being careful to keep the handle out of the ice.

- Make use of a first-aid kit immediately after an accidental cut or burn.

- Stay at home if ill. Colds can be passed on to fellow employees or customers by merely breathing on utensils.

- Use a clean fork or spoon every time you taste food. To taste a liquid, ladle a small amount into a dish or saucer before tasting.

- Make certain that all equipment and utensils are clean and ready for use.

- Use only clean and sanitary side towels.

- Keep your fingers at the edge of the plate when serving. Some restaurants require all but soiled plates to be handled with serviettes.

- Always carry clean tableware on a tray or plate, covered with a clean napkin.

- Always handle flatware and glassware by the handle, base, or stem.

- Never reuse perishable items, such as cream, butter, or bread, from a bused table. They could have been contaminated. The exception may be individually wrapped coffee cream or butter that has been kept on ice.

- Never touch food with the bare hands unless it is going to be cooked or reheated. Bread, butter, and fruit garnishes should be handled with utensils or plastic-gloved hands.

Foot Care

Because service personnel are required to stand for such long periods of time, special care must be taken to keep the feet and legs comfortable. Well-fitting, sturdy shoes will prove to be a worthwhile investment. Shoes should have ample room for toe movement and provide adequate arch support. Support hose and cushioned insoles provide extra comfort. During long work periods, changing shoes and socks will refresh tired feet, and the application of foot powder or spray will help reduce perspiration. Having several pairs of work shoes prevents having to wear the same shoes two days in a row.

After work, muscle tension can be relieved by that old standby, a warm bath. When soaking the feet, very hot water should be avoided, since tired feet may not accurately gauge the temperature of the water and can be scalded.

Dishwashing

Regular, effective cleaning of china, glassware, and flatware will prevent the spread of disease and infection. County, city, and state health regulations vary from place to place. Contact the local health department to ensure compliance with local requirements, water properties, and temperature levels.

Washing Glasses and Flatware

Glass washing is, no doubt, the most difficult part of the dishwashing operation. For best results, glassware should be run through the machine before other dishes or in a separate washing operation, if possible. Prior to washing, glasses should be examined for lipstick or any other foreign material, which should be removed manually, since it may not come off in the wash cycle.

All chipped or cracked china and glassware should be replaced. Not only are they difficult to clean and sanitize properly, but they may injure the patron as well. Some places do not allow employees to take chipped items home, feeling that this may lead to an increase in damage in service ware.

Flatware should be placed in warm water and detergent for presoaking in order to loosen any food particles. Then it should be run through the machine on a wire rack in single layers for effective cleaning. Flatware should not be sorted and

STEPS TO FOLLOW WITH AUTOMATIC DISHWASHERS

An automatic dishwashing machine can maintain clean and sterile dishes only if it is operated properly. Certain basic steps must be followed in order to achieve clean dishes:

1 Scrape all dishes thoroughly.

2 Prerinse.

3 Stack the dishes ready for racking.

4 Rack but do not overload. Invert cups, glasses, and bowls. Spread flatware in a single layer.

5 Make sure enough detergent is used.

6 Maintain the proper water temperature—a minimum of 120°F for washing, and 190°F for sterilization. Where equipment or facilities cannot reliably produce or maintain these temperatures, chemical sanitizers can be injected during the rinse cycle.

7 Drain, dry, and stack prior to storing in a clean cabinet.

8 Do not handle service ware more than necessary.

placed into divider cups; it can become nested, preventing washing liquids from reaching all parts of the flatware. Flatware should be air-dried and stored with the handles protruding to prevent any contamination.

After the completion of all dishwashing, the area around the dish table and the machine must be thoroughly cleaned. Screens, spray arms, and rinse pipes should be removed and cleaned thoroughly. All water should be drained dry and the tank and machine properly cleaned inside and outside.

Polishing

Even the best dishwashing equipment may leave water spots. Consequently, glassware and flatware may need polishing before service. Certain rinse agents and proper adjustments to the machine may improve this situation.

Silver: Since silverware tarnishes, it may need to be polished with silver polish prior to washing. Since most metal polishes can stain linens, paper towels or special polishing cloths should be used. Silver should be stored in airtight containers or silver bags if not used daily.

Flatware: Stainless-steel flatware should be dipped in hot water and wiped dry with clean wiping cloths and transferred to the tables or drawers on a clean napkin or tray.

Glassware: Racks of clean glasses may be placed over chafing dishes of hot water and wiped dry with clean wiping cloths if local health authorities permit. Linen supply companies can provide lint-free wiping cloths. Cotton napkins should not be used; they may leave lint.

Cleanliness

Surveys conducted by the National Restaurant Association have consistently ranked cleanliness as one of the most important customer considerations when choosing a restaurant. Here are a few areas that need a systematic approach to maintaining a positive public image:

Salt and pepper shakers and sugar bowls: Every week these should be emptied and run through the dishwasher as an evening closing duty, preferably on separate nights. Drying them overnight will enable an opening server to fill them at the beginning of the following shift. Salt and pepper shakers should be filled and wiped off daily; make sure the caps are tight.

Coffee cups: Since these become stained from tea and coffee, they may need to be soaked in special stain-removing chemicals available from detergent suppliers. Bleach should not be used to remove the stains; it can etch the enamel coating of the china, eventually allowing the stains to become permanent.

Coffeepots: Pots used for serving coffee should be polished and clean at all times. Coffee oil residues on the inside may be removed with special coffee stain remover. The brewing pots can be washed with soap and water, ice cubes, and salt, or soaked with the stain remover. Proper rinsing is crucial.

Table bases: Visible table bases should be checked for chips and soil. Dirty bases or those in need of paint can negatively affect the dining experience.

Table tents: Table tents and other promotional materials should be checked for cleanliness and wear. They should be wiped clean or replaced as needed.

Windows and doors: All glass should be cleaned thoroughly before service. Doorknobs should be wiped clean, since germs collect on them and can be transferred to staff and guests.

Rest rooms: A male employee and a female employee, preferably management personnel, should be assigned to check the rest rooms on a regular basis for cleanliness and necessary supplies.

Food Safety

Food safety issues, while not as frequent as in the kitchen, are equally important in the dining room. Tasting is important. To taste in a sanitary manner, a utensil should be washed after each use. If several sauces are to be tasted, a spoon may be reused only if the sauces are poured onto the tasting spoon (never over any other food).

Snacking during service is not allowed, since it involves placing the fingers in or near the mouth. Those fingers then touch guest plates, bar fruit, glasses, and numerous other items that could spread germs. In fact, those fingers have probably touched menus, doorknobs, and coffeepot handles, all potentially laden with other people's germs, before they went to the server's mouth, possibly exposing the server to disease. These are good reasons to frequently wash the hands with soap and hot water.

It is suggested that servers quench their thirst with beverages in closed containers that are kept in an appropriate area, away from the dining room. Each container should be clearly marked with the owner's name. An uncovered container can spill and contaminate food, surfaces, or serving utensils.

Many items needed for service are kept in the walk-in refrigerator along with kitchen items. Raw meat products (such as chicken, beef, pork, and fish) should be stored below other items so that they do not drip on, and possibly contaminate, other food items. Milk, butter, lemons, and other server needs should be stored on higher shelves, above the meat.

With more and more concern about health and sanitation, many restaurants have developed HACCP (hazard analysis critical control point) plans for perishable items, designed to reduce the possibilities of food-borne illnesses. While HACCP plans were originally created for use in the kitchen, systems may be set up for dairy products. For example, an inventory list may be developed for the replenishment of pantry items for each day's service. This list could include a place to record the temperature of the refrigerator and next to each item (for example, the half-and-half) a column for the expiration date listed on the carton. This becomes a constant reminder for servers to check on critical information. Spoiled milk may not make someone ill, but it reflects poorly on the restaurant when it curdles in a guest's coffee.

Sanitation is also an issue when serving take-out or doggie bags. Since the restaurant has no idea how the guests will handle the food when it leaves, written instructions can be helpful. Even a verbal reminder to guests not to leave the leftover food in a hot car while shopping will be appreciated.

For additional information, contact:

National Restaurant Association
1200 17th Street, NW
Washington, DC 20036
Telephone: (202) 331-5900
Fax: (202) 331-2429
E-mail: isal@restaurant.org
Web site: http://www.restaurant.org

There are also many local sources of information that restaurateurs can (and in some cases must) consult to address problems of health and safety—for example, state and local health departments, local Red Cross units (which may provide safety procedure information or seminars), and the local fire department.

Conclusion

This entire book has been about ways to provide Remarkable Service to restaurant guests, the kind of service that will make them want to come back and that will encourage them to tell their friends about the wonderful time they spent in the restaurant. Safety and sanitation may not seem like the most glamorous aspects of the business, but if the goal is to provide caring service, can anything be more important? Guests will not become repeat customers if they are injured or become ill during a visit to a restaurant.

Afterword

"WE ARE LADIES AND GENTLEMEN
SERVING LADIES AND GENTLEMEN"

Earlier in this book, the authors introduced two important quotations (Reynière's "The host whose guest is obliged to ask for anything is a dishonored man" and Brillat-Savarin's "To entertain a guest is to be answerable for his happiness so long as he is beneath your roof." These two statements, which epitomize the spirit of Remarkable Service, are worth repeating. A modern-day restatement of these guiding principles can be seen in the Ritz-Carlton Hotel's credo:

- The Ritz-Carlton Hotel is a place where the genuine care and comfort of our guests is our highest mission.

- We pledge to provide the finest personal service and facilities for our guests who will always enjoy a warm, relaxed yet refined ambience.

- The Ritz-Carlton experience enlivens the senses, instills well-being, and fulfills even the unexpressed wishes and needs of our guests.

The Ritz-Carlton's approach to hospitality is not limited to hotel service. It should be adopted by all professional servers, from the bus person in a diner to the maître d' in a five-star restaurant, from a waiter in a country club to the bartender in a bistro, from the reservationist to the sommelier. Ultimately every employee in a restaurant has but one task: to provide Remarkable Service. The Ritz-Carlton posts, everywhere, its Three Steps of Service as reminders for all employees:

- A warm and sincere greeting. Use the guest name, if and when possible.

- Anticipation of and compliance with guest needs.

- Fond farewell. Give them a warm good-bye and use their names, if and when possible.

The hotel's policies reflect a simple but profound understanding of the meaning of hospitality, one that should be adopted by all who aspire to deliver Remarkable Service. This book has introduced the skills and techniques needed by today's professional servers. Along the way it has shown some of the traditions associated with the profession, why these traditional methods and terminology were created, and how they have evolved into the kind of service we see in the best restaurants today.

Servers are not machines serving other machines. They are intelligent, skilled, and caring human beings, and as such, they recognize that of all the Nine Basic Principles of Hospitality and Service, the one that states "Remarkable Service is flexible" is at the core of their professionalism. Servers need to work constantly to improve their skills and appearance, increase their knowledge, and find more efficient ways to do their jobs. They must also have the confidence to change the ways they normally do things, if that is what is required to provide the very best service possible. They know this because they are ladies and gentlemen serving ladies and gentlemen.

Appendix A
Glossaries

Glossaries

This appendix contains a number of resources that can help readers of this book to become more remarkable servers. The glossary of technical terms defines some of the terminology that is unique to the profession. Because some of these terms sound very like one another, a second glossary of frequently confused culinary terms has been included. A third listing, of restaurant slang, is included to clarify some of the more mysterious, and sometimes amusing, aspects of professional jargon.

GLOSSARY OF TECHNICAL TERMS

Abalone A mollusk with a single shell and a large, edible adductor muscle similar to that of scallops.

Aboyeur (Fr.) Expediter or announcer; a station in the brigade system. The aboyeur accepts orders from the dining room, relays them to the appropriate stations of the kitchen, and checks each plate before it leaves the kitchen.

Aïoli (Fr.) Garlic mayonnaise. (Also, in Italian, *allioli*; in Spanish, *aliolio*.)

À la carte (Fr.) Type of service in which guests compose their own meal by selecting from the menu, where each item is priced separately.

À la minute (Fr.) Cooked at the moment.

À la serviette (Fr.) Served with a fancy folded napkin on china.

Al dente (It.) Literally, "to the tooth"; to cook an item, such as pasta or vegetables, until it is tender but still firm, not soft.

Albumen The major protein in egg whites.

Allumette Vegetables, potatoes, or other items cut into pieces the size and shape of matchsticks, ⅛ inch by ⅛ inch by 1 to 2 inches is the standard.

Amuse-gueule/bouche (Fr.) Either term is commonly used to refer to a small complimentary canapé or hors d'oeuvre served after the order has been taken. Both *gueule* and *bouche* refer to the mouth.

Angel food cake A type of sponge cake made with egg whites that are beaten until stiff.

AP/as-purchased weight The weight of an item before trimming or other preparation (as opposed to edible portion weight or EP).

Aperitif (Fr.) Literally, "to open"; the first drink offered. It should be dry since it is meant to enhance the appetite, rather than sweet, which would satiate the appetite. Dry fortified or aromatized wines, bitters, vermouths, or wine cocktails such as kir and kir royale are most common.

Appareil A prepared mixture of ingredients used alone or as an ingredient in another preparation.

Appetizer Light foods served before a meal. These may be hot or cold, plated or served as finger food.

Aquaculture The cultivation or farm raising of fish or shellfish.

Aromatics Plant ingredients, such as herbs and spices, used to enhance the flavor and fragrance of food.

Arrowroot A powdered starch made from a tropical root. Used primarily as a thickener. Remains clear when cooked.

Aspic A clear jelly made from stock (or occasionally from fruit or vegetable juices) thickened with gelatin. Used to coat foods or cubed and used as a garnish.

Assiette (Fr.) Plate, dish.

Au plateau (Fr.) Served on a platter.

Bain-marie A water bath used to cook foods gently by surrounding the cooking vessel with simmering water. Also, a set of nesting pots with single, long handles used as a double boiler. Also, steam table inserts.

Banquet service Type(s) of service used to serve parties, i.e., Russian, American, butler, buffet, French, or any combination of the above.

Barbecue A cooking method involving grilling food over a wood or charcoal fire. Usually some sort of marinade or sauce is brushed on the item during cooking.

Barquette A boat-shaped tart or tartlet, which may have a sweet or savory filling.

Baste To moisten food during cooking with pan drippings, sauce, or other liquid. Basting prevents food from drying out.

Baton/batonnet (Fr.) Literally, "stick/small stick." Items cut into pieces somewhat larger than allumette or julienne; ¼ inch by ¼ inch by 2 to 2½ inches is the standard.

Batter A mixture of flour and liquid, sometimes including other ingredients. Batters vary in thickness but are generally semiliquid and thinner than doughs. Used in such preparations as cakes, quick breads, pancakes, and crêpes.

Bavarian cream/bavaroise A type of custard made from heavy cream and eggs; it is sweetened, flavored, and stabilized with gelatin.

Béarnaise A classic emulsion sauce similar to hollandaise made with egg yolks; a reduction of white wine, shallots, and tarragon; and butter; finished with tarragon and chervil.

Béchamel A white sauce made of milk thickened with light roux and flavored with onion. It is one of the grand sauces.

Beurre blanc (Fr.) Literally, "white butter." A classic emulsified sauce made with a reduction of white wine and shallots thickened with whole butter and possibly finished with fresh herbs or other seasonings.

Beurre manié (Fr.) Literally, "kneaded butter." A mixture of equal parts by weight of whole butter and flour, used to thicken gravies and sauces.

Beurre noir (Fr.) Literally, "black butter." Butter that has been cooked to a very dark brown or nearly black; a sauce made with browned butter, vinegar, chopped parsley, and capers. It is usually served with fish.

Beurre noisette (Fr.) Literally, "hazelnut butter." Whole butter that has been heated until browned. Also called *browned butter*.

Bi-metal Heavy-gauge oval or round pan with white metal inside and copper outside; used for tableside cooking and service.

Binder An ingredient or appareil used to thicken a sauce or hold together another mixture of ingredients.

Bisque A soup based on crustaceans or a vegetable purée. It is classically thickened with rice and usually finished with cream.

Bivalve A mollusk with two hinged shells. Examples are clams and oysters.

Blanch To cook an item briefly in boiling water or hot fat before finishing or storing it.

Blanquette A white stew, usually of veal but sometimes of chicken or lamb. It is served after the sauce has been thickened with a liaison.

Boil A cooking method in which items are immersed in liquid at or above the boiling point (212°F/100°C).

Bolster A collar or shank at the point on a knife where the blade meets the handle.

Boning knife A thin-bladed knife used for separating raw meat from the bone; its blade is usually about 6 inches long.

Boucher (Fr.) Butcher.

Bouillabaisse A hearty fish and shellfish stew flavored with saffron. A traditional specialty of Marseilles, France.

Bouillon (Fr.) Broth.

Boulanger (Fr.) Baker, specifically of breads and other unsweetened doughs.

Bouquet garni A small bundle of herbs tied with string. It is used to flavor stocks, braises, and other preparations. Usually contains bay leaf, parsley, thyme, and possibly other aromatics.

Braise A cooking method in which the main item, usually meat, is seared in fat, then simmered in stock or another liquid in a covered vessel.

Bran The outer layer of a cereal grain and the part highest in fiber.

Brazier/brasier A pan, designed specifically for braising, that usually has two handles and a tight-fitting lid. Often is round but may be square or rectangular.

Brigade system The kitchen organization system instituted by Auguste Escoffier. Each position has a station and well-defined responsibilities.

Brine A solution of salt, water, and seasonings, used to preserve foods.

Brioche A rich yeast dough traditionally baked in a fluted pan with a distinctive topknot of dough.

Brisket A cut of beef from the lower forequarter, best suited for long-cooking preparations such as braising. Corned beef is cured beef brisket.

Broil A cooking method in which items are cooked by a radiant heat source placed above the food.

Broth A flavorful, aromatic liquid made by simmering water or stock with meat, vegetables, and/or spices and herbs.

Brown stock An amber liquid produced by simmering browned bones and meat (usually veal or beef) with vegetables and aromatics (including caramelized mirepoix).

Brunoise (Fr.) Small dice; ⅛-inch square is the standard. For a brunoise cut, items are first cut in julienne, then cut crosswise. For a fine brunoise, ¹⁄₁₆-inch square, cut items first in fine julienne.

Brut Very dry sparkling wine.

Bussing Clearing off tables and dining areas.

Butcher A chef or purveyor who is responsible for butchering meats, poultry, and occasionally fish. In the brigade system, the butcher may also be responsible for breading meat and fish items and other mise en place operations involving meat.

Buttercream A mixture of butter, sugar, and eggs or custard; it is used to garnish cakes and pastries.

Butterfly To cut an item (usually meat or seafood) and open out the edges like a book or the wings of a butterfly.

Buttermilk A dairy beverage liquid with a slightly sour flavor similar to that of yogurt. Traditionally, the liquid by-product of butter churning, now usually made by culturing skim milk

Canapé An hors d'oeuvre consisting of a small piece of bread or toast, often cut in a decorative shape, garnished with a savory spread or topping.

Capitainne (Fr.) Captain in French service; working captain in charge of a maximum of three rings; seats customers, oversees service, and actively helps on the floor with the preparations when needed.

Capon A castrated male chicken, slaughtered at under 8 months of age and weighing 5 to 8 pounds (2.3 to 3.6 kilograms). Very tender, it is usually roasted or poêléed.

Caramelization The process of browning sugar in the presence of heat. The temperature range in which sugar caramelizes is approximately 320° to 360°F (160° to 182°C).

Carbohydrate One of the basic nutrients used by the body as a source of energy; types include simple (sugars) and complex (starches and fibers).

Carryover cooking Heat retained in cooked foods that allows them to continue cooking even after removal from the cooking medium. Especially important to roasted foods.

Carte des mets (Fr.) À la carte menu.

Carte des vins (Fr.) Wine list.

Carving Applies to an array of preparations on the dining room floor, replacing several French classical terms: (1) slicing charcuterie or pâtés, "*couper à travers*"; (2) slicing meat, "*couper en tranches*"; (3) portioning small game or poultry, "*decoupage*"; (4) deboning and filleting fish, "*desossage*"; (5) peeling and cutting fruit, "*épluchage.*"

Casing A synthetic or natural membrane (usually pig or sheep intestines) used to enclose sausage forcemeat.

Casserole/en casserole (Fr.) A lidded cooking vessel that is used in the oven; usually round with two handles. Also, foods cooked in a casserole.

Cassoulet A stew of beans baked with pork or other meats, duck or goose confit, and seasonings.

Caul fat A fatty membrane from a pig or sheep intestine that resembles fine netting; used to bard roasts and pâtés and to encase sausage forcemeat.

Cephalopod Marine creatures whose tentacles and arms are attached directly to their heads; includes squid and octopus.

Chafing dish A metal dish with a heating unit (flame or electric) used to keep foods warm and to cook foods at the table side or during buffet service.

Champagne A sparkling white wine produced in the Champagne region of France; the term is sometimes incorrectly applied to other sparkling wines.

Charcuterie (Fr.) The preparation of pork and other meat items, such as hams, terrines, sausages, pâtés, and other forcemeats.

Charcutière (Fr.) In the style of the butcher's wife. Items (usually grilled meat) are served with sauce Robert and finished with a julienne of gherkins.

Chasseur (Fr.) Hunter's style. A mushroom-tomato sauce made with a white wine reduction and demi-glace, and finished with butter and parsley.

Cheese board Can be any shape or material depending on needs but ought to be big enough to offer between four and eight cheeses. A variety of cheese should be offered, totaling about five ounces per serving.

Cheesecloth A light, fine mesh gauze used for straining liquids and making sachets.

Chef de partie (Fr.) Station chef. In the brigade system, these are the line-cook positions, such as saucier, grillardin, etc.

Chef de salle (Fr.) Head waiter.

Chef de service (Fr.) Director of service.

Chef de vin (Fr.) Wine steward.

Chef's knife An all-purpose knife used for chopping, slicing, and mincing; its blade is usually between 8 and 14 inches long.

Chef's potato All-purpose potato.

Chiffonade Leafy vegetables or herbs cut into fine shreds; often used as a garnish.

Chili powder Dried, ground, or crushed chilies, often with other ground spices and herbs.

Chili/chile The fruit of certain types of capsicum peppers (not related to black pepper), used fresh and dry as a seasoning. Chilies come in many types (for example, jalapeño, serrano, poblano) and varying degrees of spiciness.

Chine Backbone. A cut of meat that includes the backbone; in butchering, to separate the backbone and ribs to facilitate carving.

Chinoise A conical sieve used for straining and puréeing foods.

Chop To cut into pieces of roughly the same size. Also, a small cut of meat including part of the rib.

Choron Sauce béarnaise finished with tomato purée.

Choucroute (Fr.) Sauerkraut. *Choucroute garni* is sauerkraut garnished with various meats.

Chowder A thick soup that may be made from a variety of ingredients but usually contains potatoes.

Cioppino (It.) A fish stew usually made with white wine and tomatoes, believed to have originated in Genoa.

Clarification The process of removing solid impurities from a liquid (such as butter or stock). Also, a mixture of ground meat, egg whites, mirepoix, tomato purée, herbs, and spices used to clarify broth for consommé.

Clarified butter Butter from which the milk solids and water have been removed, leaving pure butterfat. Has a higher smoking point than whole butter but less butter flavor.

Coarse chop To cut into pieces of roughly the same size; used for items such as mirepoix, where appearance is not important.

Cocoa The pods of the cacao tree, processed to remove the cocoa butter and ground into powder. Used as a flavoring.

Cocotte (Fr.) Casserole. A cooking dish with a tight-fitting lid for braising or stewing. Also, a small ramekin used for cooking eggs. (*En cocotte* is often interchangeable with *en casserole*).

Coddled eggs Eggs cooked in simmering water, in their shells or in ramekins or coddlers, until set.

Colander A perforated bowl, with or without a base or legs, used to strain foods.

Combination method A cooking method that involves the application of both moist and dry heat to the main item (for example, braising or stewing).

Commis débarasseur (Fr.) In French service the closest position to a bus person. Duties include getting hot and cold plates, getting guéridons, replacing soiled utensils and equipment, and getting other mise en place for the station, e.g., wine buckets, fuel, napkins, etc. Does not clear the table until the guest has left.

Commis de rang (Fr.) In charge of the station ("*rang*"); orchestrates the service, welcomes guests and makes them comfortable, takes the orders, prepares and plates the food, and presents the check; never leaves the floor during service.

Commis de suite (Fr.) The runner in French service; brings the suitard aperitif order to the bar and the subsequent food orders to the kitchen, brings drinks and food to the *commis de rang,* sets up the guéridon as needed, gets all food and beverage, helps clear, and assists the *commis de rang* in general.

Communard (Fr.) The kitchen position responsible for preparing staff meals.

Complex carbohydrate A large molecule made up of long chains of sugar molecules. In food, these molecules are found in starches and fiber.

Compote A dish of fruit—fresh or dried—cooked in syrup flavored with spices or liqueur.

Compound butter Whole butter combined with herbs or other seasonings and usually used to sauce grilled or broiled items or vegetables.

Concassé/concasser (Fr.) To pound or chop coarsely. Usually refers to tomatoes that have been peeled, seeded, and chopped.

Condiment An aromatic mixture, such as pickles, chutney, and some sauces and relishes, that accompanies food (usually kept on the table throughout service).

Conduction A method of heat transfer in which heat is transmitted through another substance. In cooking, when heat is transmitted to food through a pot or pan, oven walls, or racks.

Confiserie/confiseur (Fr.) Confectionery/confectioner. A pâtissier specializing in, and responsible for, the production of candies and related items, such as petits fours.

Confit Meat (usually goose, duck, or pork) cooked and preserved in its own fat.

Consommé Broth that has been clarified using a mixture of ground meat, egg whites, and other ingredients that trap impurities.

Convection A method of heat transfer in which heat is transmitted through the circulation of air or water.

Convection oven An oven that employs convection currents by forcing hot air through fans so that it circulates around food, cooking it quickly and evenly.

Coquilles Saint-Jacques (Fr.) Scallops. Also, a dish of broiled scallops with any of several garnishes.

Coral Lobster roe, which is red or coral-colored when cooked.

Corned beef Beef brisket preserved with salt and spices. The term *corned* refers to the chunks of salt spread over the brisket during the corning process.

Cornichon (Fr.) A small, sour pickled cucumber.

Cornstarch A fine white powder milled from dried corn; used primarily as a thickener for sauce and occasionally as an ingredient in batters.

Coulibiac (Fr.) A preparation of fish (usually salmon), kasha or rice, onion, mushrooms, and herbs, baked in a pastry crust. (Also in Russian, *kulibyaka*.)

Coulis A thick purée, usually of vegetables but possibly of fruit. (Traditionally meat, fish, or shellfish purée; meat jus; or certain thick soups.)

Country-style A forcemeat that is coarse in texture, usually made from pork, pork fat, liver, and various garnishes.

Court bouillon (Fr.) Literally, "short broth." An aromatic vegetable broth that usually includes an acidic ingredient, such as wine or vinegar; most commonly used for poaching fish.

Couscous Pellets of semolina usually cooked by steaming, traditionally in a couscoussière. Also, the stew with which this grain is traditionally served.

Couscoussière A set of nesting pots similar to a steamer used to cook couscous.

Covert (Cover) (Fr.) Individual setup for one guest. In countries other than the United States, an automatic cover charge is added to the total of the check to cover the expense of the mise en place (bread, butter, linen).

Couverture Fine semisweet chocolate used for coating and decorating. Its high cocoa butter content gives it a glossy appearance after tempering.

Cream The fatty component of milk; available with various fat contents. Also, a mixing method for batter cakes.

Cream puff A pastry made with pâte á choux, filled with crème pâtissière, and usually glazed. (Also in French, *profiterole*.)

Cream soup Traditionally a soup based on a béchamel sauce. Loosely, any soup finished with cream, a cream variant such as sour cream, or a liaison; these soups are usually based on béchamel or velouté.

Crème anglaise (Fr.) Custard.

Crème brûlée (Fr.) Custard topped with sugar and caramelized under the broiler before service.

Crème fraîche (Fr.) Heavy cream cultured to give it a thick consistency and a slightly tangy flavor; used in hot preparations, since it is less likely to curdle when heated than sour cream or yogurt.

Crème pâtisserie (Fr.) Literally, "pastry cream." Custard made with eggs, flour or other starches, milk, sugar, and flavorings, used to fill and garnish pastries or as the base for puddings, soufflés, and creams.

Crêpe A thin pancake made with egg batter; used in sweet and savory preparations.

Croissant A pastry consisting of a yeast dough with a butter roll-in, traditionally rolled in a crescent shape.

Cross-contamination The transference of disease-causing elements from one source to another through physical contact.

Croûte, en (Fr.) Encased in a bread or pastry crust.

Croûton (Fr.) A bread or pastry garnish, usually toasted or sautéed until crisp.

Crudités (Fr.) Small cuts of fresh vegetables offered with a dip as a stationary canapé.

Crumb A term used to describe the texture of baked goods; for example, an item can be said to have a fine or coarse crumb.

Crustacean A class of hard-shelled arthropods, primarily aquatic, which includes edible species such as lobster, crab, shrimp, and crayfish.

Cuisson (Fr.) Poaching liquid, including stock, fumet, court bouillon, or other liquid, which may be reduced and used as a base for the poached item's sauce.

Cure To preserve a food by salting, smoking, and/or drying.

Curing salt A mixture of 94 percent table salt (sodium chloride) and 6 percent sodium nitrite, used to preserve meats. (Also known as *tinted curing mixture*, or *TCM*.)

Curry A mixture of spices used primarily in Indian cuisine; may include turmeric, coriander, cumin, cayenne or other chilies, cardamom, cinnamon, clove, fennel, fenugreek, ginger, and garlic. Also, a dish seasoned with curry.

Custard A mixture of milk, beaten egg, and possibly other ingredients, such as sweet or savory flavorings, which is cooked with gentle heat, often in a bain-marie or double boiler.

Danger zone The temperature range from 45° to 140°F (7° to 60°C), the most favorable condition for rapid growth of many pathogens.

Danish pastry A pastry consisting of rich yeast dough with a butter roll-in, possibly filled with nuts, fruit, or other ingredients and iced. This pastry originated in Denmark.

Daube A meat stew braised in red wine, traditionally in a daubière, a specialized casserole with a tight-fitting lid and indentations to hold hot coals.

Debarrassage (Fr.) Clear off.

Deck oven A variant of the conventional oven, in which the heat source is located underneath the deck or floor of the oven and the food is placed directly on the deck instead of on a rack.

Découpage (Fr.) To disjoint and portion; refers to poultry and flying game served via French service.

Decrumbing Cleaning the guest's table of bread crumbs and other debris. In all types of service this should be done at least once during the meal, usually before dessert; the crumber or a rolled napkin is used, and debris is swept onto a service plate.

Deep-fry A cooking method in which foods are cooked by immersion in hot fat; deep-fried foods are often coated with bread crumbs or batter before being cooked.

Deglaze/déglacer To use a liquid, such as wine, water, or stock, to dissolve food particles and/or caramelized drippings left in a pan after roasting or sautéing.

Degrease/Dégraisser To skim the fat off the surface of a liquid, such as a stock or sauce.

Dégustation (Fr.) Tasting of wines and sometimes food.

Demi-glace (Fr.) Literally, "half glaze." A mixture of equal proportions of brown stock and brown sauce that has been reduced by half. One of the grand sauces.

Demi-sec (Fr.) Half-sweet, in reference to sparking wine.

Démitasse (Fr.) Literally, "half cup"; a small cup used for espresso.

Dépouillage (Fr.) To skim the surface of a cooking liquid, such as a stock or sauce. This action is simplified by placing the pot off center on the burner and skimming impurities as they collect at one side of the pot.

Deviled Meat, poultry, or other food seasoned with mustard, vinegar, and possibly other seasonings; coated with bread crumbs; and grilled.

Dice To cut ingredients into small cubes (¼ inch for small, ½ inch for medium, ¾ inch for large standard).

Direct heat A method of heat transfer in which heat radiates from a source (for example, an open burner or grill) and travels directly to the item being heated with no conductor between heat source and food. Examples are grilling, broiling, and toasting.

Drawn A whole fish that has been scaled and gutted but still has its head, fins, and tail.

Dredge To coat food with a dry ingredient such as flour or bread crumbs.

Dressed Prepared for cooking; a dressed fish is gutted and scaled, and its head, tail, and fins are removed (same as *pan-dressed*). Dressed poultry is plucked, drawn, singed, trimmed, and trussed. Also, coated with dressing, as in a salad.

Dry cure A combination of salts and spices used usually before smoking to process meats and forcemeats.

Dry sauté To sauté without fat, usually using a nonstick pan.

Dumpling Any of a number of small soft dough or batter items, which are steamed, poached, or simmered (possibly on top of a stew); may be filled or plain.

Durum A species of hard wheat primarily milled into semolina flour for use in dried pasta.

Dutch oven A kettle, usually of cast iron, used for stewing and braising on the stovetop or in the oven.

Duxelle An appareil of finely chopped mushrooms and shallots sautéed gently in butter.

Egg wash A mixture of beaten eggs (whole eggs, yolks, or whites) and a liquid, usually milk or water, used to coat baked goods to give them a sheen.

Emulsion A mixture of two or more liquids, one of which is a fat or oil and the other of which is water-based, so that tiny globules of one are suspended in the other. This may involve the use of stabilizers, such as egg or mustard. Emulsions may be temporary, permanent, or semipermanent.

Entrecôte (Fr.) Literally, "between the ribs"; a cut of meat; sized from petite to double; carved like Chateaubriand when large.

Entrée (Fr.) In the United States, the main course of the meal. In Europe, an entrée is a separate course served before the main course. An entrée can be any of the following: vegetable dish; eggs; farinaceous; offal; composed salad; fish, shellfish, mollusk; white meat or poultry; red meat or game.

Entremet (Fr.) Literally, "between courses"; simple sweet course made from fruits, puddings, mousses, pies, bavarians, tarts, simple cakes, sherbet, sorbet, ice cream, or any combination of the above. These can be made by someone without patisserie skills.

Entremetier (Fr.) Vegetable chef/station. The position responsible for hot appetizers and often soups, vegetables, starches, and pastas; may also be responsible for egg dishes.

EP/edible portion The weight of an item after trimming and preparation (as opposed to as-purchased weight or AP).

Escalope (Fr.) Same as *scallop*; a small boneless piece of meat or fish of uniform thickness.

Espagnole sauce (Fr.) Literally, "Spanish sauce." Brown sauce made with brown stock, caramelized mirepoix and tomato purée, and seasonings.

Essence A concentrated flavoring extracted from an item, usually by infusion or distillation; includes items such as vanilla and other extracts, concentrated stocks, and fumets.

Estouffade (Fr.) Stew. Also, a type of brown stock based on pork knuckle and veal and beef bones that is often used in braises.

Etouffé (Fr.) Literally, "smothered." A cooking method similar to braising in which items are cooked with little or no added liquid in a pan with a tight-fitting lid. (Also *étuver*, *á l'étuvée*.)

Extrusion/extruding machine A machine used to shape pasta. The dough is pushed out through perforated plates rather than being rolled.

Fabrication The butchering, cutting, and trimming of meat, poultry, fish, and game.

Farce (Fr.) Forcemeat or stuffing; *farci* means "stuffed."

FIFO/first in, first out A fundamental storage principle based on stock rotation. Products are stored and used so that the oldest product is always used first.

Filé A thickener made from ground dried sassafras leaves; used primarily in gumbos.

Fillet/filet A boneless cut of meat, fish, or poultry.

Filleting knife A flexible-bladed knife used for filleting fish; similar in size and shape to a boning knife.

Fines herbes A mixture of herbs, usually parsley, chervil, tarragon, and chives.

Fish poacher A long, narrow pot with straight sides and possibly a perforated rack, used for poaching whole fish.

Flat fish A fish skeletal type characterized by its flat body and both eyes on one side of its head (for example, sole, plaice, and halibut).

Flat-top A thick plate of cast iron or steel set over the heat source on a range; diffuses heat, making it more even than an open burner.

Flatware Service eating utensils; "silverware" implies that the utensils are silver rather than stainless.

Fond (Fr.) Stock.

Fondant An icing made with sugar, water, and glucose; used primarily for pastry and confectionery.

Food-borne illness An illness in humans caused by the consumption of an adulterated food product. In order for a food-borne illness to be considered official, it must involve two or more people who have eaten the same food and it must be confirmed by health officials.

Food mill A type of strainer with a crank-operated, curved blade. It is used to purée soft foods.

Food processor A machine with interchangeable blades and disks and a removable bowl and lid separate from the motor housing. It can be used for a variety of tasks, including chopping, grinding, puréeing, emulsifying, kneading, slicing, shredding, and cutting julienne.

Forcemeat A mixture of chopped or ground meat and other ingredients used for pâtés, sausages, and other preparations.

Fortified wine Wine to which a spirit, usually brandy, has been added (for example, port or sherry).

Free-range Livestock that is raised unconfined.

French knife See *chef's knife*.

Fricassée (Fr.) A stew of poultry or other white meat with a white sauce.

Fritter Sweet or savory foods coated or mixed into batter and deep-fried (also in French, *beignet*).

Friturier (Fr.) Fry chef/station. The position responsible for all fried foods; it may be combined with the rôtisseur position.

Fumet (Fr.) A type of stock in which the main flavoring ingredient is allowed to smother with wine and aromatics; fish fumet is the most common type.

Génoise (Fr.) A sponge cake made with whole eggs, used for petits fours, layer cakes, and other desserts.

Galantine Boned meat (usually poultry) that is stuffed, rolled, poached, and served cold, usually in aspic.

Ganache A filling made of heavy cream, chocolate, and/or other flavorings.

Garbure (Fr.) A thick vegetable soup usually containing beans, cabbage, and/or potatoes.

Garde manger (Fr.) Pantry chef/station. The position responsible for cold food preparations, including salads, cold appetizers, pâtés, etc.

Garni (Fr.) Garnished.

Garnish An edible decoration or accompaniment to a dish.

Gherkin A small pickled cucumber.

Giblets Organs and other trim from poultry, including the liver, heart, gizzard, and neck.

Glace (Fr.) Reduced stock; ice cream; icing.

Glacé (Fr.) Glazed or iced.

Glaze To give an item a shiny surface by brushing it with sauce, aspic, icing, or another appareil. For meat, to coat with sauce and then brown in an oven or salamander.

Goujonette (Fr.) Fish fillet cut in strips and usually breaded or batter-coated and then deep-fried.

Grand sauce One of several basic sauces that are used in the preparation of many other small sauces. The grand sauces are demi-glace, velouté, béchamel, hollandaise, and tomato. Also called *mother sauce*.

Gratin A tasty crust that forms on a dish that is usually topped with cheese and browned under the salamander or broiler.

Gratiné (Fr.) Browned in an oven or under a salamander (*au gratin, gratin de*). *Gratin* can also refer to a forcemeat in which some portion of the dominant meat is sautéed and cooled before grinding.

Gratinée (Fr.) French onion soup. The term is often used in place of the more appropriate gratin.

Griddle A heavy metal surface, which may be either fitted with handles, built into a stove, or heated by its own gas or electric element. Cooking is done directly on the griddle.

Grill pan A skillet with ridges that is used to simulate grilling on the stovetop.

Grill A cooking technique in which foods are cooked by a radiant heat source placed below the food. Also, the piece of equipment on which grilling is done. Grills may be fueled by gas, electricity, charcoal, or wood.

Grillardin (Fr.) Grill chef/station. The position responsible for all grilled foods; may be combined with rôtisseur.

Griswold A pot, similar to a rondeau, made of cast iron; may have a single short handle rather than the usual loop handles.

Guéridon (Fr.) A rolling service cart.

Guinea hen/fowl A bird related to the pheasant. It is slaughtered at about 6 months of age and weighs ¾ to 1½ pounds (350 to 700 grams). Its tender meat is suitable to most techniques.

Gumbo filé powder See *filé*.

Gumbo A Creole soup/stew thickened with filé or okra.

Haricot (Fr.) Literally, "bean." *Haricots verts* are green beans.

Hash Chopped, cooked meat, usually with potatoes and/or other vegetables, which is seasoned, bound with a sauce, and sautéed. Also, to chop.

Heimlich maneuver First aid for choking; the application of sudden, upward pressure on the upper abdomen to force a foreign object from the windpipe.

Hollandaise A classic emulsion sauce made with a vinegar reduction, egg yolks, and melted butter flavored with lemon juice. It is one of the grand sauces.

Holloware Generally, service items of significant depth or volume, such as soup terrines, water pitchers, coffeepots, large bowls, platters, and silver trays.

Hollow-ground A type of knife blade made by fusing two sheets of metal and beveling or fluting the edge.

Hominy Corn that has been milled or treated with a lye solution to remove the bran and germ.

Hors d'oeuvre (Fr.) Literally, "outside the work." Traditionally a warm appetizer, but often includes any tidbit served before the meal, either passed butler style, served at a station where the food is carved or prepared, or presented in a stationary display.

Hotel pan A rectangular, metal pan, in any of a number of standard sizes, with a lip that allows it to rest in a storage shelf or steam table.

Hygiene Conditions and practices followed to maintain health, including sanitation and personal cleanliness.

Incident report A form used to generate a report and follow-through on circumstances in which a guest or an employee suffers an injury, such as foodborne illness. All pertinent facts, such as date, time, and foods eaten, should be recorded before the form is forwarded to the manager.

Infection Contamination by a disease-causing agent, such as bacteria.

Infusion Steeping an aromatic or other item in liquid to extract its flavor. Also, the liquid resulting from this process.

Instant-read thermometer A thermometer used to measure the internal temperature of foods. The stem is inserted in the food, producing an instant temperature readout.

Intermezzo An intermission between courses of a long meal, traditionally after the fish course. Usually a small glass of ice, sorbet, or *trou normande*. Used to cleanse the palate or ease digestion.

Intoxication Poisoning. A state of being tainted with toxins, particularly those produced by microorganisms that have infected food.

Julienne Vegetables, potatoes, or other items cut into thin strips; ⅛-inch square by 1 to 2 inches is standard. Fine julienne is 1/16-inch square.

Jus (Fr.) Juice. *Jus de viande* is meat gravy. Meat served au jus is served with its own juice or *jus lié*.

Jus lié (Fr.) Meat juice thickened lightly with arrowroot or cornstarch.

Kasha (Russ.) Buckwheat groats that have been hulled and crushed; usually prepared by boiling.

Kosher Prepared in accordance with Jewish dietary laws.

Kosher salt Pure, refined rock salt used for pickling because it does not contain magnesium carbonate and thus does not cloud brine solutions. Also used to kosher items. (Also known as *coarse salt* or *pickling salt*.)

Lard Rendered pork fat used for pastry and frying.

Lardon (Fr.) A strip of fat used for larding; may be seasoned. (Also *lardoon*.)

Legume The seeds of certain plants, including beans and peas, which are eaten for their earthy flavors and high nutritional value. *Légume* is the French word for "vegetable."

Liaison A mixture of egg yolks and cream used to thicken and enrich sauces. (Also loosely applied to any appareil used as a thickener.)

Linen Or *nappery*, any cloth used by the servers or on the tables or side stands; napkins, tablecloths, serviettes.

Liqueur A spirit flavored with fruit, spices, nuts, herbs, and/or seeds and usually sweetened.

Little neck Small, hard-shell clams often eaten raw on the half shell.

Littleneck A Pacific coast clam, usually steamed. (Also known as *manila clam*.)

Logbook Calendar book kept in restaurants for forecasting; contains common information, number of covers, weather, or events that may affect business.

Low-fat milk Milk containing less than 2 percent fat.

Lox Salt-cured salmon.

Lyonnaise (Fr.) Lyons style; with onions and usually butter, white wine, vinegar, and demi-glace.

Macaroni (It.) Pasta.

Madeira A Portuguese fortified wine that is treated with heat as it ages, giving it a distinctive flavor and brownish color.

Madère (Fr.) A sauce made with demi-glace flavored with Madeira.

Mahi mahi A firm-fleshed Pacific fish with a light, delicate flavor, suitable to all cooking methods. Also called *dolphin fish*.

Mandoline A slicing device of stainless steel with carbon steel blades. The blades may be adjusted to cut items into various cuts and thicknesses.

Maître d'hôtel (Fr.) Dining room manager or food and beverage manager, informally called *maître d'*. This position oversees the dining room or front-of-the-house staff. Also, a compound butter flavored with chopped parsley and lemon juice.

Marbling The intramuscular fat found in meat that makes the meat tender and juicy.

Marinade An appareil used before cooking to flavor and moisten foods; may be liquid or dry. Liquid marinades are usually based on an acidic ingredient, such as wine or vinegar; dry marinades are usually salt-based.

Marmite See *stockpot*.

Marzipan A paste of ground almonds, sugar, and egg whites that is used to fill and decorate pastries.

Matelote (Fr.) A fish stew traditionally made with eel.

Matignon (Fr.) An edible mirepoix that is often used in poêléed dishes and is usually served with the finished dish. Typically, matignon includes two parts carrot, one part celery, one part leek, one part onion, one part mushroom (optional), and one part ham or bacon.

Mayonnaise A cold emulsion sauce made of oil, egg yolks, vinegar, mustard, and seasonings.

Medallion (Fr.) A small, round scallop of meat.

Meringue (Fr.) Egg whites beaten until they are stiff, then sweetened and possibly baked until stiff. Three types are regular or common, Italian, and Swiss.

Meunière, à la A cooking technique for fish.

Microwave A method of heat transfer in which electromagnetic waves (similar to radio waves) generated by a device called a magnetron penetrate food and cause the water molecules in it to oscillate. This rapid molecular motion generates heat, which cooks the food.

Mie (Fr.) The soft part of bread (not the crust); *mie de pain* is fresh white bread crumbs.

Mignardises (Fr.) The sweetest of the sweets, served with coffee; include truffles, chocolates, caramels, dipped fruits and nuts, macaroons, mints, and small cookies.

Millet A small, round, glutenless grain that is boiled or ground into flour.

Mince To chop into very small pieces.

Mirepoix A combination of chopped aromatic vegetables—usually two parts onion, one part carrot, and one part celery—used to flavor stocks, soups, braises, and stews.

Mise en place (Fr.) Literally, "put in place." The preparation and assembly of ingredients, pans, utensils, and plates or serving pieces needed for a particular dish or service period.

Mode, à la (Fr.) Literally, "in the style of" (usually followed by a descriptive phrase). *Boeuf à la mode* is braised beef; *pie à la mode* is pie served with ice cream.

Molasses The dark brown, sweet syrup that is a by-product of sugar cane refining.

Molleton On a table, undercloth used to absorb noise and spills; also known as a *silence cloth.*

Mollusk Any of a number of invertebrate animals with soft, unsegmented bodies usually enclosed in a hard shell; included are clams, oysters, and snails.

Monosodium glutamate (MSG) A flavor enhancer without a distinct flavor of its own; used primarily in Chinese and processed foods. It may cause allergic reactions in some people.

Monté au beurre (Fr.) Literally, "lifted with butter." A technique used to enrich sauces, thicken them slightly, and give them a glossy appearance by whisking in whole butter.

Mother sauce See *grand sauce.*

Mousse (Fr.) A dish made with beaten egg whites and/or whipped cream folded into a flavored base appareil; may be sweet or savory.

Mousseline (Fr.) A mousse; a sauce made by folding whipped cream into hollandaise; or a very light forcemeat based on white meat or seafood lightened with cream and eggs.

Napoleon A pastry made of layered puff pastry rectangles filled with pastry cream and glazed with fondant.

Nappe (Fr.) Tablecloth.

Napper/nappé (Fr.) To coat with sauce; thickened.

Napperon (Fr.) Topcloth.

Nature (Fr.) Ungarnished or plain. *Pommes natures* are boiled potatoes.

Navarin (Fr.) A stew, traditionally of lamb, with potatoes, onions, and possibly other vegetables.

New potato A small, waxy potato that is usually prepared by boiling or steaming and is often eaten with its skin.

Noisette (Fr.) Hazelnut. Also, a small portion of meat cut from the rib. *Pommes noisette* are tournéed potatoes browned in butter. *Beurre noisette* is browned butter.

Nonbony fish Fish whose skeletons are made of cartilage rather than hard bone (for example, shark, skate). Also called *cartilaginous fish.*

Nouvelle cuisine (Fr.) Literally, "new cooking." A culinary movement emphasizing freshness and lightness of ingredients, classical preparations, and innovative combinations and presentation.

N.V. Nonvintage, in reference to wines.

Oblique/roll cut A knife cut used primarily with long, cylindrical vegetables such as carrots. The item is cut on a diagonal, rolled 180 degrees, then cut on the same diagonal, producing a piece with two angled edges.

Oeuf (Fr.) Egg.

Offal Variety meats, including organs (brains, heart, kidneys, lights or lungs, sweetbreads, tripe, tongue), head meat, tail, and feet.

Offset spatula A hand tool with a wide, bent blade set in a short handle, used to turn or lift foods from grills, broilers, or griddles.

Oignon brûlé (Fr.) Literally, "burnt onion." A peeled, halved onion seared on a flat-top or in a skillet and used to enhance the color of stock and consommé.

Oignon piqué (Fr.) Literally, "pricked onion." A whole, peeled onion to which a bay leaf is attached, using a whole clove as a tack. It is used to flavor béchamel sauce and some soups.

Omelet Beaten egg that is cooked in butter in a specialized pan or skillet and then rolled or folded into an oval. Omelets may be filled with a variety of ingredients before or after rolling.

Organ meat Meat from an organ rather than muscle tissue.

Paella A Spanish dish of rice cooked with onion, tomato, garlic, vegetables, and various meats, including chicken, chorizo, shellfish, and possibly other types.

Paella pan A specialized pan for cooking paella; it is wide and shallow and usually has two loop handles.

Paillarde (Fr.) A scallop of meat pounded until thin; usually grilled.

Palette knife A flexible, round-tipped knife used to turn pancakes and grilled foods and to spread fillings and glazes; may have a serrated edge. (Also called a metal spatula.)

Pan gravy A sauce made by deglazing pan drippings from a roast and combining them with a roux or other starch and additional stock.

Panada An appareil based on starch (such as flour or crumbs), moistened with a liquid, that is used as a binder.

Pan-broil A cooking method similar to dry sautéing that simulates broiling by cooking an item in a hot pan with little or no fat.

Pan-dressed See *dressed*.

Pan-fry A cooking method in which items are cooked in deep fat in a skillet; this generally involves more fat than sautéing or stir-frying but less than deep-frying.

Papillote, en (Fr.) A moist-heat cooking method similar to steaming, in which items are enclosed in parchment and cooked in the oven.

Parchment Heat-resistant paper used in cooking for such preparations as lining baking pans, cooking items en papillote, and covering items during shallow poaching.

Parcook To partially cook an item before storing or finishing by another method; may be the same as blanching.

Paring knife A short knife used for paring and trimming fruits and vegetables; its blade is usually 2 to 4 inches long.

Parisienne scoop A small tool used for scooping balls out of vegetable or fruit. (Also called a *melon baller*.)

Parstock The amount of food and other supplies necessary to cover operating needs between deliveries.

Pasta (It.) Dough/paste; noodles made from a dough of flour (often semolina) and water or eggs. This dough is kneaded, rolled, and cut or extruded, then cooked by boiling.

Pastry bag A bag—usually made of plastic, canvas, or nylon—that can be fitted with plain or decorative tips and used to pipe out icings and puréed foods.

Pâte (Fr.) Noodles or pasta; dough or batter.

Pâté (Fr.) A rich forcemeat of meat, game, poultry, seafood, and/or vegetables, baked in pastry or in a mold or dish.

Pâte á choux Cream puff paste, made by boiling a mixture of water, butter, and flour, then beating in whole eggs.

Pâté de campagne Country-style pâté, with a coarse texture.

Pâté en croûte Pâté baked in a pastry crust.

Pâte feuilletée Puff pastry.

Pâtissier (Fr.) Pastry chef. This station is responsible for baked items, pastries, and desserts. This is often a separate area of the kitchen.

Paupiette A fillet or scallop of fish or meat that is rolled up around a stuffing and poached or braised.

Pesto (It.) A thick, puréed mixture of an herb, traditionally basil, and oil used as a sauce for pasta and other foods and as a garnish for soup. Pesto may also contain grated cheese, nuts or seeds, and other seasonings.

Phyllo dough Pastry made with very thin sheets of a flour-and-water dough layered with butter and/or crumbs; similar to strudel. (Also called *filo*.)

Pickling spice A mixture of herbs and spices used to season pickles, often includes dill weed and/or seed, coriander seed, cinnamon stick, peppercorns, bay leaves, and others.

Pilaf A technique for cooking grains in which the grain is sautéed briefly in butter, then simmered in stock or water with various seasonings. (Also called *pilau, pilaw, pullao, pilav.*)

Pincé (Fr.) To caramelize an item by sautéing; usually refers to a tomato product.

Place setting Individual setup for a guest; see *couvert.*

Plat (Fr.) Dish, plate.

Plateau (Fr.) Platter.

Poach A method in which items are cooked gently in simmering liquid.

Poêlé A method in which items are cooked in their own juices (usually with the addition of a matignon, other aromatics, and melted butter) in a covered pot, usually in the oven. (Also called *butter roasting.*)

Point system A system of distributing gratuities according to seniority or rank in the service brigade; more common in Europe.

Poisson (Fr.) Fish.

Poissonier (Fr.) Fish chef/station. The position responsible for fish items and their sauces; may be combined with the saucier position.

Port A fortified dessert wine. *Vintage port* is high-quality, unblended wine aged in the bottle for at least 12 years; *ruby port* may be blended and is aged in wood for a short time; *white port* is made with white grapes.

Poussin (Fr.) Young hen.

Prawn A crustacean that closely resembles shrimp; often used as a general term for large shrimp.

Pressure steamer A machine that cooks food using steam produced by heating water under pressure in a sealed compartment, allowing it to reach higher than boiling temperature (212°F/100°C). The food is placed into a sealed chamber that cannot be opened until the pressure has been released and the steam properly vented from the chamber.

Primal cuts The portions produced by the initial cutting of an animal carcass. Cuts are determined standards that may vary by country and animal type. Primal cuts are further broken down into smaller, more manageable cuts.

Protocol Set of rules concerning priorities in arriving, seating, and sequence of service during official or casual events, such as state dinners or dining in a restaurant. Social: children first, then elderly ladies, ladies, elderly gentlemen, gentlemen by age; diplomatic: by rank; corporate: by importance; clergy: by hierarchy. Usually the guest of honor is the first and the host is the last to be seated and served. The host tastes the wine first and is served last.

Purée To process food (by mashing, straining, or chopping it very finely) in order to make it a smooth paste. Also, a product produced using this technique.

Quahog A hard-shell clam larger than 3 inches in diameter, usually used for chowder or fritters. (Also called *quahaug*.)

Quenelle (Fr.) A light, poached dumpling based on a forcemeat (usually chicken, veal, seafood, or game) bound with eggs that is shaped in an oval by using two spoons.

Quick bread Bread made with chemical leaveners, which work more quickly than yeast. (Also called *batter bread*.)

Radiant heat See *direct heat*.

Raft A mixture of ingredients used to clarify consommé (see *clarification*). The term refers to the fact that the ingredients rise to the surface and form a floating mass.

Ragoût (Fr.) Stew.

Ramekin A small, ovenproof dish, usually ceramic. (Also in French, *ramequin*.)

Reach-in refrigerator A refrigeration unit, or set of units, with pass-through doors. They are often used in the pantry area for storage of salads, cold hors d'oeuvres, and other frequently used items.

Réchaud (Fr.) Hot plate, food warmer, cooking utensil used mostly for guéridon service.

Recommended Dietary Allowance (RDA) A standard recommendation of the amounts of certain nutrients that should be included in the diet in order to prevent deficiencies.

Redresser (Fr.) To plate and garnish dishes with food taken from pans, platters, or bowls.

Reduce To decrease the volume of a liquid by simmering or boiling; used to provide a thicker consistency and/or concentrated flavors.

Reduction The product that results when a liquid is reduced.

Refresh To plunge an item into, or run under, cold water after blanching to prevent further cooking.

Render To melt fat and clarify the drippings for use in sautéing or pan-frying.

Reservation book A means of recording reservation information, including but not limited to the guest's name, number of guests, reservation number, special requests, telephone number, and cancellations.

Rince-doigts (Fr.) Fingerbowl.

Ring-top A flat-top with removable plates that can be opened to varying degrees to expose more or less direct heat.

Risotto Rice that is sautéed briefly in butter with onions and possibly other aromatics, then combined with stock, which is added in several additions and stirred constantly, producing a creamy texture with grains that are still al dente.

Roast A cooking method in which items are cooked in an oven or on a spit over a fire.

Roe Fish or shellfish eggs.

Rondeau A shallow, wide, straight-sided pot with two loop handles.

Rondelle A knife cut that produces flat round or oval pieces; used on cylindrical vegetables or items trimmed into cylinders before cutting.

Rôti (Fr.) Roasted.

Rôtisseur (Fr.) Roast chef/station. The position is responsible for all roasted foods and related sauces.

Roulade (Fr.) A slice of meat or fish rolled around a stuffing; also, filled and rolled sponge cake.

Round A cut of beef from the hindquarter that includes the top and bottom round, eye, and top sirloin. It is lean and usually braised or roasted. Also, in baking, to shape pieces of yeast dough into balls to ensure even rising and a smooth crust.

Round fish A classification of fish based on skeletal type, characterized by a rounded body and eyes on opposite sides of its head.

Roux (Fr.) An appareil containing equal parts of flour and fat (usually butter) used to thicken liquids. Roux is cooked to varying degrees (white, pale/blond, or brown), depending on its intended use.

Royale (Fr.) A consommé garnish made of unsweetened custard cut into decorative shapes.

Sabayon (Fr.) Wine custard. Sweetened egg yolks flavored with Marsala or other wine or liqueur, beaten in a double boiler until frothy. (The Italian name is *zabaglione*.)

Sachet d'épices (Fr.) Literally, "bag of spices." Aromatic ingredients, encased in cheesecloth, that are used to flavor stocks and other liquids. A standard sachet contains parsley stems, cracked peppercorns, dried thyme, and a bay leaf.

Salamander See *broiler*.

Salé (Fr) Salted or pickled.

Sanitation The preparation and distribution of food in a clean environment by healthy food service workers.

Sanitize The killing of pathogenic organisms by chemicals and/or moist heat.

Sauceboat China or silver holloware container for sauce served on the side.

Saucier (Fr.) Sauté chef/station. The chef de partie responsible for all sautéed items and their sauces.

Sauté A cooking method in which items are cooked quickly in a small amount of fat in a pan (see *sauteuse, sautoir*) on the range top.

Sauteuse A shallow skillet with sloping sides and a single, long handle. Used for sautéing and referred to generically as a *sauté pan*.

Sautoir A shallow skillet with straight sides and a single, long handle. Used for sautéing and referred to generically as a *sauté pan*.

Savories Salted seeded bread or rolls.

Savory Not sweet. Also, the name of a course served after dessert and before port in traditional British meals. Also, a family of herbs (including summer and winter savory).

Savouries Salty hors d'oeuvre served in lounges, pubs, and bars used to increase liquor sales.

Scald To heat a liquid, usually milk or cream, to just below the boiling point. May also refer to blanching fruits and vegetables.

Scale/scaling To measure ingredients by weighing; to divide dough or batter into portions by weight.

Scallop A bivalve whose adductor muscle (the muscle that keeps its shells closed) and roe are eaten. Also, a thin slice of meat. (See *escalope*.)

Score To cut the surface of an item at regular intervals to allow it to cook evenly.

Scrapple A boiled mixture of pork trimmings, buckwheat, and cornmeal.

Sea salt Salt produced by evaporating seawater. Available refined or unrefined, crystallized or ground. (Also *sel gris*, French for "gray salt.")

Sear To brown the surface of food in fat over high heat before finishing by another method (for example, braising) in order to add flavor.

Semolina The coarsely milled hard wheat endosperm used for gnocchi, some pasta, and couscous.

Sequence of service The established order and timing of the various courses that make up a meal.

Service plate A plate with a napkin folded in four on top. It is used to bring serviceware to the table. Sometimes referred to as *STP* (service transport plate).

Service set Set of serving fork and spoon.

Service towel A napkin folded in three parts lengthwise that hangs around the left arm during service. It is used to handle clean or hot items and should be replaced if soiled.

Serviette (Fr.) Napkin.

Setting-in The act of placing food and beverages before a guest. May be done from the left or the right, depening on the style of service or circumstance.

Shallow poach A method in which items are cooked gently in a shallow pan of simmering liquid. The liquid is often reduced and used as the basis of a sauce.

Shelf life The amount of time in storage that a product can maintain quality.

Shellfish Various types of marine life consumed as food including univalves, bivalves, cephalopods, and crustaceans.

Sherbet Frozen fruit juice with sugar and with milk, cream, or egg.

Shirred egg An egg cooked with butter (and often cream) in a ramekin.

Side stand A small cabinet, discreetly located in the dining room, that contains supplies needed during meal service, including but not limited to condiments, silverware, napkins, and other serviceware.

Sieve A container made of a perforated material, such as wire mesh, used to drain, rice, or purée foods.

Silver Silver or silver-plated flatware.

Silverskin The tough, connective tissue that surrounds certain muscles.

Simmer To maintain the temperature of a liquid just below boiling. Also, a cooking method in which items are cooked in simmering liquid.

Skim milk Milk from which all but 0.5 percent of the milkfat has been removed.

Skim To remove impurities from the surface of a liquid, such as stock or soup, during cooking.

Slurry Starch dispersed in cold liquid to prevent it from forming lumps when added to hot liquid as a thickener.

Small sauce A sauce that is a derivative of any of the grand sauces.

Smoke-roasting A method for roasting foods in which items are placed on a rack in a pan containing wood chips that smolder, emitting smoke, when the pan is placed on the range top or in the oven.

Smoking Any of several methods for preserving and flavoring foods by exposing them to smoke. Methods include cold smoking (in which smoked items are not fully cooked), hot smoking (in which the items are cooked), and smoke-roasting.

Smoking point The temperature at which a fat begins to break when heated.

Smorgasbord Scandinavian-style buffet; also known as hors d'oeuvre buffet.

Smother To cook in a covered pan with little liquid over low heat.

Soigné (Fr.) Literally, "caring" or "excellent." French term for *service*.

Sommelier (Fr.) Wine steward.

Sorbet (Fr.) A frozen dessert made with fruit juice or another flavoring, a sweetener (usually sugar), and beaten egg whites, which prevent the formation of large ice crystals. Used as an intermezzo after the fish course to cleanse the palate for the next course. Replaced the *trou normande*.

Soufflé (Fr.) Literally, "puffed." A preparation made with a sauce base (usually béchamel for savory soufflés or pastry cream for sweet ones), whipped egg whites, and flavorings. The egg whites cause the soufflé to puff during cooking.

Sourdough Yeast dough leavened with a fermented starter instead of, or in addition to, fresh yeast. Some starters are kept alive by "feeding" with additional flour and water.

Sous chef (Fr.) Underchef. The chef who is second in command in a kitchen; usually responsible for scheduling, filling in for the chef, and assisting the chefs de partie as necessary.

Spit-roast To roast an item on a large skewer or spit over, or in front of, an open flame or other radiant heat source.

Sponge cake A sweet-batter product that is leavened with a beaten egg foam. (Also called a *génoise*.)

Sponge A thick yeast batter that is allowed to ferment and develop a light, spongy consistency and is then combined with other ingredients to form a yeast dough.

Squab A domesticated pigeon that has not yet begun to fly. It is slaughtered at 3 to 4 weeks old, weighing under 1 pound (455 grams). Its light, tender meat is suitable for sautéing, roasting, and grilling.

Station The tables assigned to a single server or team of servers.

Statler A square table with flip-up sides to make a larger, usually round table.

Steamer A set of stacked pots with perforations in the bottom of each pot. They fit over a larger pot that is filled with boiling or simmering water. Also, a perforated insert made of metal or bamboo that can be inserted in a pot and used to steam foods.

Steaming A cooking method in which items are cooked in a vapor bath created by boiling water or other liquids.

Steel A tool used to hone knife blades. It is usually made of steel but may be ceramic, glass, or diamond-impregnated metal.

Stemware Stemmed glassware.

Stew A cooking method nearly identical to braising but generally involving smaller pieces of meat and hence a shorter cooking time. Stewed items also may be blanched, rather than seared, to give the finished product a pale color. Also, a dish prepared by using the stewing method.

Stir-fry A cooking method similar to sautéing in which items are cooked over very high heat, using little fat. Usually this is done in a wok and the food is kept moving constantly.

Stock A flavorful liquid prepared by simmering meat, poultry, seafood, and/or vegetables in water with aromatics until their flavor is extracted. It is used as a base for soups, sauces, and other preparations.

Stockpot A large, straight-sided pot that is taller than it is wide. Used for making stocks and soups. Some have spigots. Also called a *marmite*.

Stone-ground Meal or flour milled between grindstones; this method retains more nutrients than some other grinding methods.

Suprême (Fr.) The breast fillet and wing of chicken or other poultry. Sauce *suprême* is chicken velouté enriched with cream.

Sweat To cook an item, usually vegetables, in a covered pan in a small amount of fat until it softens and releases moisture.

Sweetbreads The thymus glands of young animals, usually calves, but possibly lambs or pigs. Usually sold in pairs of lobes.

Syrup Sugar that is dissolved in liquid, usually water, with possibly the addition of flavorings such as spices or citrus zests.

Table d'hôte (Fr.) Preset multicourse menu offered at a set price.

Table salt Refined, granulated rock salt. May be fortified with iodine and treated with magnesium carbonate to prevent clumping.

Tamis See *drum sieve*.

Tang The continuation of the knife blade into its handle. A full tang extends through the entire handle. A partial tang runs through only part of the knife. A rat-tail tang is thinner than the blade's spine, is encased in the handle, and is not visible at the top or bottom edge.

Taper-ground A type of knife blade forged out of a single sheet of metal, then ground so that it tapers smoothly to the cutting edge. Taper-ground knives are generally the most desirable.

Tart A pie without a top crust; may be sweet or savory.

Tartlet A small, single-serving tart.

Tea caddy Set of two pots on a small tray used for tea service. Two tea bags are placed in the pot with the long nozzle, and the pot is filled with hot water. The short-nozzled pot is filled with water so the guest can enjoy the tea to his or her liking. The service is placed to the guest's right, with the long-nozzled pot to the right and the water to the left.

Temper To heat gently and gradually. May refer to the process of incorporating hot liquid into a liaison to gradually raise its temperature. May also refer to the proper method for melting chocolate.

Tempura (Jap.) Seafood and/or vegetables that are coated with a light batter and deep-fried.

Tenderloin A cut of meat, usually beef or pork, from the hindquarter.

Terrine A loaf of forcemeat, similar to a pâté, but cooked in a covered mold in a bain-marie. Also, the mold used to cook such items, usually an oval shape made of ceramic.

Tilting kettle A large, relatively shallow, tilting pot used for braising, stewing, and, occasionally, steaming.

Timbale A small pail-shaped mold used to shape rice, custards, mousselines, and other items. Also, a preparation made in such a mold.

Tomalley Lobster liver, which is olive green in color.

Total utilization The principle advocating the use of as much of a product as possible in order to reduce waste and increase profits.

Tournant (Fr.) Roundsman or swing cook. A kitchen staff member who works as needed throughout the kitchen.

Tourné knife A small knife, similar to a paring knife, with a curved blade used to cut tournéed items.

Tourner/tourné To cut items, usually vegetables, into barrel, olive, or football shapes.

Toxin A naturally occurring poison, particularly those produced by the metabolic activity of living organisms, such as bacteria.

Trash fish Fish that have traditionally been considered unusable. (Also called *junk fish* or *underutilized fish*.)

Tripe The edible stomach lining of a cow or other ruminant. *Honeycomb tripe* comes from the second stomach and has a honeycomblike texture.

Trou normande (Fr.) A precursor to sorbet as the intermezzo, a *trou normande* was traditionally a bottle of Calvados (from Normandy) encased in a small block of ice. It was meant to "burn a hole" in one's stomach to make room for the next course. A room-temperature brandy was often substituted.

Truss To tie up meat or poultry with string before cooking it in order to give it a compact shape for more even cooking and better appearance.

Tuber The fleshy root, stem, or rhizome of a plant that is able to grow into a new plant. Some, such as potatoes, are eaten as vegetables.

Tureen A large container with a ladle, holding several portions of soup; can be used for family service as well as Russian, French, or English service.

Underliner Additional larger plate on which a plated food is served.

Univalve A single-shelled mollusk, such as abalone and sea urchin.

Utility knife A smaller, lighter version of the chef's knife; its blade is usually between 5 and 7 inches long.

Variety meat Meat from a part of an animal other than the muscle; for example, organs.

Velouté A sauce of white stock (chicken, veal, seafood) thickened with white roux; one of the grand sauces. Also, a cream soup made with a velouté sauce base and flavorings (usually puréed) that is usually finished with a liaison.

Venison Meat from large game animals; often used to refer specifically to deer meat.

Vinaigrette (Fr.) A cold sauce of oil and vinegar, usually with various flavorings; it is a temporary emulsion sauce. (The standard proportion is three parts oil to one part vinegar.)

Waffle A crisp, pancakelike batter product that is cooked in a specialized iron that gives the finished product a textured pattern, usually a grid. Also a special vegetable cut which produces a grid or basketweave pattern.

Walk-in refrigerator A refrigeration unit large enough to walk into. It is occasionally large enough to maintain zones of varying temperature and humidity to store a variety of foods properly. Some have reach-in doors as well. Some are large enough to accommodate rolling carts as well as many shelves of goods.

Whip To beat an item, such as cream or egg whites, to incorporate air. Also, a special tool for whipping made of looped wire attached to a handle.

White chocolate Cocoa butter flavored with sugar and milk solids. It does not contain any cocoa solids, so it does not have the characteristic brown color of regular chocolate.

White mirepoix Mirepoix that does not include carrots and may include chopped mushrooms or mushroom trimmings. It is used for pale or white sauces and stocks.

White stock A light-colored stock made with bones that have not been browned.

Whole-wheat flour Flour milled from the whole grain, including the bran and germ. Graham flour is a whole-wheat flour named after Sylvester Graham, a nineteenth-century American dietary reformer.

Wok (Chin.) A round-bottomed pan, usually made of rolled steel, that is used for nearly all cooking methods.

Yam A large tuber that grows in tropical and subtropical climates; it has starchy, pale yellow flesh and is often confused with the sweet potato.

Yeast Microscopic fungus whose metabolic processes are responsible for fermentation. It is used for leavening bread and in the making of cheese, beer, and wine.

Yogurt Milk cultured with bacteria to give it a slightly thick consistency and sour flavor.

Zabaglione See *sabayon*.

Zest The thin, brightly colored outer part of citrus rind. It contains volatile oils, making it ideal for use as a flavoring.

FREQUENTLY CONFUSED CULINARY TERMS

darphin Shredded potatoes formed into a flat round pancake and sautéed in oil, then baked.

dauphine Puréed potatoes rolled into a ball and deep-fried.

dauphinoise Thinly sliced potatoes layered with cream and butter and baked. Similar to American scalloped potatoes.

nappe Tablecloth.

napper To coat with a sauce.

napperon Top cloth.

pâte Batter used for baking, as in *pâte á choux*. In plural, noodles.

pâté Mixture of seasoned ground meats molded in a terrine and baked.

poisson Fish.

poussin Very young chicken.

terrine A container for making pâté, a slice of which is itself often referred to as a *terrine*.

tureen A large container with ladle holding several portions of soup.

darphin

dauphine

dauphinoise

terrine

tureen

GLOSSARY OF RESTAURANT SLANG TERMS

86 1. No longer available, as in "86 veal chop" for communicating to the service staff. 2. No longer of any use, so to be thrown away, as in "86 it." *Supposed origin(s):* 1. Possibly from the Depression era: Soup pots held 85 cups of soup, so when the pot was empty, the cook called out, "86 soup." 2. Possibly from a nautical term: The ship must be at 86 fathoms before garbage can be thrown overboard. 3. Possibly from the last stop on a Chicago train line, "86—all out." 4. According to Mary and William Morris (*Morris Dictionary of Word and Phrase Origins,* 2nd ed., New York: HarperCollins, 1988), the term originated in soda fountains during the 1920s. All of the soda jerks' codes were numeric, such as "55" for root beer, "99" for the boss, "98" for the second in command, and "87½" for "there's a good-looking girl out front."

68 The item is once again available. For example, if the veal was delivered late, the service staff would be notified, as in "68 veal chop."

ace A single diner at a table.

all day A total count of a certain menu item by adding up all the dupes.

cover 1. A single place setting. 2. A guest, as in the number of covers served.

deuce A table for two; also *two-top*.

drop To serve or present the item, as in "Drop the check on table 21."

dupe Abbreviation for duplicate, can be handwritten or computer generated. Sometimes referred to as a *chit*.

F & B The food and beverage department.

Fire Start preparing the next course, as in "Fire main course on table 16." Appetizers and desserts are generally automatically fired when ordered unless otherwise indicated by the server. Courses can be fired by the service staff or chef/expediter, depending on house procedures.

four-top A table for four. Similar uses include *six-top* for a table for six and *eight-top* for a table for eight.

in the weeds Having more tasks than can be handled; needing to be in several places at once. Also referred to as *weeded*. Result of being slammed (q.v.).

on the fly Needed right away, usually as a result of an error or miscommunication, as in "One trout on the fly."

pick up Announcing to kitchen line that the table is ready and flatware in place for the next course, as in "Pick up pasta course on table 34."

reach-in A free-standing refrigerator unit. If below a countertop, it may be referred to as a lowboy.

slammed Having all the tables in a station seated at once. This often results in slamming the kitchen as well, which can be avoided by getting the order to the kitchen as each order is taken, rather than delivering all the orders at once.

SOS Sauce on the side.

Stiff To leave a restaurant without leaving a tip.

STP Silverware transport plate. A plate with a folded napkin used to take clean flatware to a table.

walk-in 1. A large refrigerator that you can stand up in. Usually stores butter and milk products for front of house. 2. A guest without a reservation.

walk-out A guest who leaves the restaurant without paying.

Appendix B
Sample Forms

GIFT CERTIFICATE ORDER FORM

Manager's initials: _____

Restaurant name: _____

Address: _____

Telephone number: (___)_____ Fax number: (___)_____

Name of recipient/reservation: _____

Description of gift: _____ Amount: $_____

Special comment or occasion: _____

From: _____

Bill to credit card holder: _____

Telephone number: (___)_____ Fax number:(___)_____

Would you like us to mail you a receipt? (circle) Yes   No

Address: _____

Credit card: (circle) Amex Visa MC Other:

Credit card number: _____ Expiration date: _____

Signature _____

Please mail the gift certificate to (circle) Purchaser   Recipient

Address: _____

Please fax or send this form to _____ when completed.
(restaurant name)
Thank you.

CAKE ORDER FORM

Name of recipient/reservation: _____

Date of reservation: _____ Time of reservation: _____

Number of people: _____

Name of person ordering cake: _____

Telephone number: (___)_____ Fax number: (___)_____

Any allergies? _____ Alcohol? (circle) Yes   No

Specific dislikes: _____ Special requests: _____

Any inscription on cake? _____

Total amount ($ ____ per person) / Deposit ($____ per person)

Should we add this amount to the check? (circle) Yes   No

Telephone number: (___)_____ Fax number: (___)_____

Would you like us to mail you a receipt? (circle) Yes   No

Address: _____

Credit card: (circle) Amex Visa MC Other: _____

Credit card number: _____ Expiration date: _____

Any cancellation must be made 24 hours in advance.

Signature: _____

Please fax or send this form to _____ when completed.

Thank you.
                        (restaurant name)

HOLIDAY REGISTRATION FORM

Restaurant name: _____

Address: _____

Telephone number: (___)_____ Fax number: (___)_____

Name of party: _____

Date of party: _____ Time of reservation: _____

Party of (number of people): _____

Contact person: _____

Telephone number: (___)_____ Fax number: (___)_____

Menu sent by date: _____ Any allergies? _____

Specific dislikes: _____ Special requests: _____

Full names of guests in party (including your own) _____

The price for dinner is $_____ per person. Deposit $_____ per person.
Cancellation must be made 48 hours in advance for refund of deposit.
How would you like us to handle the payment? (check one)

    Present at table

    Hold at front desk for your signature

    Charge to credit card and mail receipt to your address

Name of credit card holder: _____

Credit card: (circle) Amex Visa MC Other: _____

Credit card number: _____ Expiration date: _____

Signature: _____

Please fax or send this form to _____ when completed.
                                 (restaurant name)

Thank you.

FOOD SERVICE INCIDENT REPORT

Your Name: _____ Date: _____

Time: _____ Location: _____ ext: _____

Be sympathetic, not apologetic. Tell the caller that our sanitation representative will call them in an hour (or the next work day if after office hours.) It is therefore crucial that you take as much of the following information as possible. Please print clearly.

Caller's Name: _____

Daytime Telephone number: (___)_____ Evening: (___)_____

Name of Ill Person: _____

Address: _____

Daytime Telephone number: (___)_____ Evening: (___)_____

Relationship to Caller: _____

Date of Incident: _____ Location: _____ Time: _____

Time when symptoms began_____

Description of Complaint/Meal: _____

_____

_____

_____

_____

Current Status: _____

_____

Medical Facility/Physician: _____

Medical Facility Phone Number: (___)_____ Location: (___)_____

Hand deliver this form immediately to Food & Beverage Operations

Received by: _____ Date: _____ Time: _____

FOOD SERVICE INCIDENT REPORT

You play a very important role if you receive a phone call from someone who thinks they have "food poisoning." If someone calls complaining that they have become ill from eating in one of our facilities, do not become defensive. Explain to the caller that you need to write down some information so that a representative can call them back. Our representative will try to reach them within an hour or the beginning of the next working day.

DO	DON'T
Be sympathetic	Be apologetic
Tell them you're sorry they are ill	Tell them you're sorry our food made them ill
Get all the information you can	Suggest symptoms
Make additional notes	Offer medical advice
Get the form to F&B office immediately	Deny it

Procedure:

A) The form is filled out by the person receiving the phone call.

B) Form is immediately hand delivered to the Food & Beverage office who will:

    1) Contact the GM.

    2) Notify the Accounting Department.

    3) Speak with the maitre d'hôtel and chef of the restaurant in question.

    4) Speak with person who received call (if necessary.)

    5) Collect, bag, and refrigerate any food in question.

    6) Reproduce the guest check.

    7) Obtain menu abstract to determine quantity served of item in question.

C) Contact Health Department and complainant after information is gathered from F&B director.

Sample Filled-in Form 4070 from Publication 1244

Form 4070 (Rev. July 1996) Department of the Treasury Internal Revenue Service	**Employee's Report** **of Tips to Employer** ▶ For Paperwork Reduction Act Notice, see back of form. OMB No. 1545-0065

Employee's name and address
John W. Allen
117 Maple Ave.
Anytown, NY 14202

Social security number
987 00 4321

Employer's name and address (include establishment name, if different)

Diamond Restaurant
834 Main Street
Anytown, NY 14203

1 Cash tips received
1,024.00

2 Credit card tips received
519.20

3 Tips paid out
273.60

Month or shorter period in which tips were received

from October 1 , 19 97 , to October 31 , 19 97

4 Net tips (lines **1** + **2** - **3**)
1,269.60

Signature
John W. Allen

Date
Nov. 6, 1997

Penalty for not reporting tips. If you do not report tips to your employer as required, you may be subject to a penalty equal to 50% of the social security and Medicare taxes or railroad retirement tax you owe. (For information about these taxes, see *Reporting social security and Medicare taxes on tips not reported to your employer* under *Reporting Tips on Your Return*, later.) The penalty amount is in addition to the taxes you owe.

You can avoid this penalty if you can show reasonable cause for not reporting the tips to your employer. To do so, attach a statement to your return explaining why you did not report them.

Giving your employer money for taxes. Your regular pay may not be enough for your employer to withhold all the taxes you owe on your regular pay plus your reported tips. If this happens, you can give your employer money to pay the rest of the taxes, up to the close of the calendar year.

If you do not give your employer enough money, your employer will apply your regular pay and any money you give to the taxes, in the following order:

1) All taxes on your regular pay,

2) Social security and Medicare taxes or railroad retirement tax on your reported tips, and

3) Federal, state, and local income taxes on your reported tips.

Any taxes that remain unpaid may be collected by your employer from your next paycheck. If withholding taxes remain uncollected at the end of the year, you may need to make an estimated tax payment. Use **Form 1040–ES**, *Estimated Tax for Individuals.* See Publication 505, *Tax Withholding and Estimated Tax,* for more information.

 You must report on your tax return any social security and Medicare taxes or railroad retirement tax that remained uncollected at the end

of 1997. See Reporting uncollected social security and Medicare taxes on tips *under* Reporting Tips on Your Tax Return, *later. These uncollected taxes will be shown in box 13 of your Form W-2 (codes A and B).*

Reporting Tips on Your Tax Return

How to report tips. Report your tips with your wages on line 1, Form 1040EZ, or line 7, Form 1040A or Form 1040.

What tips to report. You must report all tips you received in 1997, including both cash tips and noncash tips, on your tax return. Any tips you reported to your employer for 1997 are included in the wages shown in box 1 of your Form W-2. Add to the amount in box 1 only the tips you did not report to your employer.

⚠️ *If you received $20 or more in cash and charge tips in a month and did not report all of those tips to your employer, see* Reporting social security and Medicare taxes on tips not reported to your employer, *later.*

⚠️ *If you did not keep a daily tip record as required and an amount is shown in box 8 of your Form W-2, see* Allocated Tips, *later.*

If you kept a daily tip record and reported tips to your employer as required under the rules explained earlier, add the following tips to the amount in box 1 of your Form W-2:

• Cash and charge tips you received that totaled less than $20 for any month, and

• The value of noncash tips, such as tickets, passes, or other items of value.

Form 4070A (Rev. July 1996) Department of the Treasury Internal Revenue Service	**Employee's Daily Record of Tips** This is a voluntary form provided for your convenience. See instructions for records you must keep.	OMB No. 1545-0065

Employee's name and address

Employer's name

Establishment name (if different)

Month and year

Date tips rec'd.	Date of entry	**a.** Tips received directly from customers and other employees	**b.** Credit card tips received	**c.** Tips paid out to other employees	**d.** Names of employees to whom you paid tips
1					
2					
3					
4					
5					
Subtotals					

For Paperwork Reduction Act Notice, see Instructions on the back of Form 4070.   Page 1

Bibliography

The bibliography includes a number of excellent books that can aid in the acquisition of professional knowledge. In addition, there are listings of periodicals; government, trade, and professional groups; Internet sources; and recommended videotapes.

Amendola, Joseph. *Ice Carving Made Easy.* New York: National Restaurant Association, 1969.

Andrioli, Sergio. *Tableside Cookery.* New York: Van Nostrand Reinhold, 1990.

Aresty, Esther B. The Delectable Past: *The Joys of the Table—from Rome to the Renaissance, from Queen Elizabeth I to Mrs. Beeton. The Menus, the Manners— and the Most Delectable Recipes of the Past, Masterfully Re-created for Cooking and Enjoying Today.* New York: Simon and Schuster, 1964.

Axler, Bruce H. *Profitable Catering.* Indianapolis: ITT, 1974.

Axler, Bruce H., and Carol A. Litrides. *Food and Beverage Service.* New York: Wiley, 1990.

Brett, Gerard. *Dinner Is Served: A Study in Manners.* Hamden, CT: Archon Books, 1969.

Collins, Philip. *The Art of the Cocktail: 100 Classic Cocktail Recipes.* San Francisco: Chronicle Books, 1992.

Cullen, Max O'Rell. *How to Carve Meat, Game, and Poultry.* New York: Dover Publications, 1976.

Dahmer, Sondra J. *The Waiter and Waitress Training Manual.* Boston: Cahners Books, 1974.

Dalby, Andrew, and Sally Grainger. *The Classical Cookbook.* Malibu, CA: J. Paul Getty Museum, 1996.

Fitzgibbon, Theodora. *The Pleasures of the Table.* Oxford: Oxford University Press, 1981.

Flower, Barbara, and Elizabeth Rosebaum. *The Roman Cookery Book: A Critical Translation of The Art of Cooking by Apicius for Use in the Study or Kitchen.* London and New York: Peter Nevill Ltd., 1958.

Fuller, John. *Modern Restaurant Service: A Manual for Students and Practitioners.* London: Hutchinson, 1983.

Gauntner, John. *The Sake Handbook.* Singapore: Yenbooks (Charles E. Tuttle Co.), 1997.

Giblin, James. *From Hand to Mouth, or How We Invented Knives, Forks, Spoons, and Chopsticks, and the Table Manners to Go with Them.* New York: Crowell, 1987.

Ginders, James R. *A Guide to Napkin Folding.* Boston: CBI Publishers, 1980.

Gluck, Sandra. *The Best of Coffee.* San Francisco: Collins, 1994.

Griffin, Jill. *Customer Loyalty: How to Earn It, How to Keep It.* San Francisco: Jossey-Bass, 1997.

Gutek, Barbara A. *The Dynamics of Service: Reflections on the Changing Nature of Customer/Provider Interactions.* San Francisco: Jossey-Bass, 1995.

Harris, R. Lee. *The Customer Is King!* Milwaukee: ASQC Quality Press, 1991.

Hazlitt, W. Carew. *Old Cookery Books.* London: Eliot Stock, 1886 (reissued Detroit: Gale Research Co., 1968).

Herbst, Sharon Tyler. *The New Food Lover's Companion.* 2nd ed. New York: Barron's, 1995.

Hetzer, Linda. *The Simple Art of Napkin Folding: 94 Fancy Folds for Every Tabletop Occasion.* New York: Hearst, 1991.

Illy, Francesco, and Riccardo Illy. *The Book of Coffee.* New York, London, and Paris: Abbeville, 1992.

Jenkins, Steven. *Cheese Primer.* New York: Workman, 1996.

Kahan, Nancy. *Entertaining for Business.* New York: Crown, 1990.

Kalish, Susan S. *The Art of Napkin Folding.* Philadelphia: Running Press, 1988.

Katona, Christie. *Cappuccino/Espresso: The Book of Beverages.* San Leandro, CA: Bristol, 1993.

Kemp, Jim. *Stylish Settings: The Art of Tabletop Design.* New York: Gallery Books, 1990.

Ketterer, Manfred. *How to Run a Successful Catering Business.* Rochelle Park, NJ: Hayden, 1982.

King, Carol A. *Professional Dining Room Management.* 2nd ed. New York: Van Nostrand Reinhold, 1988.

Knox, Kevin. *Coffee Basics: A Quick and Easy Guide.* New York: Wiley, 1997.

Koch, Maryjo. *Coffee: Delectables for All Seasons.* San Francisco: Collins, 1995.

Kolpan, Steven, Brian Smith, and Michael Weiss. *Exploring Wine.* New York: Wiley, 1996.

Kramer, Matt. *Making Sense of Wine.* New York: Morrow, 1989.

Labensky, Steven, Gaye G. Ingram, and Sarah R. Labensky (compilers). *Webster's New World Dictionary of Culinary Arts*. Upper Saddle River, NJ: Prentice Hall, 1997.

Lash, Linda M. *The Complete Guide to Customer Service*. New York: Wiley, 1989.

Latham, Jean. *The Pleasure of Your Company: A History of Manners and Meals*. London: A. and C. Black, 1972.

Lillicrap, Dennis R., and John A. Cousins. *Food and Beverage Service*. London: Hodder and Stoughton, 1990.

Lipinski, Robert A. *Professional Beverage Management*. New York: Van Nostrand Reinhold, 1996.

Litrides, Carol A., and Bruce H. Axler. *Restaurant Service: Beyond the Basics*. New York: Wiley, 1994.

Maresca, Tom. *The Right Wine*. New York: Grove Weidenfeld, 1990.

Marshall, A. C. *The Waiter*. 3rd ed. London: Barrie and Rockliff, 1967.

Mennell, Stephen. *All Manners of Food: Eating and Taste in England and France from the Middle Ages to the Present*. Oxford and New York: Basil Blackwell Ltd., 1985.

Michaelson, Gerald A. *Building Bridges to Customers*. Portland, OR: Productivity Press, 1995.

Müller, Marianne, and Ola Mikolasek, with Hans Tapper. *Great Napkin Folding and Table Setting*. Trans. Elisabeth R. Reinersmann. New York: Sterling, 1990.

Murphy, Claudia Quigley. *The History of the Art of Tablesetting, Ancient and Modern: From Anglo-Saxon Days to the Present Time, with Illustrations and Bibliography, For the Use of Schools, Colleges, Extension Workers, Women's Clubs, Etc., Etc.* New York: n.p., 1921.

Nantet, Bernard, et al. *Cheeses of the World*. New York: Rizzoli, 1993.

Nutley, Joyce. *Advanced Service Techniques*. London: Hodder and Stoughton, 1992.

Plotkin, Robert. *The Bartender's Companion: A Complete Drink Recipe Guide*. 3rd ed. Tucson, AZ: R. Plotkin's Barmedia, 1997.

Revel, Jean François. *Culture and Cuisine: A Journey Through the History of Food*. Trans. Helen R. Lane. Garden City, NY: Doubleday, 1982.

Root, Waverley Lewis. *Eating in America: A History*. New York: Morrow, 1976.

Rudman, Theo. *Rudman's Complete Guide to Cigars*. 3rd ed. Chicago: Triumph Books, 1996.

Ruffel, Denis. *The Professional Catering Series*. New York: Van Nostrand Reinhold, 1989.

Saint George, Amelia. *Amelia Saint George's Table Decorating Book: With 8 Pages of Pull-out Designs*. North Pomfret, VT: Trafalgar Square, 1995.

Schivelbusch, Wolfgang. *Tastes of Paradise: A Social History of Spices, Stimulants, and Intoxicants*. Trans. David Jacobson. New York: Vintage, 1993.

Simon, Joanna. *Wine with Food*. New York: Simon and Schuster, 1996.

Southey, Paul. *The Expert Carver: How to Carve Meat, Poultry, and Game*. London: Century, 1987.

Splaver, Bernard. *Successful Catering*. New York: Van Nostrand Reinhold, 1991.

Stiel, Holly. *Thank You Very Much: A Book for Anyone Who Has Ever Said "May I Help You?"* Berkeley, CA: Ten Speed Press, 1995.

Sullivan, Jim and Phil "Zoom" Roberts. *Service that Sells! The Art of Profitable Hospitality*. Denver: Pencom International, 1991.

Takahashi, Kuwako. *East Meets West Table Setting: Table Design and Food*. Tokyo: Shufunotomo, 1991.

Tannahill, Reay. *Food in History*. 2nd ed. New York: Crown, 1988.

Tapper, Hans, and Helena York. *Napkin Folding and Place Cards for Festive Tables*. Trans. Elisabeth Reinersmann. New York: Sterling, 1989.

Tuor, Conrad. *Wine and Food Handbook: Aide-Mémoire du Sommelier*. London: Hodder and Stoughton, 1977.

Ukers, William H. *The Romance of Coffee: An Outline History of Coffee and Coffee Drinking Through a Thousand Years*. New York: Tea and Coffee Trade Journal Co., 1948.

Visser, Margaret. *Much Depends on Dinner: The Extraordinary History and Mythology, Allure and Obsessions, Perils and Taboos, of an Ordinary Meal*. New York: Grove Press, 1986.

Visser, Margaret. *The Rituals of Dinner: The Origins, Evolution, Eccentricities, and Meaning of Table Manners*. New York: Grove Wiedenfeld, 1991.

Weiss, Edith, and Hal Weiss. *Catering Handbook*. New York: Van Nostrand Reinhold, 1991.

Wirth, Barbara. *The Elegant Table*. Trans. Danielle Lawrence de Froidmont. New York: Harry N. Abrams, 1988.

Wolk, Michael. *Designing for the Table: Decorative and Functional Products*. New York: Library of Applied Design, PBC International, 1992.

Zraly, Kevin. *Windows on the World Complete Wine Course*. New York: Sterling, 1998.

PERIODICALS

American Mixologist

Robert Plotkin's Barmedia

P.O. Box 14486

Tucson, AZ 85732-4486

Phone: (800) 421-7179

(520) 747-8131

Fax: (520) 747-7640

Web: www.barmedia.com/ssi/newsletter.shtml

Appellation

Appellation® Wine Country Living

1700 Soscol Avenue, Suite 2

Napa, CA 94559

Phone: (707) 255-2525

Fax: (707) 258-0473

Web: www.appellation.com/

Art Culinaire

Art Culinaire

40 Mills Street

P.O. Box 9268

Morristown, NJ 07960

Phone: (973) 993-5500

Fax: (973) 993-8779

Web: www.getartc.com/

Cater Service Journal

Cater Service Journal

P.O. Box 14776

Chicago, IL 60614

Phone: (800) 932-3632

Web: www.globalgourmet.com/food/egg/fdnews.html

Chef

The Chef's Business Magazine

Talcott Communications Corp.

20 N Wacker Drive, Suite 3230

Chicago, IL 60606-3112

Phone: (312) 849-2220

Fax: (312) 849-2184

Web: www.chefmagazine.com/index.htm

Cigar Aficionado

M. Shanken Communications, Inc.

387 Park Avenue South

New York, NY 10016

Phone: (212) 684-4224

Fax: (212) 684-5424

Web: www.cigaraficianado.com/

Coffee Journal

Tiger Oak Publications, Inc.

123 N. 3rd Street, Suite 508

Minneapolis, MN 55401-1664

Phone: (612) 338-4125

Fax: (612) 338-0532

Decanter

Decanter

1st Floor

Broadway House

2-6 Fulham Broadway

London SW6 5UE

United Kingdom

Phone: +44 (0) 20-7610-3929

Fax: +44(0) 20-7381-5282

Web: www.decanter.com/

Food Arts

Food Arts Publishing, Inc.

387 Park Avenue South

New York, NY 10016

Phone: (212) 684-4224

Fax: (212) 684-5424

Web: www.mshanken.com

Food Forum

International Association of Culinary Professionals

304 W. Liberty Street, Suite 201

Louisville, KY 40202

Phone: (502) 581-9786

Fax: (502) 589-3602

Web: www.cieh.org.uk

Hospitality

David Goymour (Editor)

69 Searles Close

Battersea

London SW11 4RQ

Phone: +44(0) 20-7228-6260

Web: www.hcima.org.uk

Nation's Restaurant News

Nation's Restaurant News

A Publication of Lebhar-Friedman Inc.

P.O. Box 5038

Brentwood, TN 37024-9411

Phone: (800) 944-4674

Web: www.nrn.com/

Restaurant Business

Restaurant Business

770 Broadway

New York, NY 10003-9595

Phone: (646) 654-7390

Web: www.foodservicetoday.com/rb/index.shtml

Restaurant Hospitality

Restaurant Hospitality

1100 Superior Avenue

Cleveland, OH 44114-2543

Phone: (216) 696-7000

Fax: (216) 696-0836

Web: subscribe.penton.com/rh/

Tea and Coffee Journal

Tea and Coffee Journal

130 W 42nd Street, Suite 1050

New York, NY 10036

Phone: (212) 391-2060

Fax: (212) 827-0945

Web: www.teaandcoffee.net/

Tea Talk

P&R Publications

P.O. Box 860

Sausolito, CA 94966

Phone: (415) 331-1557

The Wine Advocate

The Wine Advocate

P.O.Box 311

Monkton, MD 21111

Phone: (410) 329-6477

Fax: (410) 357-4504

Web: www.winetech.com/html/wineadvo.html

Wine and Food Companion

Wine and Food Companion

P.O. Box 639

Lenox Hill Station

New York, NY 10021

Phone: (800) 888-1961

Fax: (212) 737-7629

Web: www.globalgourmet.com/food/egg/fdnews.html

Wine and Spirits

Wine and Spirits

2 W 32nd Street, Suite 601

New York, NY 10001

Phone: (212) 695-4660

Web: www.wineandspiritsmagazine.com

Wine Business Monthly

Smartwired Inc.

867 W Napa Street

Sonoma, CA 95476

Phone: (707) 939-0822

Fax: (707) 939-0833

Web: smartwine.com/wbm/swwbm1.htm

Wine Spectator

Wine Spectator

387 Park Ave. South

New York, NY 10016

Phone: (212) 684-4224

Fax: (212) 684-5424

Web: www.winespectator.com/

World Coffee and Tea

GCI Publishing Group, Inc.

18011 Rockville Park, Suite 330

Rockville, MD 20852

Phone: (301) 984-4000

Fax: (301) 984-7340

GOVERNMENT, TRADE, AND PROFESSIONAL GROUPS

American Culinary Federation, Inc. (ACF)

P.O. Box 3466

10 San Bartola Drive

St. Augustine, FL 32086

Phone: (904) 824-4468

Fax: (904) 825-4758

E-mail: acf@aug.com

Web site: http://www.acfchefs.org

American Institute of Wine and Food (AIWF)

550 Bryant Street, Suite 700

San Francisco, CA 94103

Phone: (415) 255-3000

Fax: (415) 255-2874

Web site: http://www.aiwf.org/aiwfwho1.htm

Council on Hotel, Restaurant and Institutional Education (CHRIE)

1200 17th Street NW

Washington, DC 20036-3097

Phone: (202) 331-5990

Fax: (202) 785-2511

E-mail: alliance@access.digex.net

Web site: http://www.access.digex.net/~alliance/

Federation of Dining Room Professionals
115 Franklin Turnpike, #100
Mahwah, NJ 07430
Phone: (201) 995-0033
Fax: (201) 995-0433
Web site: http://www.restaurantprofessional.com

International Association of Culinary Professionals (IACP)
304 West Liberty Street, Suite 201
Louisville, KY 40202
Phone: (502) 581-9786 or (800) 928-4227
Fax: (502) 589-3602
E-mail: iacp@hqrts.com
Web site: www.iacp.com

International Association of Women Chefs and Restaurateurs
110 Sutter Street, Suite 210
San Francisco, CA 94104
Phone: (415) 362-7336
Fax: (415) 362-7335
E-mail: iawcr@well.com

International Food Information Council (IFIC)
1100 Connecticut Avenue, NW, Suite 430
Washington, DC 20036
Phone: (202) 296-6540
Fax: (202) 296-6547
E-mail: foodinfo@ific.health.org
Web site: http://ificinfo.health.org

Roundtable for Women in Foodservice
3022 West Eastwood Avenue
Chicago, IL 60625
Phone: (312) 463-3396
Fax: (312) 463-3397

Sommelier Society of America
205 East 25th Street
New York, NY 10159
Phone: (212) 679-4190

Waiters Association
1100 West Beaver Avenue
State College, PA 16801
Phone: (800) 437-7842

INTERNET SOURCES

Food and Nutrition Information Center (FNIC)
http://www.nal.usda.gov/fnic/

Robert Mondavi Winery
http://www.freerun.com/

Waiters/Waitresses: California Occupational Guide
http://www.calmis.cahwnet.gov/file/occguide/WAITER.HTM

Wait Staff News
http://www.ce.net/users/coolocea/waitstuf.htm

Wines.com
http://www.wines.com/wines.html

RECOMMENDED VIDEOTAPES

Art of Folding Table Napkins. The Food and Beverage Institute, 1997. (Available at 1-800-285-8280, ask for VT 1498)

Bar Code: How Alcohol Affects the Body. National Restaurant Association, n.d. (Available at 1-800-765-2122)

Bar Code: The Law and your Responsibility. National Restaurant Association, n.d. (Available at 1-800-765-2122)

Bar Code: Service in Difficult Situations. National Restaurant Association, n.d. (Available at 1-800-765-2122)

Bar Code: Techniques for Responsible Alcohol Service. National Restaurant Association, n.d. (Available at 1-800-765-2122)

Basic Table Service Skills, Part 1. The Culinary Institute of America, 1993. (Available at 1-800-285-8280, ask for VT 244)

Basic Table Service Skills, Part 2. The Culinary Institute of America, 1993. (Available at 1-800-285-8280, ask for VT 245)

Basic Table Service Skills, Part 3. The Culinary Institute of America, 1993. (Available at 1-800-285-8280, ask for VT 246)

Brewing Coffee. The Culinary Institute of America, 1985. (Available at 1-800-285-8280, ask for VT 191)

CARE: Controlling Alcohol Risk Effectively. Educational Foundation, 1993. (Available at 1-517-372-8800)

Espresso 101. Bellissimo, 1998. (Available at 1-800-655-3955)

Heimlich Maneuver: How to Save a Choking Victim. AIMS Multimedia, 1982. (Available at 1-800-367-2467, ask for catalog no. 20951)

How to Give Exceptional Customer Service, Volumes 1–4. Career Track, 1989. (Available at 1-800-334-1018, ask for catalog no. 40435)

Kevin Zraly Wine Tasting. The Culinary Institute of America, 1993. (Available at 1-800-285-8280, ask for VT 1115)

Kosher Catering. The Culinary Institute of America, 1979. (Available at 1-800-285-8280, ask for VT 124)

Service that Sells. Pencom International, 1998. (Available at 1-800-247-8514)

Tableside Service, Part 1: Introduction. The Culinary Institute of America, 1994. (Available at 1-800-285-8280, ask for VT 741)

Tableside Service, Part 2: Appetizers, Soups and Salads. The Culinary Institute of America, 1994. (Available at 1-800-285-8280, ask for VT 742)

Tableside Service, Part 3: Entrées, Boning and Carving. The Culinary Institute of America, 1994. (Available at 1-800-285-8280, ask for VT 743)

Tableside Service, Part 4: Desserts and Beverages. The Culinary Institute of America, 1994. (Available at 1-800-285-8280, ask for VT 744)

Wine Service. The Culinary Institute of America, 1990. (Available at 1-800-285-8280, ask for VT 232)

Index

The Institute wishes to acknowledge the following individuals and organizations for assistance provided both directly and indirectly in the preparation of this book:

RETAIL ESTABLISHMENTS
Illycaffe
John Harney & Sons Tea Company
Kimms Oriental Gifts and Home Accessories, Kingston, NY
Kingston Restaurant and Kitchen Supply, Kingston, NY
Lavazza Superior Coffees, Inc.
Lucullus Culinary Antiques, Art & Objects, New Orleans, LA
Nat Sherman Tobacconists
Pier One Imports, Kingston, NY
Serendipitea, Life, Inc., CT
The Village Antique Center at Hyde Park, Hyde Park, NY
The Alternative Baker, Essel-Hoenshell-Watson '93,
    Kingston, NY
Villeroy and Boch

MODELS AND STUDENT ASSISTANTS
Nicholas Angelakis
Jeremiah Bacon
Susan Balaban
Carter Bell
Taylor Bell
Michelle Bell
Jason Bettis
Ellen Blaich
Donna Bramble
Azariha Bramble
Simone Brown
Bryant Calbazana
Rich Carlacci
Thananyi Carr
Christopher Casale
Julie Cervone
Lou Cervone
Kathryn Conrad
Rosemarie Corbett
James Corbett Jr
Kristan Craig
Matt Craig
Sydney Culver
Felicia Dees
Sean Doherty
Vivian Duncan
Olifia Easton
Raychel Freiman
Gypsy Gifford
Kendra Glanbocky
Mark Griffin
Andrea Hagan
Jason Hall
Carol Hanscom
Todd Haramic
Debora Hartman
Siada Haylett
Jason Hill
Charles Huet
Dong Hun Kim
Saira Hussain
Atul Jain
Marisol Jaramillo
Aaliyah Johnson
Dennis Johnson
Melissa Johnson
Tatiana Johnson
Zachary Johnson
Sam Kameny
Angela Knox
Wildon Lacro
Lisa Lahey
Krista Lamphier
Justin LeClair
Joe Lefstein
Roxanne Levis
Troy MacLarty
Sylvia Matias
Phil McCain
John McKracken
Aisha Muhammad
Dena Peterson
Heather Renz
Benjamin Rottkamp
Mary Ellen Salomone
Tony Schmerge
Audrey Taylor
Anita Terrell
Adele Thaxton
Toni Tyler
Lori Villafuerte
Rose Visbeck
Andrew Young

NOTES

Scallops- Dinner Knife - Dinner Fork

Lamb - Dinner Fork

Salad - Salad Fork

Cheese — Salad Fork

Cake - Salad Fork

NOTES

NOTES

NOTES